CHICAGO STUDIES IN THE HISTORY OF AMERICAN RELIGION

Editors

JERALD C. BRAUER
AND MARTIN E. MARTY

A CARLSON PUBLISHING SERIES

For a complete listing of the titles in this series,
please see the back of this book.

Thomas Merton as Writer and Monk

A CULTURAL STUDY, 1915-1951

Peter Kountz

PREFACE BY MARTIN E. MARTY

CARLSON
Publishing Inc

BROOKLYN, NEW YORK, 1991

Please see the end of this volume for a listing of all the titles in the Carlson Publishing Series *Chicago Studies in the History of American Religion*, edited by Jerald C. Brauer and Martin E. Marty, of which this is Volume 11.

Library of Congress Cataloging-in-Publication Data

Kountz, Peter.
   Thomas Merton as writer and monk : a cultural study, 1915-1951 / Peter Kountz ; preface by Martin E. Marty.
         p.   cm. — (Chicago studies in the history of American religion ; 11)
   Includes bibliographical references and index.
   ISBN 0-926019-48-1 (alk. paper)
   1. Merton, Thomas, 1915-1968. 2. Trappists—United States--Biography. I. Title. II. Series.
BX4705.M542K68 1991
271'.12502—dc20   91-25223
[B]

Typographic design: Julian Waters

Typeface: Bitstream ITC Galliard

Case design: Alison Lew

Index prepared by Scholars Editorial Services, Inc., Madison, Wisconsin, using NL Cindex, a scholarly indexing program from the Newberry Library.

Printed on acid-free, 250-year-life paper.

Manufactured in the United States of America.

Contents

In memory of my father, FJK, whose greatest
gift was seeing things as they really are.

An Introduction to the Series

The *Chicago Studies in the History of American Religion* is a series of books that deal with topics ranging from the time of Jonathan Edwards to the 1970s. Three or four deal with colonial topics and three or four treat the very recent past. About half of them focus on the decades just before and after 1900. One deals with blacks; two concentrate on women. Revivalists, fundamentalists, theologians, life in the suburbs and life in heaven and hell, the Beecher family of old and a monk of new times, Catholics adapting to America and Protestants fighting one another—all these subjects assure that the series has scope. People of every kind of taste and curiosity about American religion will find some books to suit them. Does anything serve to characterize the series as a whole? What does the stamp of "Chicago studies" mean?

Yale historian Sydney Ahlstrom in *A Religious History of the American People*, as influential as any twentieth-century work in its field, pays respect to the "Chicago School" of American religious historians. William Warren Sweet, the pioneer in such studies (beginning in 1927) at Chicago and, in many ways, in America at large represented the culmination of "the Protestant synthesis" in this field. Ahlstrom went on to name two later generations of Chicagoans, including the seminal Sidney E. Mead and major figures like Robert T. Handy and Winthrop Hudson and ending with the two editors of this series. He saw them as often "openly rebellious" in respect to Sweet and his synthesis.

If, as Ahlstrom says, "a disproportionate number" of historians have some connection with the Chicago School, it must be said that the new generation represented in these twenty-one books carries on both the lineage of Sweet and something of the "openly rebellious" character that scholars at Chicago are encouraged to pursue. This means, for one thing, that the "Protestant synthesis" does not characterize their work. These historians question the canon of historical writing produced in the Protestant era even as many of them continue to pursue themes shaped in a Protestant culture. Few of them concentrate on the old "frontier thesis" that marked the early years of the school. The shift for most has been toward the urban and pluralist scene. They call into question, not in devastating rage but in steady patterns of inquiry, the received wisdom about who matters, and why, in American religion.

So it is that this series of books focuses on blacks, women, dispensationalists, suburbanites, members of "marginal" denominations, "ethnics" and immigrants as readily as it does on white men of progressive urban bent in mainstream denominations and of long standing in America. The authors relish religious diversity and enjoy discovering the power of people once considered weak, the centrality to the American plot of those once regarded as peripheral, and the potency of losers who were once disdained by winners. Thus this series enhances an understanding of an America overlooked by the people of Sweet's era two-thirds of a century ago when it all, or most of it, began.

Rebellion for its own sake would not long hold interest; it might tell more about the psychology of rebels and revisers than about their subject matter. Revision, better than rebellion, characterizes the scholars. Re+vision: that's it. There was an original vision that characterized the Chicago School. This was the contention that in secular America and its universities religion mattered, as a theme in the national past and as a presence in the present. Second, it argued that the study of religious history belonged not only in the seminaries and archives of denominations, but also in the rough-and-tumble of the secular university, where no religious meanings were privileged and where each historian had to make a case for the value of his or her story.

Other assumptions from the earliest days pervade the books in this series. They are uncommonly alert to the environment in which expressions of faith occur. That is, they do not take for granted that religion comes protected in self-evidently important and hermetically sealed packages. Churches and denominations are porous, even when they would be sealed off; they cannot be understood apart from the ways the social environs effect them, but their power to effect change in the environment demands equal and truly unapologetic treatment. These writers do not shuffle and mumble and make excuses for their existence or for the choice of apparently arcane subject matter. They try to present their narrative in such ways that they compel attention.

A fourth characteristic that colors these works is a refusal in most cases to be typed in a fashionable slot labeled, variously, "intellectual" or "institutional" history, "cultural" or "social" history, or whatever. While those which concentrate on magisterial thinkers such as Jonathan Edwards are necessarily busy with and devoted to his intellectual achievement, most of the books deal with figures who cannot be understood only as exemplars in a sequence of studies of "the life of the mind." Instead, their biographies and circumstances come very much into play. On the other hand, none of these writers is a reductionist who sees religion as "nothing but" this or that—"nothing but" the working out of believers' Oedipal urges or expressing the economic and class interests of the subjects. Social history becomes in its way intellectual history, even if the intellects are focused on something other than the theologians in the traditions might like to see.

Some years ago *Look* magazine interviewed leaders in various denominations. One was asked if his fellow believers considered that theirs was the only true faith. Yes, he said, but they did not believe that they were the only ones who held it. The editors of this series of studies and the contributors to it do not believe that the "Chicago School," whenever and whatever it was, is the only true approach to American religious history. And, if they did, they would not hold that Chicagoans alone held it. To do so would imply a strange solipsistic or narcissistic impulse that would be the death of collegiality in the historical field. They have welcomed the chance to be in a climate where their inquiries are given such encouragement, where they find a company of fellow scholars in the Divinity School, the History Department, and the Committee on the History of Culture, whence these studies first emerged, and elsewhere in a university that provides a congenial home for massed and massive concentration of a special sort on American religious history.

While the undersigned have been consistently involved, most often together, in all twenty-one books, we want to single out a third person mentioned in so many acknowledgment sections, historian Arthur Mann. He has been a partner in two or three dozen religious history dissertation projects through the years and has been an influential and decisive contributor to the results. We stand in his debt.

Jerald C. Brauer
Martin E. Marty

Editor's Preface

On my shelves is a book-length bibliography of the writings of Thomas Merton and of reviews and writings, many of them book-length, about the late monk and writer, or writer and monk. Merton is such an anomalous and creative figure that he has attracted enough scholars to have generated a Merton industry. On that landscape of scholarship, one is tempted to gasp an "Oh, no, not another!" when this work crosses the desk or is added to the shelves. But such an understandable if fashionable and world-weary sigh soon yields to more optimistic responses after one has given Peter Kountz a few minutes and a few pages to start making his peculiar case for Merton.

Many of the books on that shelf deal with Merton as a monk who wrote and others treat Merton as the writer who happened to be a monk; a few try to relate the two vocations, as Kountz does here. But this is a particularly nuanced study because of the way he locates the vocations in Merton's early experiences and because of the way he is informed about the history of culture, not only of monasticism or literary art. The first pages alert readers to what is to follow: Kountz reminds us that Merton was a promising and not inexperienced writer *before* he felt the call to the monastery. He might well have made his living as a professor or novelist. But he *did* become a monk, and that changed everything.

That a monk could be a writer is not all that remarkable. In what used to be called the Dark Ages, it was the monasteries that often kept the light of learning burning, and some of that learning took the form of original, imaginative writing, not mere chronicling and copying. That a writer could be deeply religious is also not all that remarkable: in Merton's own day, writers like Flannery O'Connor were utterly Catholic and impressively successful as authors.

What is important about Merton, as Kountz makes clear, is the way he never came to be serene about either half of his vocational choice. Had he been only a monk or only a writer there certainly would have been storm in his soul; he was not born for quietude or passivity. But by becoming a monk and a writer, and while attempting to fuse his two callings, Merton faced his inner storms in ways that reflect on the vocation of so many moderns who are not given the luxury to settle back and find a single direction in life.

Editor William Sloan says that we do not read autobiography while thinking, "Tell me about yourself!" We come with, "Tell me about myself, using you as mirror or exemplar." We do not read biography saying only, "Tell me about her or him!" but, "Tell me about myself by portraying a life so I can learn something of the human condition." (I don't suppose any of us put our responses into such formal terms, and Sloan does not either, but substantively they represent a transaction that is a normal response.)

"Tell us about Merton, Peter Kountz," comes to mean not only: inform us about an individual of great gifts and accomplishments; provide an account of a person who quickens curiosity for his achievements. Instead, as even a first, quick page-through suggests, we are likely to come to this to see how one representative modern, a man whose antennae were alert and whose talents were rich, lived with two pulls that are part of many lives. On the one hand, there is a call to come to terms with Being, Presence, the *Unum* or All, or whatever word we use to code the "Thou" or the "Other." On the other, each individual is busy asking how to spend a worthwhile life, how to find a vocation or a voice, a profession or career, which will matter, which will give expression to the need for communicating with or serving other people.

Most of us are given the luxury of living out that dual quest on small screens, and we do our agonizing in the loneliness of our chambers or our expressing in memos and diaries intended for no large public. The monk positions himself where all the dark nights of the soul threaten to overwhelm and the little graces stand a chance of dancing. The writer locates herself where, in the silences and stillnesses of soul and night, the words threaten to elude one but often come—and for Merton they really did come often—so that we can address others, publics, markets, readerships.

No one in our time brought together and permanently wrestled with the angels and demons of his nature and recorded it more clearly for others than did Merton. Peter Kountz looks beyond the mid-century scope of his own work, beyond 1951 when Merton seemed to have come to some temporary resolution of his discontents, to the rest of a career that suggested some peace. Yet he properly contends that we best understand the meaning of vocation by concentrating on the years of struggle. We who live quieter inner lives are likely to find elements in Merton that throw light on life in the studies of professors, the homes of homemakers, the studios of writers, and sanctuaries of people who pray or would pray, by seeing Merton, working on a high-risk scale, in action. Kountz captures Merton's intensity and recollects it with scholarly tranquility.

Martin E. Marty

Introduction

It has been only twenty-three years since Thomas Merton died in Bangkok (December 10, 1968), but Merton scholarship and general interest writing about Merton—with the accompanying conferences, newsletters, and audio- and videotapes—has become an industry. The numbers are striking. The major Merton bibliography, published in 1986,[1] lists the following: books, pamphlets, and tapes about Thomas Merton, 58 entries; theses, 97 entries; articles, essays, poems, and reviews, 985 entries; media presentations and sound recordings by and about Merton, 31 entries. Since 1976, the Thomas Merton Studies Center has published a quarterly review-newsletter called the *Merton Seasonal*. In 1987, the International Thomas Merton Society was founded by a group of Merton scholars. Merton conferences—including the annual meeting of the Merton Society—academic and nonacademic, have been held in North America, Europe, and Asia since the early 1970s. Two major biographies have been published, the second of which is the authorized biography commissioned by the Merton Legacy Trust, the executors of Merton's literary estate.

Merton's literary estate has grown as well. In his lifetime, Thomas Merton published some fifty books and booklets. Today there are well over twice as many available. In the 1986 bibliography, there are 1,263 entries in the section titled "Shorter Prose Writings (Essays, Reviews, Chapters in Books, Contributions to Periodicals, Journals, Newspapers, and Including Unpublished Essays)." Merton's "Literary Essays" have been collected and edited into a book of over 500 pages. His poetry has been collected in a volume of over 1,000 pages. There are over 700 tapes of Merton's conferences and talks, many available commercially. To date, the Merton Studies Center has files on over 1,800 of Merton's correspondents and there are three published volumes of Merton's letters, with two additional volumes in preparation. At Merton's death, the Legacy Trust placed some parts of the literary estate under a twenty-five-year restriction, which expires in 1993-94.

It is likely that additional, previously unpublished Merton materials will become available then. Amid this growing wealth of material by and about Merton, there is a set of writings that is particularly helpful in revealing the nature and directions of Merton's philosophical and spiritual explorations.

Merton on Merton

It has long been argued by Merton scholars and readers that virtually all of Thomas Merton's writings are, in some dimension, autobiographical. This is obvious, of course, with the journals. But it is less obvious in his poetry and his one published novel, *My Argument with the Gestapo* (1969). A macaronic work, the novel is in the form of a journal. With its double-talk and its crazy mixture of English, French, German, Italian, and Spanish, it is not easy to read. On the other hand, with slow and careful attention—and some awareness of Merton's premonastic life—the reader comes to understand how much Merton reveals, in this journal of the mysterious journalist-poet who returns to England to cover the war in Europe, about his (Merton's) life at Cambridge and about his search for the truths and meaning of his life. He wrote a preface in January of 1968, that gives some important context to the novel.

> The book was written in the Summer of 1941, when I was teaching English at Saint Bonaventure University. I wanted to enter the Trappists but had not yet managed to make up my mind about doing so. This novel is a kind of sardonic meditation on the world in which I then found myself; an attempt to define its predicament and my own place in it. That definition was necessarily personal. I do not claim to have gained full access to the whole myth of Europe and the West, only to my own myth. But as a child of two wars, my myth had to include that of Europe and of its falling apart; not to mention America with its built-in absurdities.[2]

One recognizes in the novel the foundation not only for Merton's very strong pacifist and antiwar principles but also his remarkable self-scrutiny and self-analysis. It is revealing, too, to realize that in 1941 Merton chose not to discuss himself directly, in a more traditional autobiography. Such was also the case with his long and perhaps equally difficult prose poem, *The Geography of Lograire*, published in 1969 as well. Here the autobiographical revelations are often hidden in the text. Even though it is more "poetic" than macaronic, it is still dependent on a kind of clever and playful mysteriousness that Merton used to veil the autobiographical elements. Like the novel, *The Geography of Lograire* is an account of a search for place, for location, for where Merton "fits." While it is more sophisticated and learned than the novel, it is still the same searching, probing Merton, twenty-seven years later. In form, neither the novel nor the poem is traditional, nor is either especially strong. But both are original, inventive, contemporary, and revealing. They are worth the difficult read.

While still the master of novices at Gethsemani, Merton began his formal life as a hermit, albeit part-time. His hermitage could be only part-time, so that he could continue his work with the novices. The journal from this period, written in 1964-65, was published in 1988 as *A Vow of Conversation*. It is a companion piece to the journal of the early sixties, *Conjectures of a Guilty Bystander*, which reveals clearly and powerfully how deeply Merton was committed to the life of a hermit and explains in some part his decision to give up the position as novice master and seek permission to live as a "full-time hermit," which permission he received in late July of 1965. This was one of those works that Merton had prepared before his death, so he knew very well what its publication would mean, especially the description of his significant conflict with the then abbot of Gethsemani, Dom James Fox. The preface to the work, written by Merton's devoted and wise literary agent of many years, Naomi Burton Stone, explains the nature of the journal and, specifically, the potential elements of controversy. Like the other published Merton journals, this is a text of beauty and of insight, another installment in his search for meaning and place.

Most Merton readers know about his fateful trip in the late fall of 1968, but it is not so widely known that Merton took many trips prior to that October 15 departure for India and Thailand. In fact, he traveled to California and New Mexico twice and also to Washington, D.C., Chicago, and Alaska. Two original notebooks/journals from these trips have been published: *Woods, Shore, Desert: A Notebook, May 1968* (1983) and *Thomas Merton in Alaska* (1989). As one might expect, Merton, ever vigilant for an opportunity for publication, carefully edited *Woods, Shore, Desert*. It is engaging and informative, but somewhat too deliberate and self-conscious. In contrast, *Thomas Merton in Alaska* was prepared by Robert Daggy, Merton scholar and director of the Merton Studies Center, and is an actual working notebook. To his credit, Daggy let the notebook be, and, as a result, it reveals Merton's depth and remarkable inventiveness. The text contains not only Merton's unedited journal entries, but also the transcripts of all of his conferences during his several-week stay, his photographs, an itinerary, his letters written to friends and colleagues, and exceptionally helpful and informative editorial notes. This is not to suggest that Robert Daggy did not edit. He did, but in a skillful and sensitive manner, taking the most provocative and authentic elements from the public and private journals. (We now know that Merton deliberately kept at least two "constant journals," one intended for publication and the other only for himself—yet another telling revelation!)

It was precisely this "blending," this time by three editors and a consulting editor, that brought the now-famous *Asian Journal of Thomas Merton*, published in 1973, to life. The Editors' Notes explain in detail Merton's habit of keeping an "A" journal (public), a "B" journal (private), and a "C" journal (a pocket notebook) and the difficulty of creating a coherent text from the three sources. To this end, the editors included a facsimile reproduction from the so-called holograph diaries. Deservedly, *The Asian Journal* generated a great deal of interest. It is an account of Merton's last and perhaps most important pilgrimage. It was the one Merton work that literally brought the reader to Merton's premature death in Bangkok on December 10, 1968. It also confirms the extraordinary power and commitment of Merton's authentic "journey" to the spiritualities of the East and of his belief that these principles and practices could actually enlarge and strengthen the faiths of the West. Many Merton commentators and critics have argued that Thomas Merton merely dabbled in the religions and customs of the East. *The Asian Journal* puts these criticisms to rest. Not only did Merton know what he was talking about, and not only was he erudite in the history of Eastern religions and religious life, but, as the text revealed, he was humble about what he knew and, thus, ever a student because of what he believed he did not yet know. While Merton did indeed dabble in any number of subjects, this was not one of them. *Zen and the Bird of Appetite* (1968) and *Mystics and Zen Masters* (1967)—in addition to *The Asian Journal*—clearly exhibit not only how much Merton knew but also what he could do with his knowledge on behalf of the Western tradition.

I come now to a brief discussion of the post-1968 Merton texts on the monastic tradition, specifically on monastic spirituality and its significance for the everyday world of nonmonastic pilgrims. There are three texts worth noting: *The Climate of Monastic Prayer* (1969), also published as *Contemplative Prayer*; *Contemplation in a World of Action* (1971); and *Love and Living* (1979). The last work appears at first glance not to be directly grounded in Merton's commitment to monastic tradition. But, in fact, the outward and very worldly character of the essays must be seen in the context of Merton's profound fidelity to his monastic vocation and in what he believed was its exceptional perspective on the madness of everyday life in twentieth-century America. It reveals how deeply Merton believed that the traditions of Western monasticism could, with careful study and constant prayer, provide a way for the ordinary spiritual citizen to make sense of his or her life.

The Climate of Monastic Prayer/Contemplative Prayer was one of those texts that Merton had ready for publication before his Asian trip. In fact, the editor of the Cistercian Press series in which the book was published received a note from Merton on December 9, the day before Merton's death. *Climate* was intended to be an essay on the nature and place of prayer. While it was certainly about monastic prayer in general, it was also very much about what the layperson could gain from the ways and means of this form of prayer. It is historical but not detached. Indeed, it is warm and engaging and, once again, it confirms the degree to which Merton had become a consummate man of prayer. It might even be thought of as a "Primer for Prayer," for very few twentieth-century religious writers knew or had experienced the elements of prayer as had Thomas Merton. This is an extraordinarily graceful book.

If there is one book that "explains" Thomas Merton in his own voice, it is, I believe, *Contemplation in a World of Action*. Once again, this collection of essays was prepared by Merton in the fall before his death. The ever-faithful Naomi Burton Stone, with help from Merton's secretary, Brother Patrick Hart, put the proper editorial touch to the final manuscript. This is truly the most compelling and convincing installment in Merton's multidimensional geography of faith. It is about monasticism in the modern world as well as about monastic renewal and Merton's learned and personal views about where monasticism ought to direct itself. These aspects alone would make *Contemplation* exceptional, but the book is much more. In explaining Merton, it reveals the integrity and strength of his monastic principles, the degree of comfort and conviction with which he lived his monastic vocation as well as the degree to which this vocation had become the core of his life, and it shows how engaged Merton had become with the world as a singular human being, a being who not only observes the world but also sensibly and sensitively participates in it. For Merton, to be fully human is to be "in God." No Merton book discloses this conviction more powerfully and beautifully than *Contemplation in a World of Action*.

Finally, I come to the Merton letters. To date, three volumes have been published. *The Hidden Ground of Love* contains letters on the subjects of "religious experience and social concerns." *The Road to Joy* includes letters on assorted topics to various friends. *The School of Charity* is devoted to "religious renewal and spiritual direction." Two additional volumes are scheduled for publication, one about writing and the life of letters and the other a more general collection. If there was any remaining doubt that he was a contemporary man of letters, the "word fellow" I discuss in this book, these letters should eradicate such uncertainties. Merton needed to write every day, and I suspect he was shrewd enough to realize that those to whom he wrote would keep his letters. He was also, by virtue of his monastic vocation, compelled to connect with people by mail. It must also be said, however, that Thomas Merton was one of those beings who was most comfortable psychologically with intimacy by mail. Such a method is safe and, as John Howard Griffin put it, allowed Merton to "keep the back door always open." Nevertheless, these letters exhibit the breadth of Merton's interests and knowledge, his generosity with the written word for even the first-time correspondent, the constancy of his authenticity of word and spirit, and the variety of those individuals with whom he corresponded. It is sometimes difficult to grasp how a contemplative monk could possibly maintain such a rich correspondence or that he would even want to. But this was the very nature of Merton as writer and monk. He lived to write as he lived to pray. The only way to begin to understand this apparent conflict is to read his letters, and, even then, it will not be entirely clear.

Writing about Merton

To comprehend a life as rich and complex as Thomas Merton's, to grasp the many chapters and meanings of the Merton story, it is necessary to study a variety of secondary sources. This book remains the only one devoted solely to the interplay between Merton the writer and Merton the monk during a specific and formative period in his life. It will be useful to the reader to know where it fits in the growing corpus of Merton interpretations. I will comment on several works written during the last twenty years, each of which provides a valuable perspective. By offering new information and new insights, these books increase our understanding of Merton. To my mind, however, there is still no one book—including this one—that fully captures the elusive Merton and the meaning of his life and work.

The first Merton biography, informal in conception and realization, was Edward Rice's *The Man in the Sycamore Tree: The Good Times and Hard Life of Thomas Merton* (1970). Rice and his publishers called the book "an entertainment" and that it was. Full of pictures and Merton drawings from his Columbia years and some fresh and not-so-delicate reminiscences, the book was the product of a strong friendship. Rice's "photograph" of Merton's life, especially his premonastic period, raises more questions than it either addresses or answers, but Rice initiated the ongoing biographical assessment of Merton.

Monica Furlong's *Merton: A Biography*, published ten years later, is well written and thoughtfully conceived. Based on the sensitive use of the then more limited number of published works by and about Merton, Furlong's perspective on the details of Merton's life continues to be appealing. Although it broke new ground in its day, this useful biography was soon superseded by the publication of Michael Mott's *The Seven Mountains of Thomas Merton* (1984).

Shortly after Merton's death, the Merton Legacy Trust asked John Howard Griffin to take on the task of writing the "official" Merton biography. In the last years of his life, Merton and Griffin had developed a rich friendship and it was believed that because he was an author, artist, kindred spirit, and Merton-like nonconformist, Griffin would produce an exceptional Merton study. Griffin went right to work and spent a great deal of preparatory time (years, in fact) "being Merton" and living in the Merton hermitage, studying manuscripts, making notes, and keeping journals. Years went by with, at least as far as the Merton Legacy Trust was concerned, very little to show for Griffin's efforts. In late 1977, after painful and awkward negotiations, Griffin was relieved of his duties as the Merton biographer and Michael Mott was appointed in early 1978.

Who Michael Mott was—a faculty member in the Department of English at Bowling Green State University in Ohio—was much less important than what it was believed he could do, that is, write a serious, heavily researched and highly detailed, and thus complete account of Thomas Merton's life. *The Seven Mountains of Thomas Merton* is certainly all of that and more. With almost 600 pages of text and just under 100 pages of notes, the work comes close to suffocating the reader with information. (To be fair to Mott, this almost obsessive attention to detail was likely what the Merton Legacy Trust wanted and what Mott could do best.) The book is not always easy to read. Many times, it is too guarded and careful. Yet, it is a remarkable piece of scholarship and Mott deserves great credit for his achievement. For what it is,

The Seven Mountains of Thomas Merton is a stunning achievement, but it is the work of one who chronicles and lists, not one who interprets and makes sense of his subject.

The smallest and shortest work on Merton is one of the most complete thus far: Henri Nouwen's, *Pray to Live: Thomas Merton Contemplative Critic* (1972). Quiet and certain, modest in scope and unencumbered in its prose, Nouwen's book uncovers what Mott misses—Merton's search for himself in God alone. Though certainly an introduction to Merton, *Pray to Live* is an inventive fusion of the biographical with the interpretive. It is engaging, insightful, and thought-provoking. In its simplicity, Nouwen's perspective gives the reader something to work with, which is exactly what Merton himself did.

Anne Carr's *A Search for Wisdom and Spirit: Thomas Merton's Theology of the Self* (1988), can be seen as an extension of the Nouwen text. Like Nouwen, Carr sees Merton as a learned and empathic "spiritual being" whose explorations take many directions: the quest for autonomy, with and in God; the pursuit of inner transformation in the monastic tradition; "self-forgetfulness"; commitment to existential dread *and* "final integration" with the world (a reference to one of Merton's essays in *Contemplation in a World of Action*); the recognition of ambiguity and paradox; the quest for the discovery of God and the discovery of self, and the recognition that one cannot be without the other; the living of the monastic life as a liberation, not as a confinement; the absence of fear of dread and the Dark Night, and the willingness to confront the dark self; and cosmic humility. Despite this careful interpretive approach, Carr shares Nouwen's lack of interest in Merton's artistic sensibility. This is unfortunate, for his artistic sensibility was perhaps Merton's greatest source of both difficulty and strength with respect to his monastic vocation.

There are, however, two texts that do address Merton's artistry and artistic sensibility. The first of these is George Woodcock's *Thomas Merton, Monk and Poet: A Critical Study* (1978). In a quasibiographical context, Woodcock examines what he believes are Merton's "trio of beings existing, different but without conflict": Merton the monk, Merton the contemplative hermit, and Merton the creative writer and artist. He identifies the major "contradictory impulses" in Merton and attempts to show that Merton was able to become "one" in his "trio of beings" and to turn the contradictory impulses into moments of insight and resolution. For Woodcock, because Merton embraced his marginality, especially the perhaps anachronistic conflict between artist and monk, between the man of God and the man of the pen, he is an essential reader and interpreter of contemporary life in the Western world.

David Cooper's *Thomas Merton's Art of Denial: The Evolution of a Radical Humanist* (1989) also examines Merton's artistic sensibility. Cooper's is perhaps the first critical analysis of Thomas Merton. Cooper argues that it was Merton's artistic sensibility that drew him out of the monastery to embrace the world and its "humanity," and that this was Merton's great achievement. He is committed to a vision of Merton's texts as primarily biographical; that is, that the powerful artistic sensibility behind the texts could only be revealed through them. Cooper's commitment to this approach produced the first intellectual biography of Merton, but the relationship between Merton the artist and Merton the monk goes unexamined.

It is as a monk, however, that Parker Palmer treats Merton in *The Active Life: A Spirituality of Work, Creativity, and Caring* (1990). Palmer is a sociologist whose life has been devoted to writing, speaking, and leading workshops and seminars about the very issues that were so important to Thomas Merton. His understanding of and intimacy with Thomas Merton—whom he discusses at great length in *The Active Life*—is remarkable and unique. He sees Merton as a gifted teacher, and he allows Merton to teach with eloquence and simplicity.

Despite the efforts of all of these authors, it is from John Howard Griffin, the man who never completed his biography of Merton, that we have the most compelling account yet produced. Griffin's three published works on Thomas Merton, *A Hidden Wholeness/The Visual World of Thomas Merton* (1970), *The Hermitage Journals: A Diary Kept While Working on the Biography of Thomas Merton* (1981), and *Follow the Ecstasy* (1983), are grounded in Merton's monasticism, in his monastic vocation. It is from that context, and that alone, that Merton worked. In fact, he worked outward from the monastic sensibility. Whereas other writers seem not to have grasped this, Griffin's three Merton works, taken as a whole, reveal that he did. What emerges is a rich appreciation of Merton's artistic gifts, his commitment to contemplation, and the complexity of his inner life. Of all the writing on Thomas Merton since his death John Howard Griffin's is, I believe unequivocally, the most penetrating, the most revealing, and the most significant.[3]

The Storyteller

How was Thomas Merton able to be a writer and a monk at the same time?[4] When he entered the Trappist monastery of Gethsemani in Kentucky in December of 1941, Merton brought with him his writing and the instincts of a writer. Had Merton not entered the Trappists, there is reason to believe, judging from his written and published work before 1941 and the substantial biographical information now available, that he would have pursued a career as a writer or would have taught writing and literature; perhaps he would have written *and* taught. But Merton did become a monk, just as he had become a writer, and when he entered Gethsemani he began the process of living with and reconciling two vocations.

The duality of monk and writer with the sensibilities of each was, in some form or another, a source of tension and conflict during the twenty-seven years of Merton's monastic life. But this duality was also a source of a remarkable creativity that powered Merton's wise view of the world. The two vocations affected each other, ultimately making the monk more worldly and the writer more contemplative (monastic). Merton became an expert, in fact, at playing the vocations against each other. He was, for example, able to use his writing sensibilities to help shape his monastic vocation just as he was able to use monastic history and spirituality as material for his writing.

At the end of his life, Merton had more or less successfully integrated these two vocations. I am interested in the *degree* of integration/reconciliation he had reached by the time he undertook his first major administrative post in the monastery (he was named master of scholastics in 1951). Therefore, this book concentrates on a limited time period—1915 (Merton's birth) to 1951, which comprises Merton's premonastic life and his first ten years as a monk. These thirty-six years are considered precisely in order to determine *why* and *how* Merton became a writer and *why* and *how* his writing influenced and guided his conversion to Catholicism and his entrance into Gethsemani. An equally important reason I study these years, especially the first ten monastic years, is my belief that to make sense of Thomas Merton one must know why and how he came to Gethsemani, for this single act explains the rest of his life.

These ten years were the most significant and most formative for Merton in the *process* of establishing and maintaining a productive and occasionally tranquil coexistence between writer and monk. I believe Merton learned to live with his dual vocation through his experiences with each, but only *after* he had admitted to himself that he was a writer and that there was nothing he could or should do about it. All this took ten years.

Because I address only the first thirty-six years of Merton's life and do so in rather strict chronological sequence, and because this book was written at a very early point in Merton scholarship (1975), it depends on a small number of published autobiographical texts. (It does not use either the unpublished "Perry Street Journal" (1939-40) or the unpublished Saint Bonaventure Journal (1940-41).) My reading of the early Merton texts is often very specific and there is a good bit of textual analysis and long quotations. Some explanation is in order.

As this work is intended to be a kind of "geography of faith" of a writer/monk, its emphasis is on the subject telling his own story—Merton on Merton. In the belief that Merton tells his own story best, even unknowingly, I work primarily with his texts. The confessional and autobiographical nature of all of Merton's writing creates an impression that Merton knows himself better than anyone else. I believe this. However, it is always risky to rely on the subject *accurately* to tell his own story. Thus, I have not given Merton full liberties; I frequently step back and comment on and evaluate a specific passage and/or text. Further, I am less interested in accuracy than in meaning. I therefore look carefully at the Merton texts, often studying them to an almost tedious degree. I am acting on my conviction that Merton's story of himself is valuable not only for *what* is said, but also *how* it is said. Merton's are remarkable truths that need to be discovered through his own account. Indeed, this is the wonder and the mystery of the autobiographical voice.

The first two chapters, then, are very much Merton on Merton, with my guidance and interpretation. The final chapter, with its speculation and more probing analysis, is meant to be a kind of "checking mechanism." Merton's voice is, therefore, the less dominant one as the text moves through a description of what I believe Merton had become: the active-contemplative writer/monk. It is this chapter that serves as the prism through which the remainder of Merton's life can be seen. In this sense, this book is a "Merton primer" and a guide to the early autobiographical writings. The outline of Merton's life is here; the later Merton studies enlarge and complete the details.

A secondary emphasis is the broader cultural context of Thomas Merton's life, an emphasis grounded in the understanding that he cannot be known and understood except through the culture in which he grew, lived, and worked. I am "using" Merton as a particular individual who is a writer and a monk and who, in the process of integrating these two vocations, can be viewed as a carrier and a representative of some of the unique Catholic intellectual and spiritual traditions developed principally in France and established, in an "American" way, by American Catholic intellectuals in the 1930s and 1940s. These traditions are examined in the context of twentieth-century America.

This book also asks what it means to be an artist—a writer—whose daemon is as worldly as it is spiritual. The assumption here is that Merton as the "spiritual artist" is a specific human type and that, as such, he is worthy of study.

Although the explicit intent of this book is to understand Thomas Merton as an artist and as a monk, and the connectedness of the two, its implicit intent is to see religion as story and, specifically, as Merton's story. My account of Merton's story is directed toward those readers who find themselves curious about the meaning and, indeed, the possibility, of an individual voyage of faith in a time and a culture such as ours. However successful my efforts, I urge the reader to remember that Merton the "word fellow" and monk is at least partially the storyteller. Such a companion and "other voice" is a wonderful gift for any author. Though certainly not an easy gift—just as Merton may not have been an easy man to live with—the gift of Merton's voice, as storyteller and teacher, has made my own writing that much easier and, I hope, that much more valuable.

Peter Kountz
Pittsburgh, August 1991

Thomas Merton
as Writer and Monk

ONE

The Evolution of a Writer: January 1915- September 1936

On June 28, 1914, Archduke Francis Ferdinand, the heir to the Austrian throne, and his wife, the Duchess of Hohenberg, were assassinated in Sarajevo, Bosnia, by an agent of a secret terrorist organization. This was the beginning of the Great War. On July 28, Austria-Hungary declared war on Serbia and by August 5, France, England, and Russia were at war with Austria-Hungary and Germany. When Thomas Merton was born on January 31, 1915, his native France was deep in the thralls of war. Already many of the 1,385,000 Frenchmen killed in this "most terrible . . . of all wars" were rotting in the trenches along the river Marne, not many hundreds of miles from Prades, the little village in the Pyrenees of southern France where Merton was born.

War had not yet ravaged the countryside of Prades and, in fact, on the Sunday of Merton's birth, the villagers, including the midwife and the doctor, were more concerned with the snow flurries, a rare occurrence that far south. War certainly was far from the minds of Ruth Jenkins Merton and her husband, Owen, Thomas Merton's parents.

Ruth Jenkins and Owen Merton had met in Paris. Ruth was an American and Owen, a New Zealander. Both had come to Paris to study art, the one from a family of Quaker pacifists and the other from a family of hearty New Zealanders (Owen Merton's father was a teacher of music). Both had struggled with their calling and when they married in 1914, though their artistic integrity was intact, they were virtually penniless. They spent their first few months of marriage living in a tent outside of Prades.

> My father came to the Pyrenees because of a dream of his own: more single, more concrete and more practical than Mother's numerous and haunting ideas of perfection. Father wanted to get some place where he could settle in France, and raise a family, and paint, and live on practically nothing. (p. 5)[1]

Ruth was a pacifist and a feminist. Hers was a love of poverty, an artistic perfection, and a sense of self.

> It seems to me . . . that Mother must have been a person full of insatiable dreams and of great ambition after perfection: perfection in art, in interior decoration, in dancing, in housekeeping, in raising children. (p. 5)

And while Ruth Jenkins Merton prepared almost fanatically for the birth of her first son by reading everything she could find on birth and on mother and child, Owen Merton made the furniture for their little house near the village church into which they had moved in late 1914.

> [My father's] vision of the world was sane, full of balance, full of veneration for structure, for the relation of masses and for all the circumstances that impress an individual identity on each created thing. (p. 3)

After Merton's birth, his mother continued her concern for his welfare, noting in her diaries everything he did and anything anybody had to say about him, and his father began to busy himself with landscape gardening so that the family would have sufficient money to live on. Both parents continued to paint and commune with the large number of friends who came from Paris or the village to visit and drink red wine. Tom, as he was officially named, did not particularly like these strangers and, in fact, only when he was in the village streets, riding in his pram, did he become friendly. Nor did he like toys or dolls.

Merton's parents were the center of his life in these early months. He observed the countryside as best a very young child could: the valley at Canigou, the monastery on the slopes of the mountain. He observed the villagers and his parents' friends. But most of all, in an almost precocious manner, he watched his mother and father.

> My father and mother were captives in [the] world, knowing they did not belong with it or in it, and yet unable to get away from it. They were in the world and not of it—not because they were saints, but in a different way—because they were artists. The integrity of an artist lifts a man above the level of the world without delivering him from it. . . . Neither of my parents

suffered from the little spooky prejudices that devour the people who know nothing but automobiles and movies and what's in the ice-box and what's in the papers and which neighbors are getting a divorce. (p. 3)

Though Merton was not exceptionally close to his parents, he did benefit greatly from his relationship with them and learned much from his observations of them in their day-to-day activity. In a real sense, they were his first ideological mentors.

> I inherited from my father his way of looking at things and some of his integrity and from my mother some of her dissatisfaction with the mess the world is in, and some of her versatility. (p. 4)

As the months progressed, so also the Great War. Owen Merton was more and more afflicted by it and began to feel that his creative energies were being destroyed by the conflict. He began to consider seriously joining the British forces but his wife's pacifism and the responsibility for his son kept him from it. This is not to imply that Ruth Merton did not suffer. In fact, her pacifism intensified her suffering, as did the concern of her parents in Long Island that the fighting might soon come to the little village of Prades.

So, early in 1916, Merton and his parents made the trip to America, departing from Bordeaux on an armed liner. In the back of everyone's mind, except little Tom's, was the anxiety about the U-boats and the chances for making it intact across the Atlantic.

America in 1916 was in the midst of an intellectual and material revolution, which some have called "the new enlightenment." And it was during the first years of the twentieth century that America was taken far beyond the nineteenth-century patterns of life. It was a revolution precipitated by the evolutionary theories of Charles Darwin and in which the scientific method gained superiority in almost every field of learning and artistic enterprise. Philosophical pragmatism, "the progressive education," more pure scientific research and the Flexner report in medicine, realism and naturalism in letters, the "little Renaissance" that began in Chicago and ended in Greenwich Village, the growing yet still timid welcome of truly American composers, the nonrepresentational (expressionism and abstraction) painters, the Ashcan school, Frank Lloyd Wright and *The Birth of a Nation*—this was part of the cultural upheaval that gripped the America to which the Merton family came.

This was the age of the "new radicalism," when cultural issues became indistinguishable and inseparable from political issues, when an American

3

intellectual occupied the White House and sent the country into the Great War "to make the world safe for democracy." This was the war that truly settled America into the twentieth century and took from its people the possibility of ever again recovering the "good old days."

Though it cannot be said that Owen, Ruth, and Tom Merton were unprepared for the America to which they came, they came from an almost contemplative environment, one that was ultimately certain to conflict with the newly emerged "American way." For the first few weeks they stayed with Ruth Merton's parents, Pop and Bonnemaman Jenkins, in Douglaston, just outside of New York City. Eventually, as if in conflict with the Jenkinses' American way, especially Pop's, they moved to their own little rented house in Flushing, still a country town, perhaps similar to Prades. During the next several months Owen painted and did a great deal of landscape gardening to support the family.

In November 1918, a week or so before the Armistice, Merton's brother, John Paul, was born.

> . . . a child with a much serener nature than mine, with not so many obscure drives and impulses. . . . Everyone was impressed by his constant and unruffled happiness. (p. 8)

While Owen Merton painted and gardened, Ruth Merton tended to her two sons. She tutored Tom and by the time he was five he could read, write, draw, and had a 500-word vocabulary in English and in French. Mrs. Merton had used a progressive method of education, which was ordered by mail from Baltimore, designed to suit the intelligent child. It was a method that reflected the principles of John Dewey.

> To imposition from above is opposed expression and cultivation of individuality; to external discipline is opposed free activity; to learning from texts and teachers, learning through experience; to acquisition of isolated skills and techniques by drill, is opposed acquisition of them as means of attaining ends which make direct vital appeal; to preparation for a more or less remote future is opposed making the most of the opportunities of present life; to static aims and materials is opposed acquaintance with a changing world.[2]

Surely a young boy of four or five is not going to respond as Dewey would have him respond under such a method and under the tutelage of his mother, but this early educational experience did have some formative effect, albeit unconscious. Merton's two favorite books that came from the "Baltimore method" were a geography text and a collection of stories called *Greek Heroes*. This text, perhaps more than any other dimension of his early educational experience, had a very strong influence on Merton.

> . . . it was from these [stories] that I unconsciously built up the vague fragments of a religion and a philosophy, which remained implicit in my acts, and which, in due time, were to assert themselves in a deep and all-embracing attachment to my own judgment and my own will and a constant turning away from subjection, toward the freedom of my ever-changing horizons. (p. 11)

What this early educational experience, and especially *Greek Heroes*, can be linked with is Merton's fierce independence.

> . . . this was intended as the fruit of my early training. Mother wanted me to be independent, and not to run with the herd. I was to be original, individual. I was to have a definite character and ideals of my own. I was not to be an article thrown together, on the common bourgeois pattern, on everybody else's assembly line. (p. 11)

Sometime in early 1921, Ruth Merton entered the hospital with stomach cancer. Owen Merton went to work as a church organist and a piano player in a local theater to raise the extra money for his wife's treatment. Often, Tom accompanied his father to the Episcopal Church in Douglaston when he played for the Sunday service. These occasions were not without reflection.

> One came out of the church with a kind of comfortable and satisfied feeling that something had been done that needed to be done, and that was all I knew about it. . . . I see that it was very good that I should have got at least that much of religion in my childhood. (p. 13)

Apparently Mrs. Merton had been ill for some time but had concealed this from the family, perhaps, as Merton suggests in his autobiography, to keep the household free from morbidity and the awareness of pending death. After his mother entered the hospital, Merton went to stay with his grandparents where he continued to cultivate independence.

> There I was allowed to do more or less as I pleased, there was plenty of food, and we had two dogs and several cats to play with. (p. 14)

Even then he was beginning to exhibit a kind of detachment, no doubt occasioned not only by his mother's illness but also by her unconscious stress during Merton's very early years on cold and detached objectivity.

Merton says that during his stay in Douglaston he did not miss his mother a great deal and was not particularly upset when he was not allowed to visit her in the hospital. Eventually, Ruth Merton sent her young son a note telling him that she was going to die and that he would never see her again.

> . . . a tremendous weight of sadness and depression settled on me. It was not the grief of a child, with pangs of sorrow and many tears. It had something of the heavy perplexity and gloom and adult grief, and was therefore all the more of a burden because it was, to that extent, unnatural. (p. 14)

Later that year Ruth Merton died and was cremated, neither of which events young Tom was allowed to be a part of, a reflection certainly on his mother's belief that death was ugliness and without meaning and that little children should not be burdened with it.

It is very difficult to determine to what extent Ruth Merton's premature death—and the way she herself dealt with its certainty—affected her son. I do not believe that it had a profound immediate effect but rather a gradual, permeating influence on the entire rest of his life. Ruth Merton's death was for young Tom a complete event, over and done with, and the cremation was simply a reinforcement of this notion that when life is finished, the body, everything, must be finished, definitely and forever.

The death of his wife left Owen Merton with complete freedom to paint, to travel, and to study to the fullest possible degree. Tom Merton, now six-going-on-seven, was old enough to accompany his father. Thus, in early spring 1922, after attending the public school in Douglaston, where he had already advanced to the second grade, Merton and his father went to Provincetown, Massachusetts, staying through the summer; then, after a few weeks in Douglaston, they traveled to Bermuda. Merton was in and out of the local school in Somerset, Bermuda, while his father painted. In a short time Owen Merton had a successful New York exhibition, which provided enough money to travel to France for more study and painting.

> It is almost impossible to make much sense out of the continual rearrangement of our lives and our plans from month to month in my childhood. Yet every new development came to me as a reasonable and worthy change. (p. 18)

This early pattern of travel—to be intensified in later years—is, it seems to me, a partial explanation for Merton's profound sense of rootlessness prior to his entrance into the monastery at Gethsemani. His schooling, especially in France and England, is additional explanation. It is important, too, to understand that Merton absorbed a great deal from every place he ever spent any length of time. For instance, consider his discussion of the few months in Provincetown:

> That summer was full of low sand dunes, and coarse grasses as sharp as wires, growing from the white sand. And the wind blew across the sand. And I saw the breakers of the grey sea come marching in towards the land, and I looked out at the ocean. Geography had begun to become a reality.
> The whole town of Provincetown smelled of dead fish, and there were countless fishing boats, of all sizes, tied up along the wharves; and you could run all day on the decks of the schooners, and no one would prevent you or chase you away. I began to know the smell of ropes and of pitch and of the salt, white wood of decks, and the curious smell of seaweed, under the docks. (p. 17)

Merton's was an insatiable curiosity and the constant travel intensified the insatiability.

In late spring 1923, Owen Merton sailed for France while Tom and his brother remained behind with their grandparents in Douglaston. It is worth noting that Douglaston was a middle-class community "of spacious but not pretentious houses, each with an individual character of its own, girded about with hedge-lined and tree-shaded walks."[3] Merton stayed with his brother and grandparents for two years, until August 1925, when he sailed for France with his father. There were many things happening in the America of the early 1920s and Tom Merton, even at the age of eight, was an impressionable witness to much of the activity.

In August 1923, President Harding died, while all around him officials were beginning to uncover his astonishing dishonesty. He was succeeded by his vice president, Calvin Coolidge, a man of integrity and extreme conservatism. Coolidge won the election of 1924, which perhaps marked "the golden interlude of prosperity" that the mid-1920s represented. America's beloved middle class embraced Coolidge's "The business of America is business" with utter seriousness. Nowhere was this clearer than in the pages of the phenomenally successful *Reader's Digest* or in Bruce Barton's *The Man Nobody Knows*.

Merton's grandfather worked for Grosset and Dunlap, publishers specializing in cheap popular novels and adventure stories for children. Grosset and

Dunlap was, like so many other American businesses of the time, instantly prosperous. Their scheme of printing the books of popular movies illustrated with stills from the films and sold in connection with publicity for the specific picture, largely the idea of Grandfather Jenkins, was a huge success and remained so throughout the 1920s.

By the early twenties, the evolution of the " 'ad-mass' or the mass-promotion-consumption society"[4] had become clear and signaled the beginning of the end for America's rural mentality and creed. There were new urban pursuits as the rise of the city continued.

On the streets appeared women with lipstick, shorter skirts and hair, and silk stockings. These women were talking more openly about sex and visiting the many clubs and roadhouses where they heard jazz and danced and who, no doubt, had read *This Side of Paradise* and *Winesburg, Ohio*.

At his grandparents' home, Merton listened to the radio, had his clothes washed in an electric washing machine, and his food kept fresh in an electric refrigerator. When he went with them on little trips out of the city he rode in their automobile. And for the whole family, the movies were a religion. The high priest and priestess were, of course, Douglas Fairbanks and Mary Pickford, duly worshipped by Merton's grandparents.

> [They] seemed to sum up every possible human ideal: in them was all perfection of beauty and wit, majesty, grace and decorum, bravery and love, gaiety and tenderness, all virtues and every admirable moral sentiment, truth, justice, honor, piety, loyalty, zeal, trust, citizenship, valor and, above all, marital fidelity. Everything that good, plain, trusting middle-class optimism could devise was gathered up into one big holocaust of praise, by my innocent and tender-hearted grandparents, and laid at the feet of Doug and Mary. (p. 22)

Approximately forty million movie tickets were being sold weekly by 1922 to films that "played a significant part in forming the mass consumer society, contributing immeasurably to the so-called revolutions in the expectations of the common man." George Mowry enlarges this notion.

> Because the majority of the movie audience had no desire to be reminded of their shabby homes and their dreary, monotonous work, most pictures dealt with carefree individuals engaged in exciting adventures and surrounded by frivolous luxuries. . . . The movie credo was one of sustained consumption, not production. And continually reiterating this theme, the industry became midwife to the birth of the leisure-seeking, pleasure-demanding, materialistic consumer society of modern America.[5]

All this is not intended to prove that Merton and his family were fast becoming part of the pleasure-demanding, materialistic consumer society of America. It is intended rather to give some indication that these early years of Merton's life in America were very much a part of the mainstream, through and because of Grandfather and Grandmother Jenkins. Perhaps it is more accurate to call these early years, years of exploration and exposure, years in which, like other children, Merton became increasingly aware of what was available to him and how to use it. But what I believe to be the most important aspect of these years with his grandparents is the intensification of Merton's curiosity, principally because his grandparents were in a position to make more (material and cultural) dimensions of life available to him. Grandfather and Grandmother Jenkins, influenced by the radio and the movies to pursue more leisure time, passed this pursuit to their young grandson who, in turn, used it to satisfy his curiosity.

Importantly too, Merton's grandparents seemed to have accepted the technological advances and the financial and sales developments of the new mass culture as well as the social results and implications of this new age. Merton's grandfather, at least as Merton describes him in the autobiography, strikes one as having a little Babbitt in him. He was apolitical, except when it came to Tammany Hall, which he abhorred; he was openly anti-Semitic and anti-Catholic, a member of a Masonic organization (the Knights Templar), a nominal, money-giving Protestant, and to a certain degree, anti-reform and antiprogressive and certainly probusiness. It is significant, too, that Merton's grandparents and younger brother vacationed in California and Hollywood in the summer of 1923 while Merton remained in Douglaston. That year was the peak year in the phenomenal decade of growth for Los Angeles County (1920-1930) when it absorbed 1,270,000 new residents, not a small number of whom came from the Middle West and found paradise and fulfillment with Sister Aimée and her Shared Happiness of Kindred Souls in the Angelus Temple. Merton's grandfather was, from all evidence, not among Sister Aimée Semple McPherson's converts, but it is possible that he was intrigued with her movement as he was with all the newness and excitement of America in these years. Merton has called his grandfather a "live-wire." In many ways, then, the Douglaston household was to provide Merton with a forum for his imagination, his impulses, and his actions, whatever they might be.

The period from the spring of 1923 to August 1925 did, I believe, hold some significance for Merton, the future writer, for it gave him further opportunity to strengthen his freedom of intelligence, what John Dewey called that "freedom of observation and of judgment exercised in behalf of purposes that are intrinsically worthwhile."[6] As artists, Merton's parents, especially his mother, allowed him a kind of freedom of mind and spirit that, rather than get him into all kinds of childhood difficulty, nurtured and sustained his gift of curiosity and interest. The circumstances of Merton's life up to 1923—including the death of his mother—served as a foundation, a basis for the growth and development of his instincts as a writer, if for no other reason than that they spared Merton what Erik Erikson has called the "mutilation of the spirit." Above all, Merton was allowed to be himself, to the degree that a young boy in his first years of life can be himself. Admittedly, there are some negative aspects of the way Merton was raised. He spent a great deal of time alone both as a result of the surrounding circumstances and personal choice. His early time alone was spent with his imaginary friends, like Jack and his dog Doolittle. Later he would enter the world of *Greek Heroes*, his favorite geography book, and the many voyages he took in the vessels he drew with his pencil and pen. Ultimately, he would sustain his aloneness in his writing.

Merton had friends and his activities were often those of a child his age; certainly, there was a kind of normalcy. But there was, too, that aloneness and independence, that originality and individuality, his mother had wanted for him. These were the basic elements of his now slowly forming vocation as a writer. The vocation would take a clearer and more definite shape in France and England, to which Merton was to journey with his father, to stay for almost ten years.

Owen Merton had gone abroad just before the summer of 1923. He debarked in France but traveled widely, living and working in southern France and then in Africa and Algeria. In late 1924, the family in Douglaston received a letter from friends of Owen Merton saying that he was seriously ill and was not expected to live. Tom Merton was "profoundly affected, filled with sorrow and with fear" (p. 27). He wondered in disbelief whether he would ever see his father again.

Though Merton does not discuss this incident in much detail in his autobiography, particularly in terms of his feelings, it is still possible to make some inferences. Merton's father was in a coma for several days and what news came to the Long Island household was not hopeful. Thus, each day brought Merton to a deeper engagement with himself, and that much closer to the writer's sensibility. But Owen Merton recovered from his unknown illness and began to paint again. He eventually went to London, where in early 1925 he had one of his most successful exhibits.

When he returned to New York City in the early summer of 1925, Owen Merton returned an artist of significance. As Merton writes of his father, he was "a very different person—more different than I realized—from the man who had taken me to Bermuda two years before" (p. 23). But Owen Merton came bearing news that initially troubled his young son. At the end of the summer, the boys and their father were going to sail to France to live. It was extremely difficult for Merton to reconcile himself to such a move.

> For by now, having become more or less acclimatized in Douglaston, after the unusual experience of remaining some two years in the same place, I was glad to be there, and liked my friends, and liked to go swimming in the bay. I had been given a small camera with which I took pictures, which my uncle caused to be developed for me at the Pennsylvania Drug Store, in the city. I possessed a baseball bat with the word "Spalding" burnt on it in large letters. I thought maybe I would like to become a Boy Scout. (p. 28)

So the normalcy that was attained those two years in Douglaston became something of Merton's past. Again, there is the devastation of being removed, of having something important and personally valuable yanked away. It was this kind of experience, this deep sense of loss, that would take Merton deeper into himself and, within a year, would have him writing novels.

Somehow, Thomas Merton came to see the positive side of returning to the land of his birth, and on August 25, 1925, he and his father sailed for France. The return to France had great meaning for Merton.

> returning to the land of my birth, I was also returning to the fountain of the intellectual and spiritual life of the world to which I belonged." (p. 30)

France would leave its mark on Merton. He was grateful that he had come back to France at this time, before it became too late. He was still much too young to understand what France, its people, and its culture gave him, but in hindsight he could both comprehend and accept the wonderful gifts.

After a long journey, Merton and his father temporarily settled in Montauban, a small town in the central part of southern France. Merton reflects on why they were there.

> It was not only that Father wanted to continue painting in the south of France. He had come back to us that year with more than a beard. Whether it was his sickness or what, I do not know, but something had made him certain that he could not leave the training and care of his sons to other people, and that he

11

> had a responsibility to make some kind of a home, somewhere, where he could at the same time carry on his work and have us living with him, growing up under his supervision. And what is more, he had become definitely aware of certain religious obligations for us as well as for himself. (p. 33)

Additionally, Merton's father had heard of the excellent reputation of the Institute Jean Calvin in Montauban. But after a visit he decided that he would not send young Merton there. Owen Merton's decision may have had something to do with the French Protestantism of the school, for he had grown interested in Catholicism and had become concerned that his sons receive solid religious training. But Owen Merton, unlike his eldest son, was never to embrace Catholicism.

Owen Merton quickly decided on the first day, in fact, that Montauban was not the place to settle. After some investigation, he and his son traveled by train to a little village northeast of Montauban, St. Antonin. There, they rented an apartment, and before long, Owen Merton had purchased land and made plans to build a house on it.

Merton writes in his autobiography that the center of St. Antonin was the village church. His remarks are of special significance for an understanding of Merton the writer.

> Here, everywhere I went, I was forced by the disposition of everything around me, to be always at least virtually conscious of the church. . . . You are forced, in spite of yourself, to be at least a virtual contemplative. (p. 37)

I believe that it was in France that Merton began to contemplate, not so much in the sense of coming to know and love God as He is, but more in Jacob Burckhardt's sense of *Anschauung*, "graphic perception." Karl Weintraub in his *Visions of Culture* clarifies this notion and allows one to see in what sense it might be applicable to young Merton.

> [Burckhardt's] contemplation was synonymous with the active viewing of the world (if one can thus circumscribe the untranslatable but, for Burckhardt, crucial term ANSCHAUUNG). Through this act of viewing, man gains access to the beauty and value of existence. . . . ANSCHAUUNG leads man to the perceptible wealth of things and of men in their context and fullness of life.[7]

Some would contend that Merton was far too young to develop such perception. On the contrary, Merton was almost eleven years old by now and the peculiar circumstances of his life to this point had brought him to a special way of looking at things around him. His insight was uncommon for one his age; he was forced to develop it as a result of his aloneness. Eventually, the contemplation, the "graphic perception," would develop into a solitude of the heart, a much quieter, less frantic state of being. In another place in his discussion of Burckhardt, Weintraub proffers what could very well be a description of Merton and his view of life in 1925, in St. Antonin. "He saw that man's greatest accomplishment was the art of forging a harmonious style of life out of life's disharmonies; he found his own style. By patiently training his eyes and his judgment, he learned to discern the comforting realities of human existence."[8] Merton's "own style" would evolve into a dialogue with himself through the written word.

Before Merton began school in the fall of 1925, he and his father spent a great deal of time traveling all over the countryside, looking for subjects to paint. They visited many villages and saw the ruins of chapels and monasteries. It was a countryside steeped in antiquity, and with the aid of his father's experience and his own sensibilities, Merton was able to gather in some of the richness for himself. As the friend and companion of his father, Merton was conditioned to see things as an adult and thus the child Merton was pushed more into the background.

Merton notes that when he began to attend the local elementary school, it was embarrassing for him because he had to sit with the very smallest and youngest children and to try to learn the language as he went along. This experience was perhaps made more difficult by the fact that his friends were those of his father (pp. 39-43). In a very real sense, Merton was living the life of an eleven-year-old adult.

By the summer of 1926, Merton spoke French well and was deep into reading about France and its culture. He and his father had bought a three-volume set of books with money sent by his grandfather, entitled *Le Pays de France*. Merton was captivated by the books:

> I shall never forget the fascination with which I studied it, and filled my mind with those cathedrals and ancient abbeys and those castles and towns and monuments of the culture that had so captivated my heart. (p. 43)

The summer of 1926 brought also the dreaded visit of Merton's grandparents and his young brother. Merton's father knew the implications of the visit and was much distressed, for it meant the disruption of the life in St. Antonin. Though it appears to have been a miserable experience,[9] it did serve to show Merton, especially through the person of his grandfather, just what he had come from and what he had come to. Since his grandfather wanted "to keep on the move" with his mountain of luggage, Merton did a great deal of traveling, often to new places. He took in a great deal of what he saw around him; there did not seem to be much he missed. One could see the experience of his relatives' visit and the resultant travels as opportunity for Merton to sharpen his maturing writer's eye, to endorse his "graphic perception."

Merton writes in his autobiography that he fell in love in the fall of 1920 with a girl named Henriette. He does not make much of it, but it is interesting that he talks of love, for how can a young boy of eleven and a half know love? But there was the adult side of Merton and in this case there may very well have been a kind of love involved. After his father's, "What's this I hear about you chasing girls at your age?" Merton settled down to what he called a "serious life."

From late summer 1926 until the first month or two of 1927, Morton worked on four or five novels, all of them adventure stories/mysteries, some profusely illustrated. The thrust of the novel-writing experience came in the middle of Merton's first year at the lycée Ingres in Montauban, which he began in late September 1926.

Initially, the lycée was a dreadful ordeal.

> Although by this time I knew French quite well, the first day in the big, gravelled yard, when I was surrounded by those fierce, cat-like little faces, dark and morose, and looked into those score of pairs of glittering and hostile eyes, I forgot every word, and could hardly answer the furious questions that were put to me. And my stupidity only irritated them all the more. They began to kick me, and to pull and twist my ears, and push me around, and shout various kinds of insults. (p. 49)

Having been kicked around "without mercy" for the first few days, Merton began to be accepted, and as he notes, "everybody . . . became quite friendly and pleasant." Nevertheless, it was a terrible experience for Merton, particularly during the long nights when he couldn't sleep and he came to know what he has called "the pangs of desolation and emptiness and abandonment."

The students of the lycée were divided into two segregated groups. Merton was among "les petits," those in the fourth class and below. Merton had some strongly negative reactions to the students.

When they were all together there seemed to be some diabolical spirit of cruelty and viciousness and obscenity and blasphemy and envy and hatred that banded them together against all goodness and against one another in mockery and fierce cruelty and in vociferous, uninhibited filthiness. (p. 50)

In *My Argument with the Gestapo*, Merton enlarged this negative view to include those aspects of the lycée experience that frightened him, that made him uncertain, and made him plead with his father to take him out of the school. But these were fears that went beyond the gates of the school, fears that bespoke Merton's uncertainty with French culture and his life with his father in southern France, though at the lycée he was very much alone. And they were the fears of a young boy trying to grow up.

> He might ask me what I was afraid of. I am afraid of the cold walls of the corridors in the Lycée. I am afraid of the gravel in the playgrounds, and of the sickly smell of the blossoming acacias in the spring. I am afraid of getting water on my knee, because when you have water on the knee they lance your knee. I am afraid of the sound of the harsh church bells, ringing in the distant town, outside the walls. I am afraid of the rain that rained all winter so that the river flooded the suburbs, and raced under the bridges, filling up their arches, carrying away trees and dead cattle.
>
> He will ask me why I fear the dark room where they teach mathematics. He will ask me why I didn't believe the fierce boys when they told me that the guillotine where the murderers were beheaded was always set up behind the Lycée, and that the next morning, about the time we awoke at dawn, one might be able to hear the knife fall with a clang, behind the walls. He will ask me why I fear the little Protestant chapel built like an empty blast furnace in one of the courts—a forge where all the fires have gone out.[10]

For Merton, the experience of living with the students at the Lycée was new. In hindsight, he saw that the "animality, and toughness and insensitivity and lack of conscience" (p. 51) that existed in his classmates existed also, to some degree, in himself. But he admitted at the same time that his French classmates "seemed to be so much tougher and more cynical and more precocious than anyone else" (p. 51) he had ever seen. And when he finally did adjust to the lycée and its atmosphere, he befriended the precocious and more intelligent children in the lower three levels.

These were the ambitious students, those with "ideals," as Merton notes, and these were the students with whom Merton wrote his novels. The resident writers of the lycée Ingres! The students walked around the grounds discussing the plots and, to a certain extent, evaluating one another's novels.

But what does it mean for a young boy of twelve to write a novel? How did the young boy come to be an artist-writer? Why did he choose writing instead of another form? What did it mean to young Merton to write at all? And, too, are we not talking about a particular artistic sensibility?

Thomas Merton was born of two artist-intellectuals, which itself had wide ramifications: "I knew something of the life of an artist and intellectual because my father was an artist and I was brought up, for better or for worse, as an intellectual."[11] When we use the terms *artist* and *intellectual* we are speaking, perhaps, of the same peculiar sensibility, that "universal human desire for self-expression . . . channelled by the will and by some clear and higher intention,"[12] and that state of thorough aliveness, thorough awareness, and complete interest. Out of this comes what can be called the artistic sensibility, a particular worldview that shapes all that the artist does and thinks. This worldview is "both constructive and critical, technical and philosophic, and in the last capacity, persistently attacks what it thinks is wrong, disorderly, and ugly; and persistently, however subtly or evasively, attempts to show what is ordered, right and comely."[13] The artist, then, is one who lives with the knowledge of what could be and with a sadness and anger at what actually is. The artist is a man of the heart for whom even the worldview becomes, at its very core, *l'affaire d'amour*. From the heart, the artist writes or paints or composes in order to create the world of the heart. The artist acting out of faith and a consuming desire for the good, creates the proverbial "substance of things hoped for; the evidence of things not seen."[14]

And so we are talking about a particular way of life and a particular way of looking at life, a weltanschauung: that of the artist/intellectual. But there is more involved here, for we are talking also of fantasy and the implementation of the imagination.

Paul Tillich speaks of his withdrawal, between the ages of fourteen and seventeen, into a life of fantasy, "imaginary worlds" that "seemed to be truer than the world outside." He describes how his imagination found delight in play—in sports, entertainment, games, and "in the playful emotion that accompanies freedom." Eventually, Tillich was brought to Art, "the highest form of play and the genuinely creative realm of the imagination."[15]

Though Tillich was not a creator or inventor of art but rather an appreciator and perhaps participant, his experience and insight are useful in considering Merton as a writer and as a novelist at the age of twelve. Merton's quest for his aloneness would bring him to a kind of fantasy world. That is, his weltanschauung of the artist/intellectual, even as a boy, would bring him to his novels as play, as imagination, and as adventure.

Stephen Spender has written of the "young writer" and his dependence on the "magic circle" around him, analogous to Merton and his fellow novel-writing students.

> . . . the young writer is someone with a mysterious sense of his own vocation, and a vision of reality which he wishes to communicate: to show, too, that in his youth he can benefit by the magic circle of those who are touched to sympathy by him, perhaps more for what he is than for what he does. His friends believe in HIM and they take his work on trust. Later on they become interested in other things—they cannot share his vocation—and he learns to be alone. But his youth has been watered by their sympathy.[16]

Merton's lycée novel-writing experience is a significant event. It was both the source of many future writing projects as it strengthened Merton's attachment to the written word and was a culminating experience that the circumstances of Merton's life, thus far, had brought him to. In this context one is reminded of Thomas Wolfe's reflections on what he calls "the foremost quality of the artist, . . . the ability to get out of his own life the power to live and work by, to derive from his own experience—as a fruit of all his seeing, feeling, living, joy and bitter anguish—the palpable and living substance of his art."[17] Wolfe was really speaking of writers—novelists—and he says that without the "foremost quality" the writer is lost. At this early age, much like Tillich, Merton had entered a kind of fantasy world through his aloneness and this very world would become the principal material for his youthful novels. As he grew in wisdom and experience, Merton would engage himself more directly with the world at large, still, however, using his own experience as the "palpable and living substance of his art." *My Argument with the Gestapo* remains the best example of this.

Merton appears to have needed to write. It was the kind of opening up of himself to himself that was most satisfying. He could sustain both his fantasy world and his "graphic perception," his contemplation of the world around him through his writing and, in the process, satisfy his need for aloneness. In a word, Merton could live his life through his writing at the same time that the act of writing made his life that much richer.

Merton's novels at this time reflect his reading materials: Jules Verne, Pierre Loti, Charles Kingsley, and Rudyard Kipling, particularly a French translation of *The Light That Failed*. These were novels of adventure and intrigue and it is hard not to compare them to the life of Merton's father, for in the winter of 1926 he was off again, this time to Murat in the old Catholic province of Auvergne.

Owen Merton boarded with an Auvergne family, the Privats, while his son stayed at the lycée (though he joined his father in Murat for the Christmas holidays). The winter was an especially long one for Merton, as he spent several weeks in the infirmary with assorted ills. Because his father was so impressed with and drawn to the Privats, he brought his son to Murat to spend several summer weeks, resting and recovering his strength.

> Those were weeks I shall never forget, and the more I think of them, the more I realize that I must certainly owe the Privats far more than butter and milk and good nourishing food for my body. I am indebted to them for much more than the kindness and care they showed me, the goodness and the delicate solicitude with which they treated me as their own child, yet without any assertive or natural familiarity. As a child, and since then too, I have always tended to resist any kind of possessive affection on the part of any other human being—there has always been this profound instinct to keep clear, to keep free. And only with truly supernatural people have I ever felt really at my ease, really at peace.
>
> That is why I was glad of the love the Privats showed me, and was ready to love them in return. It did not burn you, it did not hold you, it did not try to imprison you in demonstrations, or trap your feet in the snares of its interest. (p. 57)

Merton's words reveal his continuing quest for aloneness, perhaps even a kind of solitude. As a writer, he could communicate to and with himself as well as to and with the world at large while still avoiding personal commitments.

Merton received Protestant instructions at the lycée but his "only valuable religious and moral training" came from his father. And yet, as he told the Privats during his stay that summer of 1927, "every man should go according to his own conscience, and settle things according to his own private way of looking at things" (p. 58). Merton's private way of looking at things was, at this point in his life, not really any way at all. To maintain the freedom that he came to believe was essential to his existence, Merton kept to himself. His was the detached observation of the writer, in the world but not of it; the classic position of the writer "outside of society," a greater sense of which Merton may have absorbed from the Victorian novelists he was reading at the time.

In the fall of 1927, Merton returned to the lycée while his father went to Paris to be best man at the wedding of a friend from New Zealand. What is significant is not the wedding itself, but that Owen Merton returned to St. Antonin with the mother of his friend's bride. Young Merton called her "an impressive kind of person," but he registered some doubts.

> At first, I was secretly resentful of the great influence she at once began to exercise over our lives, and thought she was bossing our affairs too much, but even I was able to realize that her views and advice and guidance were very valuable things. But so strong was her influence that I think it was due to her more than anyone else that we gave up the idea of living permanently in St. Antonin. (p. 59)

Merton does not provide much detail about Mrs. Stratton, but since his father was again traveling a great deal, it may have been that she came to St. Antonin to tend to him. On the other hand, since he was at the lycée most of the time, it is possible that Mrs. Stratton traveled with his father to Marseilles and Cette in those early months of 1928. One wonders what effect, if any, the woman's companionship with Owen Merton had on the young boy of thirteen. Did he reflect on it? Did he resent it more than he mentions? Merton was at the lycée, "becoming more and more hard-boiled in [his] precocity, and getting accustomed to the idea of growing up as a Frenchman," so he may not have seen much of the woman.

In the spring of 1928, Owen Merton went to London for another exhibition of his paintings. When he returned in May he told his son to pack his bags, for they were moving to England, even though the house in St. Antonin was almost finished and ready for occupation. Owen Merton's decision to move to England seems impulsive and may have been influenced by Mrs. Stratton. In any case, Merton was overjoyed with his father's decision.

> I looked around me like a man who has had chains struck from his hands. How the light sang on the brick walls of the prison whose gates had just burst open before me, sprung by some invisible and beneficent power: my escape from the Lycée was, I believe, providential. (p. 60)

When Merton and his father arrived in London, they went to stay with Aunt Maud and Uncle Ben, in the house that Merton called "a fortress of nineteenth-century security." They lived in Ealing, just west of London. Merton seemed more drawn to Aunt Maud. Since it had been decided that Merton would attend Ripley Court (in Surrey), a school run by Aunt Maud's sister-in-law, a Mrs. Pearce, he would "be more and more under her [Aunt Maud's] wing."

One day, shortly after Merton had arrived, he and Aunt Maud went into London to shop for school clothes. On the return trip to Ealing, on the open bus, Aunt Maud asked Merton if he had thought at all about his future. Merton replied that he had given the matter some thought. He mentions, however, that he hesitated telling his aunt he wanted to be a novelist. He introduced the subject by asking if she thought writing would be a good profession for anyone. She responded affirmatively and, as if to let him know that she knew his secret, asked him what kind of writing he would like to do. He replied that he would like to write stories. In her gentle way, Aunt Maud cautioned Merton to remember that novelists often have a hard time making money and that perhaps he might consider some other occupation "as a means of making a living," and write in his free time. Merton responded that he could become a journalist and write for newspapers.[18] Aunt Maud replied that Merton might develop a knowledge of languages, which would enable him to become a foreign correspondent. And on and on went the conversation, all the way to Ealing.

Aunt Maud's exploration into Merton's plans may have had something to do with her uncertainty about Owen Merton, the nomad, the impractical and unstable artist. This uncertainty was affirmed somewhat by the comments of Mrs. Pearce, the headmistress of Ripley Court, whom Merton and Aunt Maud stopped to see on their way home from the London shopping trip. When Aunt Maud mentioned in a motherly way that she and young Tom had been discussing his future, Mrs. Pearce, with a certain amount of acidity, replied that she hoped young Tom would not be a dilettante like his father. When Aunt Maud said that Tom might become a journalist, Mrs. Pearce was quick to reply. Her words show clearly what kind of atmosphere Merton was now to be schooled in. He would have some new dimensions to add to his writer's weltanschauung.

> "Nonsense, . . . let him go into business and make a decent living for himself. There's no use his wasting his time deceiving himself. He might as well get some sensible ideas into his head from the very start, and prepare himself for something solid and reliable and not go out into the world with his head full of dreams. . . . Boy! Don't become a dilettante, do you hear?" (p. 63)

And so, with this initiation, Merton was received at Ripley Court even though the summer term was almost over. Because he knew no Latin, Merton "had the humiliation of once again descending to the lowest place and sitting with the smallest boys in the school and beginning at the beginning" (p. 64).

But he is quick to point out that Ripley Court was a paradise compared to the prison of the lycée.

During his two-year stay at Ripley Court, Merton immersed himself in the English prep school life and its mores. Attending the village church on Sundays, prayers before meals and before bed, readings from such texts as John Bunyan's *Pilgrim's Progress*, evenings of recollection—all these activities, and others, Merton took an active part in. Consequently, he acquired some "natural faith" and found himself frequently praying and "lifting up" his mind to God." Merton says that he became "almost sincerely religious" while at Ripley Court and, as a result, was, "to some extent, happy and at peace" (p. 65). In hindsight, Merton would call this period his "religious phase." It was a phase of some importance.

While Merton was becoming imbued with the ways of the English, his father was, as always, trudging around England and France. The two of them spent the Easter vacation of 1929 together in Canterbury, but after that Owen Merton was off again to France. The last Merton heard, his father was in Rouen.

One day in June 1929, toward the end of the term, Merton was appointed to go along with the school cricket team as scorer for their match with Durston school in Ealing. When he was told on the way to the match that his father was ill and staying with his Aunt Maud in Ealing, Merton understood why he had been appointed as scorer. During the tea break, he saw his father and got the impression that he was quite ill. When he asked his father the nature of the illness, his father replied that no one seemed to know. Merton was unsettled and a "little saddened," but he persuaded himself that his father would probably be well in a matter of weeks.

At the end of the term, Merton and his father went to Aberdeenshire, Scotland, to spend the summer with an old friend of Owen Merton. But after only a few days, Owen Merton's condition worsened and he returned to London to enter the hospital. Merton stayed in Scotland with the family and their relatives.

Merton referred to his time in Scotland as a period of "unhappy isolation." Though he does not discuss the summer in substantial detail in his autobiography, Merton provides a great deal of background in *My Argument with the Gestapo*.

Merton refers to the family he stayed with as Mr. and Mrs. Frobisher and their two nieces, age sixteen or seventeen. Theirs was a beautiful and large house, Danecape Hall, replete with tennis lawn, great garden, huge windows overlooking moors, stables, two gardeners, a cook, and two maids. Perhaps because his father was in a London hospital, Merton was treated as a kind of orphan. Merton describes the ways of the household as those of English society: morning prayers from Scripture and *The Book of Common Prayer*, food served in silver chafing dishes, family readings from Charles Kingsley's *Water Babies* led by Mr. Frobisher, and, of course, the stables. As Merton notes, "the stables were part of the education that was to make a man out of an orphan."[19] He was expected to enjoy spending part of the day grooming the ponies and cleaning out their stalls and part of his day riding them. But Merton was apathetic about the horses and this tended to make the nieces resentful and scornful of him, a cause of further isolation.

Merton's description of the situation is not without its cynicism. This is explicable through the tension between Merton the orphan and the Merton that the Frobishers and their nieces thought he should and could become (by attending with interest to such important things as riding).

> Not only was I shirking the task of grooming, but I was also quite ready to forgo the reward of riding the horse afterwards. That was a pretty gross trait. There was a lot wrong with this orphan.

The Frobishers noticed all this and before long they removed the "privilege" of Merton's riding.

> I agreed immediately, I gave up without a glum look, I dropped everything and went for a walk on the moors, through the wet heather, a long way, walking into the cold wind, to the top of a hill about three miles away, where I sat on a big stone and looked at the distant house and wondered what I was doing in Yorkshire, and how long it would be before somebody wrote to the Frobishers and got me sent back to London.
>
> I did not have to be here. I had relatives in England, as well as other parts of the world. But they were doing my dying father a favor. I was an orphan.[20]

There were other problems for Merton. Mrs. Frobisher believed that he was being rebellious and sulking over the vegetarian diet of the house. The Frobishers appear to have been the kind of people for whom sullenness has no place; it is not the mark of young gentlemen and young women. In *My Argument with the Gestapo*, Merton gives an account of one of the many "systematic sermons" he received from Mrs. Frobisher about his behavior. In this particular sermon Mrs. Frobisher spoke of Rudyard Kipling's *The Jungle Book* and the character of Mowgli. Merton would do well, according to Mrs.

Frobisher, to "run with the pack" and "hunt with the group" where everyone depended on everyone else. Everyone does his part. She compared this principle with the Three Musketeers and their motto "one for all and all for one," which she believed kept them together. (Merton, on the other hand, felt the Three Musketeers stayed together because they, quite simply, liked one another.) Mrs. Frobisher concluded with a parable about a potentially great young man who sulked.

Merton's account ends with the following passage.

> Then I went out of the house with my book in my hand and dived through the laurels and climbed into a small cedar with roomy branches where you could sit and read comfortably. And there I read how the Count of Monte Cristo, tied in a sack, hiding inside with a knife, was thrown for dead over the high bastions of the Chateau d'If into the sea.[21]

And that is how Merton spent those weeks of "unhappy isolation"—alone, in a tree or off somewhere in a field, reading Alexandre Dumas.

The novels of Dumas are in the tradition of those Victorian novels Merton had been reading a few months earlier. They are all wonderful stories, full of adventure, romance, and elaborate escape plots. As literature, they left something to be desired. But they fulfilled Merton's need to be alone and isolated, perhaps sullen, and yet intensely involved in his fantasy world. The characters of the novels were simultaneously his friends, his heroes, and himself. For instance, he notes that Athos was his favorite musketeer, the one into whom he "tended to project" himself. Athos, one recalls, was the aristocratic, somewhat reserved musketeer, very much his own person; serious, somewhat aloof, aesthetic, a dignified man of the world. (It is curious that Athos was Merton's hero, for it was Aramis who became a monk.)

Merton's own novel-writing experience of the last two years had both generated and sustained this detached life of fantasy. His reading intensified it. It is ironic that for the family readings while Merton was staying with them, Mrs. Frobisher read Kingsley's *Water Babies*, a children's book of fantasy similar to *Alice's Adventures in Wonderland*.

Later on, Merton's life of fantasy would evolve into a kind of solitude and after that into the contemplative life of the monastery. But in that summer of 1929 in Scotland, Merton was not content with his life of fantasy and isolation. Nowhere is this unhappiness more clearly exhibited than in his account of the day he received a telegram from his father in the London hospital. Merton was alone in the house when the phone rang with the telegram. It read, "Entering New York Harbor. All Well."

> I hung up the receiver and the bottom dropped out of my stomach. I walked up and down in the silent and empty house. I sat down in one of the big leather chairs in the smoking room. There was nobody there. There was nobody in the whole huge house.
>
> I sat there in the dark, unhappy room, unable to think, unable to move, with all the innumerable elements of my isolation crowding in upon me from every side: without a home, without a family, without a country, without a father, apparently without any friends, without any interior place or confidence or light or understanding of my own—without God, too, without God, without heaven, without grace, without anything. And what was happening to Father, there in London? I was unable to think of it. (pp. 71-72)

Merton had no context within which to place the telegram. He knew of his father's illness but did not know its nature. The telegram was frightening because it opened up virtually all possibilities, including mental illness. The telegram was the culmination of a difficult period and the initiation into events even more painful.

Merton returned to his aunt and uncle's home in Ealing and was told, upon his arrival, that his father had a malignant brain tumor. Soon after, he visited his father in the hospital. His father told him the doctors were going to try to operate but that they might not be able to do very much. Merton's thoughts as he left the hospital were of his father's prolonged suffering. But, as he notes, the doctors could kill him on the operating table.

With this burden, Merton began the fall 1929 term in a new school in Ruthland, England, named Oakham, chosen by his aunt and uncle. It was a good choice, for within a year he had progressed to the sixth form. He seems to have been involved with school activities, friendly with his classmates, and much less detached from the school life—but in no way any more docile or any less fiercely independent. In 1930 Merton turned fifteen and his reflections on the celebration of this passage of time reveal the strength of his determination to be his own person and to achieve independence, almost at any cost.

> . . . the way began to be prepared for my various intellectual rebellions by a sudden and very definite sense of independence, a realization of my own individuality which, while being natural at that age, took an unhealthy egotistic turn. And everything seemed to conspire to encourage me to cut myself off from

everybody else and go my own way. For a moment, in the storms and confusion of adolescence, I had been humbled by my own interior sufferings, and having a certain amount of faith and religion, I had subjected myself more or less willingly and even gladly to the authority of others and to the ways and customs of those around me.

This newfound sense of independence had some direct relationship to Merton's summer in Scotland.

> . . . in Scotland I had begun to bare my teeth and fight back against the humiliation of giving in to other people, and now I was rapidly building up a hard core of resistance against everything that displeased me: whether it was the opinions or desires of others, or their commands, or their very persons. I would think what I wanted and do what I wanted, and go my own way. If those who tried to prevent me had authority to prevent me, I would have to be at least externally polite in my resistance: but my resistance would be no less determined, and I would do my own will, have my own way. (p. 76)

This independence itself, as well as Merton's growing awareness of it, was no doubt strengthened by his relationship with F. C. Doherty, the headmaster of Oakham, under whose guidance and direction Merton came when he reached the sixth form. It was Doherty who urged (and helped) Merton to embrace the study of modern languages and literature rather than what was then the traditional study of the classics. Doherty also prepared Merton for university study and for the Cambridge scholarship exams. In a word, Doherty allowed Merton to be himself, particularly intellectually, and this intensified, among other things, Merton's desire to write.

Independence was to broaden, for in that spring of 1930, Merton's brother and grandparents came again to Europe and eventually to Oakham. At Oakham Merton's grandfather took him aside and, in effect, gave him an emancipation speech: for the next several years, neither Merton nor his brother would have to worry about financial consideration. His grandfather had established an insurance plan with the money he was to leave the two boys in his will and the interest from the insurance would be sufficient for the two of them for the next ten years or so. Not only was there this gesture, for Merton's grandfather also bought him a pipe. Merton notes that his grandfather hated smoking and that smoking was against the rules of the school,

. . . rules which I had been systematically breaking all that year, more for the sake of asserting my independence than for the pleasure of lighting and relishing those cold, biting pipefuls of Rhodesian cut-plug. (p. 78)

So Merton had, for the first time in his life, been treated like an adult, and it was now assumed that he would be able to take care of himself. Additionally, it had been decided that Merton would now spend his holidays in London, staying with his godfather, a doctor, and his wife. Tom, as he was called (Uncle Ralph/Rafe in the autobiographical novel), was an old friend of Merton's father from New Zealand and could offer to Merton even greater independence, principally through exposure to literature and the other arts. But there were material compensations too, like extra spending money and maid service.

For most of that summer in 1930, Merton was with his grandparents and brother so that they could all be near the hospital and visit his father who by now, after several operations, could no longer speak. Merton gives a moving account of a visit to his father's bedside; the first time Merton had seen his father since the previous fall.

. . . the sorrow of his great helplessness . . . fell upon me like a mountain. I was crushed by it. The tears sprang to my eyes. Nobody said anything more.

I hid my face in the blanket and cried. And poor Father wept, too. The others stood by. It was excruciatingly sad. We were completely helpless. There was nothing anyone could do. . . .

What could I make of so much suffering. There was no way for me, or for anyone else in the family, to get anything out of it. It was a raw wound for which there was no adequate relief. . . . You just had to take it, like a dumb animal. (p. 82)

Merton was aware that his father was battling cancer and that his life by now was completely a life of faith.

I do not doubt that he had very much [faith] . . . and that behind the walls of his isolation, his intelligence and his will, unimpaired, and not hampered in any way by the partial obstruction of some of his senses, were turned to God, and communed with God who was with him and in him. . . . [His] was a great soul, large, full of natural charity. He was a man of exceptional intellectual honesty and sincerity and purity of understanding. And this affliction, this terrible and frightening illness which was relentlessly pressing him down into the jaws of the tomb, was not destroying him after all. (p. 83)

As the summer progressed, Merton continued to visit his father and tried to accept his suffering and eventual death. There was little he could do, except perhaps try to lose himself in the way of life that was now his as a result of his association with his godfather.

It is not difficult to assess this period of Merton's life from the perspective of intellectual development. Oakham came at a most advantageous time, as did his new liaison with his godfather. The latter was particularly significant on Merton's development as a writer or, at this stage, a young man who began to know that he wanted to be a writer.

And, once again, the issue seems to be one of exposure and enlarged curiosity. Tom and his wife Iris (Uncle Ralph/Rafe and Aunt Melissa) appear to have been exceptionally informed people, with taste and intelligence, cosmopolitan and aristocratic, and with sufficient money to pursue the artistic and social interests of the English intelligentsia of the early 1930s. Merton's life with Tom and Iris gave him advantages of which he made full use, advantages soon reflected in his dress, his tastes, and his social, political, and intellectual awareness.

I had a good hat, I had gloves and a neat coat, and my school tie and, in my pocket, Players' cigarettes . . . when I went up in the lift, coming home to my uncle's flat.

I never rode in that lift without being aware of the way the light yellow Virginia tobacco is packed tight in those neat cigarettes. I never rode up to the flat without being aware or the neat column of theater announcements, in boxes, in THE TIMES. I was always aware of the bindings of English novels, of the names of new records, of living artists, of the cinemas where the films of René Clair would be shown. I was conscious of all the boat trains that left for Dover, Folkestone, and Newhaven from Victoria. I was conscious of Paris and London, and not obscurely. I was aware, not abstractly, but in concrete detail, of the whole civilized world.

There I woke up in the mornings of Easter vacations with the quiet light of London coming in the two curtained windows. There was a Spanish maid who every morning dressed your suit and shined your shoes. . . . She took the shoes for shining and the suit for pressing when she left the breakfast tray, on which were a small pot of coffee and a very small cup for drinking it, and small pieces of toast. The tray was light and the breakfast no less than I wanted. After I had put the tray on the floor, I would read some part of a novel, maybe Turgenev, maybe Evelyn Waugh.

During the mornings of Easter vacations I went out and walked with my pressed suit and shined shoes in the streets of the West End, believing that the world was neat and quiet and stable; perhaps, in parts, ugly and foolish, but, mostly, a happy place for the subtle.

On those mornings I knew I had in my pocket a couple of heavy half crowns and florins: and money was books, or Duke Ellington records in the mornings, while in the afternoons money meant matinees or movies.

I came home from the Times Book Club or the music shops of the West End at lunch time and watched, out of the windows, the flags on top of Selfridges. My uncle, who walked back for lunch, stood in front of the empty fireplace and lit a cigarette and held it lightly. The speech of my aunt and uncle was light and ironic.

Uncle Ralph (Rafe) respected and mocked the school certificate and the higher certificate, with which I was successively preoccupied: he was interested in scholarship examinations for Oxford and Cambridge, which I took and (in the second case) passed.

I also respected Uncle Rafe because he mocked the House of Windsor, the Frobishers in Yorkshire. I once argued with him for a few minutes that Ravel's BOLERO was not phony, but soon I saw he was right. The next time I heard Ravel's BOLERO, I knew it was phony.[22]

Tom (Uncle Ralph) was truly a worldly man and his knowledge was vast and experienced. It was this quality that gained for him Merton's respect, admiration, and attention. It was Tom's hope that his godson would join the English diplomatic corps and thus his time with Merton was part of the preparation for this vocation. His aim was no less than sensibly educating his godson to the ways of the world and thereby enlarge the young man's weltanschauung.

Supposing I made a list of the things that I heard of, first of all, from Uncle Rafe? It would be very long.

It would be made up of the names of books, or painters, of cities, of kinds of wine, of curious facts about all the people in the world, about races and about languages and about writing. Only from my father did I learn what would make a longer list than that of the things I first heard from Uncle Rafe.

From him I first heard of Evelyn Waugh, of Céline's *Journey to the End of Night*, of the picture Galleries in the Rue de La Boetie, in Paris, or the paintings of Chagall, the films of René Clair, the films the Russians once made that were good; of Joyce, of Scriabin's POEME DE L'EXTASE, of flamenco music; of the kind of country Spain was; of all these things, some were important, some were merely curious, like the story of D. H. Lawrence being sick all over the table, at the banquet given for him at the Café Royal.

But from my father I had already heard of Blake, and Cézanne, and Picasso, and Gregorian music, and Dante, and the legends of saints, and the story of Saint Peter's denial of Christ. . . .[23]

Certainly one can think of Merton as a young artist collecting materials for his art, as a young writer collecting subjects on which to write. Books, records, films, and paintings as much as writers, musicians, filmmakers and directors, and painters. Merton's godfather was the kind of person who knew the importance of these "materials" and saw to it that his young godson had a chance to make them his own. One might even go so far as to say that Tom provided the means whereby his young charge could seek and find the symbols of his art.[24]

During the Christmas holidays of 1930, Merton spent most of his time in Strasbourg under the unofficial tutelage of a professor at the university studying French and German. His godfather had made the arrangements and one cannot help but think it was another effort to widen Merton's perspectives, to provide him more "materials."

Professor Hering (Professor H. as he is called in *My Argument with the Gestapo*) seems to have been an interesting fellow with whom Merton was not unimpressed. Merton thought him to be a holy man, "with a certain profound interior peace" (p. 84). Merton speculates that this peace perhaps came from his study of the Church fathers. In the autobiographical novel, Merton notes that the professor admired the works of Blake, Jacob Boehme, Gautama Buddha, Karl Barth, "and many others too numerous to mention."[25] It is interesting to note that while in Strasbourg, Merton stayed in a Protestant student hostel so he did have some opportunity to talk religion with the students. Oddly enough, however, he did not talk a great deal with Professor Hering about religion. While he read his copies of Plato's *Apologia* and Goethe's *Tasso* (the two books he brought with him from London) and some texts on Soviet Russia, Merton attended to the matter of the languages. But he also took time to attend the Josephine Baker revue in one of the Strasbourg theaters.

In early January 1931, Merton returned to Oakham and was there only a week when he was notified of his father's death.

> The sorry business was over. And my mind made nothing of it. There was nothing I seemed to be able to grasp. Here was a man with a wonderful mind and a great talent and great heart: and, what was more, he was the man who had brought me into the world, and had nourished me and cared for me and had shaped my soul and to whom I was bound by every possible bond or affection and attachment and admiration and reverence: killed by a growth on his brain. (p. 84)

Like his mother, Merton's father was cremated. Merton writes that he was "sad and depressed" for two or three months after his father's death. But his ultimate reaction seems to have been an intensified search for greater freedom and independence; to become absolutely self-dependent with no ties to or with anyone and no responsibilities to anyone but himself. In a sense, this marked the beginning of Merton's quest to become the twentieth-century man of pleasure, of limitless good times and boundless freedom, a quest that lasted for several years.

In the months immediately after his father's death, Merton became interested in and carefully studied William Blake. Merton notes that his father had always liked Blake and had tried to explain him to Merton when he was ten. It is then not surprising that he should approach Blake with such intensity. But there was something more to it. "I was trying to establish what manner of man he was. Where did he stand? What did he believe? What did he preach?" (p. 86).

Blake was both a revolutionary and a mystic, and this attracted Merton very much. Blake was also a man of great integrity, one who steadfastly maintained his person and beliefs in the face of all opposition. And, as artist and poet, Blake was a man of passion at the same time that he was rationalistic and deliberate. In sum, he was a man who would attract Merton throughout his life. Now Merton's attraction to Blake was more humanistic than spiritual, more curiosity than comprehension. But Blake ultimately would hold profound meaning for Merton and would greatly assist him in his struggle for faith.

In the summer of 1931, at the age of sixteen, Merton went back to Long Island at the request of his grandfather. This was the summer in which Merton "matured like a weed." One suspects that part of the maturity came by way of a painful (at least for Merton) love affair with a woman twice his age, which occurred on the boat going home.

Merton properly identifies the relationship as "the love of adolescence" but nonetheless it brought him great anguish.

> I would rather spend two years in a hospital than go through that anguish again! That devouring, emotional passionate love of adolescence that sinks its claws into you and consumes you day and night and eats into the vitals of your soul! All the self-tortures of doubt and anxiety and imagination and hope and despair that you go through when you are a child, trying to break out of your shell, only to find yourself in the middle of a legion of full-armed emotions against which you have no defense! It is like being flayed alive. No one can go through it twice. This kind of love affair can really happen only once in a man's

life. After that he is calloused. He is no longer capable of so many torments. He can suffer, but not from so many matters of no account. After one such crisis he has experience and the possibility of a second time no longer exists, because the secret of the anguish was his own utter guilelessness. He is no longer capable of such complete and absurd surprises. No matter how simple a man may be, the obvious cannot go on astonishing him for ever. (pp. 88-89)

Of course, the affair was to last for only the duration of the trip; when the boat finally entered New York harbor, it was over. Merton had declared his love and was rebuffed. The effect was no slight one, for his misery carried over to his time with his brother and grandparents. The whole experience may well have been intensified by Merton's own conflict about getting involved in the first place. On the one hand, he wanted to be his own man, with attachments and responsibilities to no one, and on the other hand was his declaration, "On the boat I am going to meet a beautiful girl, and I am going to fall in love" (p. 88).

Merton had opened himself up and was, once again, spurned, though eventually this incident was much easier to understand and accept. Yet from this perspective of rejected love, however adolescent it may have been, Merton's indolence and reticence during his time with his family is more explicable. All during this period Merton was keeping a diary so his experiences did not go unrecorded. The writer's eye was ever at work.

Again, too, this summer of 1931 was one in which Merton was left completely to his own devices. He would go into New York City and not come home for meals, never telling his family where he had been. While in the city, he would walk the streets, go to movies, observe the people, and "eat hot dogs and drink orange juice." He did get inside a dive once and for a period afterward made quite a deal of it. But Merton observes that his family suffered from his silence and detachment and must have had strange thoughts about what the young man was up to. "But the only wickedness I was up to was that I roamed around the city smoking cigarettes and hugging my own sweet sense of independence" (p. 91).

Merton, as always, read a great deal that summer, especially since his grandfather's company was publishing reprints of the works of many contemporary novelists, men to whom he had been introduced by his godfather, like Huxley, Hemingway, and Lawrence. He very likely read the texts attentively, for Merton mentions his frequent use of his uncle's dictionary.

At the end of the summer, Merton returned to England on the same boat on which he had come to America. This time, he made friends with some girls from Bryn Mawr and Vassar and together they seemed to have had quite a time, including a rather large bar bill. They listened to Duke Ellington, smoked and drank, and Merton himself got into arguments about communism, as he had begun to think of himself as a Communist. This embracing of such a political philosophy was, for Merton, at this time more a matter of what he called "decor" than a matter of philosophical commitment. Merton remarks, in fact, that the Communist Manifesto was one of many pamphlets that he kept in his study that fall of 1931 at Oakham only because he felt "it fitted in nicely with the decor in which [he] now moved in all [his] imaginings" (p. 93).

When Merton returned to Oakham in his gangster suit and his gray hat over his eye (several days after the term had begun), he seemed to be floating in the clouds. "I was convinced that I was the only one in the place who knew anything about life, from the Headmaster on down" (p. 93). But at Oakham there was a great deal of new activity for Merton, which would strengthen his view of himself as a "great rebel." He had become both a house prefect and the editor of the school magazine, and with the former position came much larger living quarters, including a study, on the walls of which hung prints of Manet and other impressionists and various photographs of Greco-Roman venuses. He continued to listen to his Duke Ellington records, read T. S. Eliot, and discuss religion and politics with his classmates. Merton also tried to write a poem based on a character from Homer, Elpenor.

Merton was one of *the* men at Oakham, much as he would be at Columbia. Successful and debonair, "marching into the future," consumed with a desire to be a writer as with the determination to take advice from no one. Faith was not one of Merton's concerns, nor was the notion of an ethical life part of his vocabulary of conscience. For now, Merton was the man of the world taking as much as he could gather in, almost as if to make up for lost time.

As his seventeenth birthday passed, Merton was more and more engrossed in the study of philosophy. The attraction was due to the encouragement and guidance of F. C. Doherty, as had been Merton's study of languages. Since there were no philosophy courses at Oakham, the students were left to their own philosophical interests and pursuits. On his own time and in his own way, Merton could be quite serious about his philosophical inquiry, as he was during the Easter holiday of 1932 when he hiked in Germany, alone, reading his Everyman Library edition of Spinoza, "earnestly and zealously . . . trying to figure out" (p. 94) the philosopher's thought. However, as one might have expected, Merton soon turned more to novels than to Spinoza, primarily because the novels were easier to understand. While he pursued his own desires, Merton remained alone in his pursuit.

Merton's grandparents were again in Paris that spring so on his way back to England he spent some time with them. During his travels, Merton had developed some kind of infection under one of his toenails. (In fact, the infection had made walking difficult so he spent several days in a room over a beer hall in Koblenz, Germany, reading his novels and Spinoza.) When he returned to school, he began to feel ill after a few days. Because he had a toothache, he went to the school dentist. The dentist extracted Merton's tooth and found it gangrenous, probably as a result of the toe infection. Evidently, Merton had developed blood poisoning, which worsened after the tooth was pulled.

Merton was quite ill and the second night in the infirmary he had a "death-watch," perhaps out of delirium but also perhaps out of a peculiar sense of his own self-destruction.

> The room was very quiet. It was rather dark, too. And as I lay in bed, in my weariness and disgust, I felt for a moment the shadow of another visitor pass into the room. It was death, that came to stand by my bed. I kept my eyes closed, more out of apathy than anything else. But anyway, there was no need to open one's eyes to see the visitor, to see death. Death is someone you see very clearly with eyes in the center of your heart: eyes that see not by reacting to light, but by reacting to a kind of chill within the marrow of your own life. And with those eyes, those interior eyes, open upon that coldness, I lay half asleep and looked at the visitor, death. What did I think? All I remember was that I was filled with a deep and tremendous apathy. I felt so sick and disgusted that I did not very much care whether I died or lived. Perhaps death did not come very close to me, or give me a good look at the nearness of his coldness and darkness, or I would have been more afraid. (p. 97)

There would be other such experiences during the next few years. This incident marked a certain level of awareness, but Merton was yet unable to transfer the awareness to the actions of his life. Even his several-week stay in the school sanitorium did not have a substantial effect on the tenor of his life.

But his period of recuperation was by no means unproductive. Merton wrote a lengthy essay on the contemporary novel, including the work of Hemingway, Dos Passos, Gide, Dreiser, and Jules Romains, for the school's Bailey English Prize competition, which he won. One would suspect, too, that Merton worked on the materials for the summer term, 1932, edition of *The Oakhamian*, which in addition to his editorial, held a Merton poem and a short piece on the potential election of Adolf Hitler and its implications in January 1933. Of course, he continued to read what he calls his "filthy novels" free of prohibition "because nobody else had heard of the authors" (p. 85).

Two attempts were made to bring him to more refined listening and reading, one of which was to stay with him the rest of his life. The music master lent him his recording of Bach's *Mass in B Minor*, which Merton says he enjoyed but did not listen to as much as his American jazz records. F. C. Doherty, the headmaster, sent Merton a book of the poems of Gerard Manley Hopkins, which Merton read from cover to cover. Though he could not decide whether he liked Hopkins, Merton never forgot him and later allowed Hopkins to have no small part in his conversion to Catholicism.

After his recuperation, Merton went back to his school activities, which now included preparations for the higher certificate examinations that came at the end of June. Merton took his in languages (Latin, German, and French) since this was his concentration in the Oakham curriculum. After sitting for the examinations, he joined his brother and his grandparents for a summer sojourn in Bournemouth, the resort city southwest of London on the English Channel. There he spent his vacation in a "big, dreary, hotel" while involving himself in another love affair, though this time the involvement seems to have been a bit greater than the experience on the boat to America. Merton makes only passing reference to this relationship in the autobiography, and no direct reference in *My Argument with the Gestapo*, so we can't know how seriously he took it. At the end of the summer he was off again with his rucksack and pup tent, this time hiking into the New Forest, in Hampshire, on the southern coast. Merton notes that he had many arguments with his girl friend that summer and when he did he would wander around for an entire day, alone, trying to regain his "equilibrium." Perhaps, then, it is not surprising that he would remove himself at the end of the summer and hike and live in a tent for a period of introspection and sulking. He roamed around for a period, "copiously pitying [himself] for [his] boredom and for the loneliness of immature love" (p. 101).

Merton ended up in the Isle of Wight, at the house of his Oakham friend Andrew (Andrews in *My Argument with the Gestapo*) and there, in that September 1932, was informed that he had passed the higher certificate examinations. It was with his friend Andrew that Merton studied *The Outline of Modern Knowledge*, which, for Merton, held special interest because of the information it provided on psychoanalysis. For a period at Cambridge, psychoanalysis would serve Merton as a life philosophy. It was apparently during this time with Andrew and his family that Merton renewed his friendship with the young woman, B., of whom he talks so much in his autobiographical novel.[26]

In December 1932, Merton sat for the Cambridge scholarship exams. In between exam sessions Merton notes that he "read reverently" one of D. H. Lawrence's psychoanalytical studies, *Fantasia of the Unconscious.* Merton's study of languages and literature served him well, for he wrote on such figures as Goethe and Schiller, Hugo, Balzac, Molière, and Racine, and did well enough to become an exhibitioner at Clare College, Cambridge, while his friend Andrew and another Oakham classmate won similar positions at St. Catherine's and St. John's, respectively. And, as before, Merton saw his success as a means to greater independence.

> My satisfaction was very great. . . . Now, at last, I imagined that I really was grown up and independent, and I could stretch out my hands and take all the things I wanted. (p. 103)

After a Christmas holiday of great merrymaking, party-going, and his eighteenth birthday celebration,[27] Merton was off again, on his own, for the third time in less than a year. His intent was to cover as much of Italy as he could. By the time he reached the French resort areas, he realized that he would need money even before he reached Italy. At Avignon, he wrote his godfather for funds. He was on his way with his rucksack, his trusty novels, and a flask of rum to Marseilles, Cassis, La Ciotat, and Hyères, where he received the money from his godfather. But Merton also received a "humiliating letter" rebuking him for spending so much money and generally criticizing his erratic behavior. Merton notes that it was the first time, after a month of traveling and freedom, that he could not always do what he wanted without hurting someone. He would express this idea again on the occasion of his humbling departure from Cambridge (and England) to America.

Merton soon was hiking again, though a bit sad and lonely and "more weary and depressed" (p. 104) from Hyères to Cavalaire and Saint Tropez, where, armed with a letter of introduction, he stayed with an acquaintance of his godfather's. As a result of his stay in Saint Tropez, he was invited to stay at a rented villa of some Americans he had met, when he arrived in Cannes.

One evening in Cannes, Merton went to a club for English chauffeurs and sailors. While eating ham and eggs there, he "grew depressed at the smell of London that lingered in the room—the smell of English cigarettes and English beer. It reminded me of the fogs I thought I had escaped" (p. 104). Was Merton running from something, some idea, from London and the English life that he was showing signs of growing to despise, or from himself? Whatever, he continued to run, though admitting boredom.

He took the train to Genoa only to discover, the morning after he arrived, a large boil on his elbow. Then, on to Florence, after cashing a letter of credit for more money, to stay with a sculptor to whom he had a letter of introduction. He treated his boil with some positive results so he was on his way to Rome. It was reminiscent of Owen Merton, running from site to site, trying to find subjects to paint. Was the one a compulsive painter and the other a compulsive writer?[28]

When Merton arrived in Rome he had not only the boil, but also a fever and a toothache. He had the tooth pulled—worrying about blood poisoning, as before—and again treated his own boil. With his physical state improved, Merton settled in for some serious explorations of Rome: the ruined places, temples and baths, museums, libraries, and bookstores. In the evenings he read: poetry and prose of John Dryden, the poetry of D. H. Lawrence, Joyce's *Ulysses*, and the novels of the German writer and publisher Christian Bernnard Von Tauchnitz. Apparently, too, Merton had begun to write another novel, from all evidence his first one in a long time. Unfortunately, no known record of the novel exists.

One wonders about Merton's fiction. The only known fictional piece to have survived his many moves is *My Argument with the Gestapo*, written in the summer of 1941, long after his adolescent fiction. It certainly has serious weaknesses as a novel. Its structure is all but buried in the journalistic parameters, and the characters are weak and more suggestive than developed. But the book is remarkable for its wealth of autobiographical material and the writing touches both quiet and noisy beauty. One cannot help but think of the fiction of Malcolm Lowry and his surrogate father Conrad Aiken, both of whom wrote predominantly autobiographical fiction. Was this autobiographical dimension the essence of Merton's fiction also? Edward Rice has suggested that Merton's novel of the summer of 1939, *The Labyrinth*, which Merton tried to have published several times and which he destroyed before entering Gethsemani, was "very autobiographical,"[29] and Merton himself supports this suggestion by his brief description of the novel (pp. 220-21).

It is possible that Merton the writer, the real artist, was the Merton who wrote nonfiction in the late forties, fifties, and sixties. In his provocative biography of Malcolm Lowry, Douglas Day quotes a passage from Carl Jung's essay "Psychology and Literature" that proffers some substance for this speculation.

> The essence of a work of art is not to be found in the personal idiosyncrasies that creep into it—indeed the more there are of them, the less it is a work of art—but in its rising above the personal and speaking from the mind and heart of the artist to the mind and heart of mankind. The personal aspect of art is a limitation, and even a vice. Art that is only personal, or predominantly so, truly deserves to be treated as neurosis.[30]

The issue of neurosis notwithstanding, Jung makes sense in terms of Merton's development as a writer. When Merton began to bring the monastic quest together with the quest to be a writer, he was able to begin to free himself from his writings, no doubt very much because of the monastic life and its varied austerities.

For a week or so Merton followed the same routine. Then he began to look into the churches of Rome rather than the ruins. His fascination for Byzantine mosaics developed and he thus sought out those churches in which he would find such art. Indirectly, he visited just about all the Christian shrines and became a pilgrim in the sense that he was truly instructed by the shrines. Both the art and the architecture of the churches reached and moved Merton.

> And now for the first time in my life I began to find out something of Who this Person was that men called Christ. It was obscure, but it was a true knowledge of Him, in some sense, truer than I knew and truer than I would admit. But it was in Rome that my conception of Christ was formed. It was there I first saw Him. (p. 109)

He put down his D. H. Lawrence, after experiencing exasperation and disgust at the Four Evangelist poems, and took up the New Testament. He returned again and again to the churches, now attracted more by an "interior peace" that he experienced there than by the art. His favorite shrine was Saint Peter in Chains with its Moses of Michelangelo, though Merton was neither particularly moved by nor impressed with the piece. His will was not reached. He did not have a conversion experience and, as yet, nothing had shaken the "iron tyranny of moral corruption" that controlled his being. A second epiphany, however, began to break the bonds.

I was in my room. It was night. The light was on. Suddenly it seemed to me that Father, who had now been dead more than a year, was there with me. The sense of his presence was as vivid and as real and as startling as if he had touched my arm or spoken to me. The whole thing passed in a flash, but in that flash, instantly, I was overwhelmed with a sudden and profound insight into the misery and corruption of my own soul, and I was pierced deeply with a light that made me realize something of the condition I was in, and I was filled with horror at what I saw, and my whole being rose up in revolt against what was within me, and my soul desired escape and liberation and freedom from all this with an intensity and an urgency unlike anything I had ever known before. And now I think for the first time in my whole life I really began to pray—praying not with my lips and with my intellect and my imagination, but praying out of the very roots of my life and my being, and praying to the God I had never known, to reach down towards me out of His darkness and to help me get free of the thousand terrible things that held my will in slavery. (p. 111)

Merton offers some explanation for this incident, though he stays away from any lengthy psychological discussion. It is too easy to talk of debilitating guilt, Merton's obsession with what his father would have wanted him to do, how he would have wanted him to behave. There is also, of course, the psycho-physiological dimension, which Merton himself seems to allow. The point is that this was a genuine experience—intimately connected with Merton's thoughts about and awareness of his dead father—which, to some degree, turned Merton around morally and spiritually. He goes so far as to call the incident "a great grace" (p. 112).

He remained in Rome for another ten days or so, continuing his reading and visitations as well as traveling out of the city to San Paolo and to the Trappist monastery of Tre Fontane where he decided one afternoon, perhaps in a kind of reckless enthusiasm, that he should like to be a Trappist monk.

Merton's grandparents had been writing him from Long Island, urging him to come to America for the spring and summer. After a few more days in Rome, Merton sailed for America, though with a heavy heart, for Rome had been a moving and significant experience for him.

He was still uncertain about his religious zeal. He notes that he read the Scriptures "surreptitiously" while at his grandparents' Douglaston house for fear someone might make fun of him. Nor did Merton pray any longer on his knees as he had begun to do in Rome. What he experienced in Rome would be difficult for him to maintain.

In the early summer, Merton boarded a train for Chicago where he planned to see the World's Fair of 1933. He ended up as a barker for a sideshow in the "Streets of Paris" part of the fair. This Chicago experience was not particularly satisfying but it was enough to undo almost completely his "religious fervor."

He returned to New York, only to become part of the religion of New York, New York itself, and the surrounding cults. He went to the burlesque shows as well as spent a great deal of time with the painter Reginald Marsh, an old friend of his father's. Marsh and Merton spent a great deal of time together during Merton's remaining time in New York, "hanging around" Fourteenth Street and Marsh's studio, going to parties, and to Coney Island.

Marsh was a painter with an artistic vision and a weltanschauung, with whom young Merton could share memories and lost moments. One wonders to what extent Merton was influenced by Marsh's particular "duality" and whether, through the relationship, Merton was able to clarify his own artistic vision as well as his emotional perspective on his father's death. Certainly, as Merton himself notes in the autobiography, Marsh's zest for life was infectious and to the degree that one profits from such infectiousness, Merton certainly did so.

With September came Merton's departure for London and his first and only year at Cambridge. Merton recalls his time at Cambridge as a "dizzy business," a time when "I was breaking my neck to get everything out of life that you think you can get out of it when you are eighteen" (p. 119). Though the autobiography provides some detail about the year at Cambridge, the autobiographical novel is richer in the particulars of Merton's many and varied experiences. Both accounts, however, reveal a grave dissatisfaction with Cambridge and Clare College as well as a sarcastic bitterness about the whole experience there. In the autobiography, Merton remembers the

> sweet stench of corruption . . . the keen, thin scent of decay that pervades everything and accuses with a terrible accusation the superficial youthfulness, the abounding undergraduate noise that fills those ancient buildings . . . a rotten fruit. (p. 118)

Merton's reflections from *My Argument with the Gestapo* are more penetrating in their bitterness and more revealing in their specificity and are worth quoting in their entirety. The reflections have a certain starkness because, in the text, Merton juxtaposes them with the reflections of another former Cambridge student whose time there was more pleasant and full of a strange kind of contentment.

Cambridge, you cry out to me from the past like the waiting rooms of dentists, you swear in my memory like the gas geysers with their big copper tanks heating a shilling's worth of hot water for a bath.

You look in, forever, to my mind the way ten o'clock in the morning comes through an unwashed windowpane on the grayest days, and the eyes of your tradition make me still the green and fragile and dim light of sixpenny gas mantles under a globe.

Oh, peering Cambridge, I taste you in the broken skin of my lips like the bloody leather of a twelve-ounce boxing glove, I constantly hear the dried scraps of putty falling from your windows onto the linoleum floor, I smell the awful cleanness of soap in the dank showers underneath the College Buttery, where the soccer player hanged himself.

The thought of Cambridge takes fire, feverishly, in my mind, like the things that appeared to be cakes of solidified oatmeal they used for lighting fires in the slick grates of Clare New Court.

The thought of you empties like old gin out of a glass that has been standing several days, among the clean plates.

You are as pompous in my mind as the framed paling documents certifying that the landlady's husband was one of the war dead (1914-1918): such documents hang, like the lithograph portrait of the old queen, in the darkness of hallways.

The wind sings in the shadows of Senate House passage with the sound of a vacuum cleaner, and rain falls on the roofs of Caius as ominously as the motors of a bus.

The bells of a big Victorian church cast down in the midst of Station Road, the ringing of their artificial past; these bells, neither new nor old, pretending to be very old!

The bald, scared houses grow along the narrow Cam beyond the railroad bridge, among their own turnips; and Cambridge fears the country all around it, bare as steel.

The sun falls on the stone of the King's Parade and colors it like the parchment skin of dying protestant bishops, but the voices of the different Victorian additions to the colleges make no more noise than clothes.

Yet everywhere, Cambridge, your real voice speaks as weary as the imitation heroines of the worst films made in Elstree, and rings forever in my mind like bravery and pathos in an empty theater.

Cambridge, you are as quiet as teashops but as blue as clinics, and I will never forget the town girls' starved laughter ringing along the narrow gutters of the Cury.

Cambridge, you are restrained as postmarks on a letter, but you are as disquieting as syphilis or cancer.[31]

Merton's sadness and disgust with his Cambridge experience seem to be tied very much to the whole of his time in England, especially in London. He notes in the autobiography that the London (and England) he had known in his younger days was not the London (and England) of his time at Cambridge. There was an emptiness, a charade, a play at being alive, an act; the England Merton was to leave in the fall of 1934 was, for him, a "blank, moral vacuum."

Part of this profound disillusionment came with the onset of the war. Merton was increasingly grieved over this pending conflict and, in fact, the writing of *My Argument with the Gestapo* was his attempt to establish and to understand the relationship between the England that so saddened him and the England of the war. In the midst of the London air raids, Merton's thoughts—in fictional forms—express the relationship he was searching for.

> I will bring to mind all the places where I ever tried to sleep, in the old days, in London, when there was supposed to be peace. The nightmares I had then may make comprehensible these raids. . . . Perhaps the things I remember in nightmares are the things everybody is really fighting for.[32]

Symbolically and realistically, then, there were two Londons, two Englands for Merton.

> The first city was as pure and kind as the music of Purcell: but it no longer existed, except in the mind, the minds of some who believed in it, and believed in things that London had been forced to forget. But the second city, which was suddenly revealed at a definite time in my life, and perhaps everybody else's was as terrible as no music at all, as dark as chaos, as inescapable as Fear.[33]

In stressing the second city of fear, the impression inadvertently may have been left that Cambridge was a deadening experience for Merton during which very little, if anything at all, of a positive nature was accomplished. To the contrary, one suspects that Cambridge was, on intellectual, artistic, and social levels—from the point of view of exposure and experience—a beneficial time. In a worldly manner, the period at Cambridge was broadening for Merton and a most important part of his development.

From every indication, Merton continued to write while at Cambridge. He had two short pieces appear in *Granta*, a Cambridge undergraduate publication, the first, "Paris in Chicago" in the November 29, 1933, edition and the second, "A Crust for Egoists" in the April 25, 1934, edition. There were also cartoons for both *Granta* and *Gownsman*, another undergraduate publication. He had a poem rejected by the Clare College magazine, *Lady Clare*.

Merton was at Clare College, Cambridge, to read modern languages, so his reading reflected this: for example, Jean Cocteau's *Thomas l'Imposter*, Flaubert's *L'Education Sentimentale*, Stendhal's *De l'Amour*, Plutarch's *Lives* in the Dryden translation (which he lost in the Lion Inn, a pub he frequented), modern French poets, and Dante. Merton called his acquaintance with Dante, "the one great benefit . . . , the greatest grace in the positive order" (pp. 122-23) that he got out of Cambridge. Merton's favorable impressions of Dante seem to have been more intellectual than spiritual, more a reaction to Dante's structural art than to his ideological dimensions. It is significant that Merton gained a respect for Dante and remained at least somewhat open to the poet's point of view.

Merton also delved thoroughly into the psychoanalytical literature of Freud, Jung, and Adler. His reflections on this pursuit are negative, but they indicate the extent to which he actually studied the literature.

> . . . [I studied] with all the patience and application which my hangovers allowed me, the mysteries of sex-repression and complexes and introversion and extroversion and all the rest. I, whose chief trouble was that my soul and all its faculties were going to seed because there was nothing to control my appetites—and they were pouring themselves out in an incoherent riot of undirected passion—came to the conclusion that the cause of all my unhappiness was sex-repression! And, to make the thing more subtly intolerable, I came to the conclusion that one of the biggest crimes in this world was introversion, and, in my efforts to be an extrovert, I entered upon a course of reflections and constant self-examinations, studying all my responses and analyzing the quality of all my emotions and reactions in such a way that I could not help becoming just what I did not want to be: an introvert. . . .
>
> I don't know if I ever got close to needing a padded cell; but if I had ever gone crazy, I think psychoanalysis would have been the one thing chiefly responsible for it. (p. 124)

This negativity is most interesting when one considers the extent to which Merton embraced psychoanalytic thought end implemented it in his monastic responsibilities with the young scholastics and novices and in his later writing, especially various critical essays.[34] But the autobiography was written several years after the fact, in the midst of an intense cathartic experience with the monastic life, in a monastery that itself had little use for psychoanalysis and psychoanalytic thought.

Judging from all his activities around Cambridge, one would hardly think Merton an introvert. It was around Armistice Day, November 11, after he had come to know about "two hundred different people" that Merton joined the marginal Cambridge crowd, those fringe people who drifted in and out of campus activities but occupied themselves mainly with off-campus goings-on. Merton spent a good bit of time in two drinking and eating spots very close to the campus, the Lion Inn and the Red Cow, the latter a favorite of Malcolm Lowry, who graduated from St. Catherine's College, Cambridge, in May 1932.

Merton was grounded twice, and one of the times caused him to miss the New Theatre appearance of Louis Armstrong. But he did manage to see every play presented by the Festival Theatre repertory company during the 1933-1934 academic year as well as a West African native dance program and the Marlowe Society's *Antony and Cleopatra*.

Merton contributed his share of pranks, too, not a small number of which seemed to have been the result of drinking: like throwing a brick through a shop window or being arrested for riding on the running board of a car or getting drunk at a bump supper. There were other activities, like playing the drums in an amateur public competition at a dance hall and signing a petition to have an expelled Communist reinstated at the London School of Economics. He also forgot to go to social events and ran up bills he could not or would not pay. He spent a great deal of time seeing French films at the Cosmopolitan Cinema, near the campus. And on the walls of the rooms (in a house in which Queen Elizabeth had slept) Merton hung several reproductions: Gauguin's *Women on a Beach*, Manet's *River at Argenteuil*, Cézanne's *Mont Sainte Victoire*, and van Gogh's *Fishing Boats*, in addition to two etchings by Reginald Marsh (signed and given in friendship by the artist) and some photographs of persons whose names Merton does not reveal. This was Merton's Cambridge during those months of 1933-1935.

Merton's Aunt Maud died in November 1933.

> They committed the thin body of my poor Victorian angel to the clay of Ealing, and buried my childhood with her. . . . She it was who had presided in a certain sense over my most innocent days. And now I saw those days buried with her in the ground.
> Indeed the England I had seen through the clear eyes of her own simplicity, that too had died for me here. (p. 121)

It is worth noting the relationship in time between the death of Merton's aunt and Armistice Day, the date he gives to mark the beginning of his relationship with the fringe crowd. Did his innocence, or what he saw as his innocence, go to the grave with Aunt Maud? Was she the last obstacle to his complete and reckless independence, of Merton's doing anything he wanted to do? One would perhaps think this when these two incidents are placed in the larger context of the entire Cambridge year, for Merton's experiences and thoughts at year's end reveal a sensitivity to the horrors of the year, horrors due mostly to his own behavior.

In March or April 1934, Merton was called to London by his godfather and guardian Tom to explain why he had been doing so much playing around and not attending to the more important matter of his studies. The meeting was the "most painful and distressing" few minutes he had ever experienced.

> The thing that made me suffer was that he asked me very bluntly and coldly for an explanation or my conduct and left me to writhe. For as soon as I was placed in the position of having to give some kind of positive explanation or defense of so much stupidity and unpleasantness . . . the whole bitterness and emptiness of it became very evident to me, and my tongue would hardly function. (p. 125)

But the confrontation seems to have had little actual effect because things went on just as they had been; in fact, they worsened. After the Easter holiday Merton was called in by his tutor, Mr. Telfer, to explain why he was cutting so many of his lectures, and "a few other things besides." Merton was apparently confident about his upcoming exams—which is evidently what Telfer was concerned about—the modern language tripos in French and Italian. He got a second-level pass on both, which put him in the middle third of his class but was not sufficient for him to keep his scholarship.

Merton had already left for America and his summer stay there by the time the results of the exams were released, so a friend wired him the results on the boat. He had planned to return to Cambridge in the fall but a letter from Tom suggested that he would do well to give up the idea of the Diplomatic Corps (and thus Cambridge) and that he might just as well stay in America permanently. Merton was in agreement and so he returned to England at the end of the summer and stayed long enough to get on the quota.

My Argument with the Gestapo provides a poignant and moving account of Merton's last few days in England and reveals the depth of the sadness and confusion with which he left Cambridge. After returning to England, Merton spent some time at Cambridge visiting friends and then came down to London for the last time on the train on November 29, 1934, the day of the wedding of Prince George and Princess Marina of Greece. He had no time on this last full day in England to say goodbye to anyone, except by phone, including those special friends he had seen earlier, including his godfather and guardian, Tom and his family, whom he promised he would stop in and see on this last day. But he realized he could not and decided to call. He ended up in a pub near Oxford Circle. In the pub were several of his Cambridge friends in London for the wedding and together they stood around joking, reminiscing about Cambridge, talking about what Merton would do, and getting drunk.

From the dialogue Merton constructs in the novel, it seems that he was flippant and jocular in his answers to questions about what he would do, e.g., be a planter in the West Indies, planting novels, dramas, and tragicomedies. Merton reveals himself with a comment that precedes the dialogue: "I don't know what I am saying anymore; I don't know what I believe. Everybody that asks me a question gets a different answer."[35]

After getting fairly drunk, Merton gathered his change and went to the phone to make his calls. He had made a list of the people to call: Elaine,[36] the people he stayed with in Scotland that summer whom he called the Frobishers, a couple of other people, and Tom (Uncle Rafe). He says he made the call to his godfather first.

> I put the coin in the box and dial the number, and the words are already in my mind. "Rushing through London. Afraid I must apologize for saying good-by this way, finally. Apologize for everything else, too. Sorry about Cambridge. Good-by."
> Aunt Melissa [his godfather's wife] will answer.
> I wait for the ringing to stop.
> Then, "Hello." I try to say it all very fast and hang up before she realizes I am drunk. I forget what I have said, but it is all over. She obviously knows I am drunk, and I am leaving without saying good-by. . . .

And then, immediately following, is Merton's soliloquy, full of remorse and sadness and a kind of disbelief sheathed in a strange paralysis.

> I had learned in the novels that questions of right and wrong didn't exist. I had learned from the laughter of the English in the corners of bars and from the presence or so many whores in London that pleasure was what was applauded. I had learned from somewhere, maybe from the parsons, that it was all right to have a good time so long as you didn't interfere with the good time of anybody else.

Now I found out that, in practice, I was not able to realize how much my pleasures might hurt somebody else until too late.

But I didn't know how to say so, because problems or right and wrong didn't exist, as everybody knew. We were merely put on earth to enjoy ourselves without hurting anybody else.

When it came time for them to take away my scholarship at Cambridge, and when it came time for me to go away from England for good, I wanted to say I was wrong, but didn't know how, because the word wrong didn't exist, no, not in the novels.

When it came time for me to say good-by, and say I was sorry because I had lost my scholarship at Cambridge (which included being sorry for a year that would make the saddest novel you ever heard of), I could not say it, because I hadn't any words to say it with. I wanted to say I was sorry, but the word sorry is the one you use when you step on someone's foot, in the bus. I wanted to confess that I had done wrong, but confession is ill bred, and embarrassing for everyone concerned in it, the one who makes and the one who has to hear the confession. I wanted to say I had sinned, but there was no such thing as sin: sin was a morbid concept, it would poison you entirely and you would go crazy.

But what most of all had struck me dumb were the two questions that I even feared to ask myself: If I am here to have a good time without hurting other people, why is it, first, that you can't have the pleasures everybody believes in without hurting somebody? And why is it, second, that you never get the pleasure you expect anyway?

So, I had nothing to say, and sat like a man ready to be shot.[37]

Thus, with a sense of relief—as well as sadness and confusion—that he was leaving a Europe full of forebodings of war and death, Merton boarded a liner on the evening of November 30, 1934, to return forever to America, an America now of Franklin Roosevelt, who was "convinced that he [could] transform the country physically and morally in his time."[38]

One suspects that Merton's personal vision was not unlike that which Roosevelt held for his country and that, for each man, there was quite a lot of toil and suffering to go through before they could get out of hell. Both men hoped, though Merton was less certain of his hope than was FDR. But November 1934 was a kind of beginning for both men, though one was faced with the prospects of saving a country while the other faced the awesomeness of saving himself.

Merton's initial response—the first involved response would perhaps be more accurate—to his painful end to Cambridge took the form of a conversion to communism. He realized that he was a "mess" and that he must attempt to make some kind of radical change to bring order to his life.

So now, when the time came for me to take spiritual stock of myself, it was natural that I should do so by projecting my whole spiritual condition into the sphere of economic history and the class struggle. In other words, the conclusion I came to was that it was not so much I myself that was to blame for my unhappiness but the society in which I lived. (pp. 132-33)

Communism became for Merton a "handy religion." In rhetoric typical of the autobiography, Merton describes why communism was so easy.

The thing that made Communism seem so plausible to me was my own lack of logic which failed to distinguish between the reality of the EVILS which Communism was trying to overcome and the validity of its diagnosis and the chosen cure. (p. 135)

But there was some good for him in the Communist experience because it was his way of admitting his past behavior and trying to make some kind of positive response or reparation to it "by developing some kind of social and political consciousness" (p. 136). Merton was as genuine about this "conversion" as he could be. He was truly concerned about the potential of war and the destruction of peace and believed that he could do something about it by aligning himself with a vocal and active group that fought bourgeois capitalism, a root cause of war.

Merton was to pursue his Communist interests as a three-month member of the Young Communist League, under the party name of Frank Swift. He picketed the Casa Italiana, took part in the Columbia Peace Strike, sold newspapers and pamphlets, and even gave a speech on communism in England about which he admitted knowing very little. Though he believed he was truly contributing to the antiwar effort and that he was making, by his public actions, a kind of confession of faith, his days as a self-proclaimed revolutionary came to an end around the end of April 1935.

. . . my inspiration to do something for the good of mankind had been pretty feeble and abstract from the start. I was still interested in doing good for only one person in the world—myself. (p. 148)

After some thought, Merton had registered and begun classes at Columbia University in early February 1935. Columbia, after Cambridge, was a virtual Arcadia. It was open, alive, and full of "intellectual vitality."

Columbia was for me a microcosm, a little world, where I exhausted myself in time. Had I waited until after graduation it would have been too late. During the few years in which I was there I managed to do so many wrong things that I was ready to blow my mind. But fortunately I learned, in so doing, that this was good. . . . I always felt at Columbia that people around me, half amused and perhaps at times half incredulous, were happy to let me be myself. (I add that I seldom felt this way at Cambridge.) The thing I always liked best about Columbia was the sense that the University was, on the whole, glad to turn me loose in its library, its classrooms, and among its distinguished faculty, and let me make what I liked out of it all. I did.[39]

One of the distinguished faculty whose course in English literature Merton took that first semester was Mark Van Doren. Van Doren was more than a passing influence on Merton, as Van Doren himself has indicated.[40] Merton's own reflections suggest that it was Van Doren who offered him encouragement and guidance that clarified his intellectual interests and pursuits and ultimately brought him closer to the Catholic Church.

As far as I can see, the influence of Mark's sober and sincere intellect, and his manner of dealing with his subject with perfect honesty and objectivity and without evasions, was remotely preparing my mind to receive the good seed of scholastic philosophy. . . .

It was a very good thing for me that I ran into someone like Mark Van Doren at that particular time, because in my new reverence for Communism, I was in danger of socially accepting any kind of stupidity, provided I thought it was something that paved the way to the Elysian fields of classless society. (p. 140-41)

However much Van Doren influenced and helped shape Merton intellectually, he could not change what he himself had called Merton's "playful" mind. Merton continued to read playfully such things as a text on aesthetics and the *Enneads* of Plotinus in Latin. But strangely enough (or perhaps not so strangely) Merton began to study intensely the life of Daniel Defoe and his works. In returning to these eighteenth-century adventure-romance writings, was Merton again escaping, climbing back into his own private world? It is possible that Merton found uncomplicated pleasure in these books, a way—not necessarily escapist or neurotic—of relaxing. He also was reading Jonathan Swift, presumably *Gulliver's Travels*, certainly more explicable than the works of Daniel Defoe.

It was in this spring of 1935 that Merton began his association with the fourth floor of John Jay Hall, the offices of the student publications, by doing some of the artwork for *The Jester*, the undergraduate magazine. During the academic year 1936-37 he would become the magazine's art editor, and would be partially responsible by his cartoons for the magazine's award as America's Best College Humor Magazine from the American Association of College Comics and *Judge* magazine. Eventually, Merton would write for the student paper, *The Spectator*, edit the yearbook, *The Columbian*, contribute reviews, essays, and fictional pieces to the literary magazine, *The Columbia Review*, all in addition to his artwork for *The Jester*.

Merton spent the summer of 1935 in Douglaston with his family, including his brother John Paul, with whom he and his friends swam, listened to records, and went to the movies almost every evening; Merton notes that he must have seen all the movies made between 1934 and 1937. Because Merton went day after day, "The movies soon turned into a kind of hell for me." But

We could not keep away from them. We were hypnotised by those yellow flickering lights and the big posters. . . . Yet as soon as we got inside, the suffering of having to sit and look at such colossal stupidities became so acute that we sometimes actually felt physically sick. In the end, it got so I could hardly sit through a show. It was like lighting cigarettes and taking a few puffs and throwing them away, appalled by the vile taste in one's mouth.

Perhaps Merton was coming to face the reality of his life and movies no longer were able to help him avoid this reality.

In 1935 and 1936, without my realizing it, life was slowly, once more, becoming almost intolerable. (p. 149)

For the moment, Merton looked to his writing for satisfaction and fulfillment. That fall of 1935, when he returned to Columbia, he went to work again for *The Jester* and also took on new positions with *The Review*, *The Spectator*, and the yearbook, and by the September issue of *The Jester* he was on his way. His "Katabolism of an Englishman" appeared in that issue and from then on it was one cartoon, critical essay, regular column, fictional piece, review, news story, poem, after another.[41] "At the Corner," a semifictional piece, serves as a good example of Merton at this time.

There were the two cars, ripped open and twisted into two piles of junk under the dim street lights. Everything else was deliberately distorted. The telephone pole did not stand up straight, and the two trees on the dark lawn leaned and bowed in different directions. The people walked around quietly and did not touch anything. The cop stood there and said nothing.

Over on one side of the street was the Packard, and the wrecked taxi blocked the road at a right angle, leaning over where the wheels lay pressed flat against the tar road. The roof had caved in. The back seat had folded up in a heap of broken glass and twisted metal. The street glittered with tiny fragments of the pane.

The man was lying there in the road with a newspaper over his face. His two hands, half open at his sides looked like wax. The thick blood lay like fresh unmixed paint where it had spilled out on the streets. Near his right hand was a full pack of cigarettes soaked in blood and gas. The wrapper was torn open. In these last seconds of his life he was going to have a smoke on the way home. Now his body lay there, a cold, objective thing, separate and meaningless.

Finally three men came, and one of them was pale. He hesitated, then bent down stiffly and lifted the paper for a mere second. "That's him," he said, and turned away, groping in his pockets for a smoke.

When the ambulance came there was no hurry, no screaming of sirens. It pulled up quietly, and silently they lifted him in.

In the street lay the smear of thick blood, like unmixed paint, and a pack of cigarettes.[42]

Was this Merton's America or was it simply a Merton creation? At this point in his life, is this how he viewed things, with such violence and the seemingly inevitable "smoke"? This piece may have been based on an accident Merton witnessed and, as such, would not seem to have unusual significance. But why would Merton choose to write about such an accident? Or why create the piece from his imagination? Why would he write about the genuine horror and violent sadness of an automobile crash, all the time cynically mentioning the pack of cigarettes and "the smoke on the way home"?

One suspects that Merton was revealing something significant about the intolerability of his life. Was his tale any different from the peculiar violence he saw in the films or the violence he knew was coming with the war, a war that he could connect with incidents such as auto wrecks and the senseless killings and maimings that go with them? Merton was telling us in "At the Corner" a great deal about the American way of life in 1936 at the same time that he was revealing his growing dissatisfaction with his own life.

The tale reveals a strange paralysis, for no one did much of anything; few words and few actions except those words and actions which bred the accident itself. There is much behind Merton's tale, particularly his sense of moral decay and dehumanization not only around him but in him. There is his sense of emptiness and despair with his life and yet an inability to do anything about it. Everything functions but nothing of any real consequence is accomplished.

Perhaps it was in his writing that Merton sought to work things out for himself: once again, to sort out the problems and find the solutions. In a sense, Merton's writing was his only way of dealing with the chaos around him and in him. Certainly, he did not yet have the self in order enough to rise completely above Jung's predominantly "personal art," but one suspects Merton was moving more and more toward that art which speaks "from the mind and heart of the artist to the mind and heart of mankind."

As a kind of catalyst, Merton's writing would, in a matter of years, lead him on another part of his journey. His writing would lead him to a monastery where he could become a monk and then a writer-monk.

But Merton's writing was not, in any fashion, directly responsible for his entering a monastery. Columbia had given to Merton the gift of himself. It had given back to him, in a sense, what Cambridge had taken away. Thus he was brought to the point of facing himself without any masks or diversions. He was unhappy and disturbed with what he saw. Yet he did not turn away. He turned inward and with courage and sometimes surprising strength faced what he saw. And in the ensuing ordeal, Merton retained his art and his artistic vision.

Let us turn now to an account of the ordeal.

TWO

The Evolution of a Monk: November 1936- December 1941

One day, in the fall of 1936, Thomas Merton became ill on the Long Island train coming into New York City. He became concerned and went to see the house physician in the Pennsylvania Hotel. The doctor examined Merton—with no findings—and suggested that he take a room in the hotel and sleep until he felt better and then go home.

> I lay on the bed and listened to the blood pounding rapidly inside my head. I could hardly keep my eyes closed. Yet I did not want to open them, either. I was afraid that if I even looked at the window, the strange spinning inside my head would begin again. . . . And far, far away in my mind was a little dry, mocking voice that said: "What if you threw yourself out of that window. . . ." I thought to myself: "I wonder if I am having a nervous breakdown." (p. 163)

The context in which this "psychosomatic epiphany" occurs is important to note. During 1935 and 1936 Merton was taking at least eighteen hours of course work at Columbia per semester, was active in a fraternity, Alpha Delta Phi, on the staffs of *The Columbia Review*, *The Jester*, *The Spectator*, editor of the yearbook, a member of the cross-country team (only for a period), held outside jobs including private tutoring, and led an active social life.

> I had never done so many different things at the same time or with such apparent success. I had discovered in myself something of a capacity for work and for activity and for enjoyment that I had never dreamed of. And everything began to come easy as the saying goes. (p. 154)

Merton's furious activity had conflicted with his impressionable emotions and deep sensitivity and produced a kind of psychosomatic explosion. As if related to this "nervous breakdown," Merton developed gastritis and what appeared to be the beginnings of a stomach ulcer for which he was put on a diet and medication.

> Now my life was dominated by something I had never really known before: fear. . . . I had refused to pay any attention to the moral laws upon which all our vitality and sanity depend: and so now I was reduced to the condition of a silly old woman, worrying about a lot of imaginary rules of health, standards of food-value and a thousand minute details of conduct that were in themselves completely ridiculous and stupid, and yet which haunted me with vague and terrific sanctions. (p. 163)

It was as if Merton's whole life had come to rest in front of his eyes and demanded that he makes some response. He had been going at a frantic pace, punishing not only his body but his emotions and what was, even then, a conscience. And as the body reacted, so did the emotions and the conscience.

> Here I was, scarcely four years after I had left Oakham and walked out into the world that I thought I was going to ransack and rob of all its pleasures and satisfactions. I had done what I intended, and now I found that it was I who was emptied, and robbed and gutted. What a strange thing! In filling myself, I had emptied myself. In grasping things, I had lost everything. In devouring pleasures and joys, I had found distress and anguish and fear. (pp. 163-64)

In the same section of *The Seven Storey Mountain* from which these quotes come, Merton talks of his death as a hero, as the "great man" he wanted to be. Everyone knew him at Columbia and those who did not soon would when they saw his pictures in the yearbook. He considered himself full of "dumb, self-satisfaction and ignominious vanity." At this point in his life, he was a man wounded by his discovery of self.

> The wounds within me were, I suppose, enough. I was bleeding to death.
> If my nature had been more stubborn in clinging to the pleasures that disgusted me: if I had refused to admit that I was beaten by this futile search for satisfaction where it could not be found, and if my moral and nervous constitution had not caved in under the weight of my own emptiness, who can tell what would eventually have happened to me? Who could tell where I would have ended?

> I had come very far, to find myself in this blind-alley: but the very anguish and helplessness of my position was something to which I rapidly succumbed. And it is my defeat that was to be the occasion of my rescue. (pp. 164-65)

The condition that Merton describes here is, I believe, the beginning of his monastic vocation. From the cave-in of his moral and nervous constitution he progressed to an awareness of God's presence in his own life. This awareness intensified to assume a central position in Merton's daily life and, as if to terminate the intensification, Merton became a Catholic and, eventually, a monk. But what is significant is that Merton, as a result of his psychosomatic epiphany, began to operate from a position of need; he had become acutely aware of an absence of contentment in his life. As he describes the epiphany, one is inclined to think that the absence was one of religion, of a set of organized beliefs. I do not believe this was so. Rather, Merton awoke to the awareness that his life as a whole was an empty shell and that he had created the shell by abusing both body and soul. To put the matter another way, I believe that Merton found his soul through his body; his bodily upheaval led him to his hollow soul.

Merton's was a deliberate and systematic journey to monasticism, comprised of many steps and many plateaus, of which his psychosomatic epiphany was the first of great significance. He was now in a position to be receptive to outside influences and directives. He had, in a sense, prepared himself for the signs to come, signs that would lead him first to Catholicism and then to Gethsemani.

The new semester in 1937 found Merton taking a course in French medieval literature.

> My mind was turning back, in a way, to the things I remembered from the old days in Saint Antonin. The deep, naive, rich simplicity of the 12th and 13th centuries was beginning to speak to me again. I had written a paper on a legend of a "Jongleur de Notre Dame," compared with a story from the Fathers of the Desert in Migne's *Latin Patrology*. I was being drawn back into the Catholic atmosphere, and I could feel the health of it, even in the merely natural order, working already within me. (p. 171)

As if in response to this course, one day in February 1937 Merton purchased a copy of Étienne Gilson's *The Spirit of Medieval Philosophy* from Scribner's Fifth Avenue bookstore. Initially, he was overcome with the "feeling of disgust and deception" because of the "Nihil Obstat . . . Imprimatur," the official sanction of the Catholic Church that a specific text is free from doctrinal error and "non-Catholic" statements.

> . . . the imprimatur told me that what I read would be in full conformity with that fearsome and mysterious thing, Catholic Dogma, and the fact struck me with an impact against which everything in me reacted with repugnance and fear.

But Merton did read the book and was very much influenced by it, perhaps even more than he allows.

> . . . I consider that it was surely a real grace that, instead of getting rid of the book I actually read it. Not all of it, it is true: but more than I used to read of books that deep. . . . I am more astounded than ever at the fact that I actually read this one: and what is more, I remembered it.
>
> And the one big concept which I got out of its pages was something that was to revolutionize my whole life. It is all contained in . . . the word *Aseitas*. In this one word, which can be applied to God alone, and which expresses His most characteristic attribute, I discovered an entirely new concept of God—a concept which showed me at once that the belief of Catholics was by no means the vague and rather superstitious hangover from an unscientific age that I had believed it to be. On the contrary, here was a notion of God that was at the same time deep, precise, simple and accurate and, what is more, charged with implications which I could not even begin to appreciate, but which I could at least dimly estimate, even with my own lack of philosophical training. (p. 172)

Gilson's explanation of *Aseitas* (aseity) is useful for understanding the nature of Merton's attraction to it.

> To say that God is Being is equivalent to asserting his aseity. We must . . . be quite clear as to the meaning of this last term. God exists in virtue of Himself (per se) in an absolute sense, that is to say as Being He enjoys complete independence not only as regards everything without but also as regards everything within Himself. Just as His existence is not derived from the other than Himself, so neither does he depend on any kind of internal essence, which would have in itself the power to bring itself into existence.[1]

There is no question that Merton was very moved—albeit more intellectually than spiritually—by this notion.

> What a relief it was for me, now to discover not only that no idea of ours, let alone any image, could adequately represent God, but also that we *should not* allow ourselves to be satisfied with any such knowledge of Him. (p. 175)

But I believe that Merton was more substantially moved by the nature of *The Spirit of Medieval Philosophy* itself. Gilson is a highly learned and extremely competent Catholic philosopher and his book, though very much a part of the tradition of Catholic philosophy, was something much more.

> It will be found . . . that all these lectures (on which the book is based) converge to this conclusion: that the Middle Ages produced, besides a Christian literature and a Christian art as everyone admits, this very Christian Philosophy which is a matter of dispute. . . . The true questions are, first, whether we can form the concept of a Christian philosophy, and secondly, whether medieval philosophy, in its best representations at any rate, is not precisely its most adequate historical expression.
>
> As understood here, then, the spirit of medieval philosophy is the spirit of Christianity penetrating the Greek tradition, working within it, drawing out of it a certain view of the world, a *Weltanschauung*, specifically Christian.[2]

I believe that Gilson was writing a kind of cultural history with a strong philosophical basis, which would be exactly the kind of scholarship that Merton, with his own academic training, would respond to. The philosophical basis of Gilson's history provided a system for Merton, a system of stability, integrity, and consistency of thought, something that Merton earnestly sought in his own life.[3] In many respects, the purchase and reading of *The Spirit of Medieval Philosophy* was, for Merton, the principal intellectual step toward Catholicism and, ultimately, toward Gethsemani. That Gilson was a Catholic made a great deal of difference to Merton because he was sensitive to how and why an author wrote what he did. Merton perceived that Gilson believed what he wrote and that perhaps he led his own life the way Merton would hope to lead his.

So where did all this take Merton? What was the immediate impact of *The Spirit of Medieval Philosophy* as evidenced in Merton's daily life?

> The result was that I at once acquired an immense respect for Catholic Philosophy and the Catholic Faith. . . . I now . . . recognized that faith was something that had a very definite meaning and a most cogent necessity. . . .
>
> When I put this book down, and had ceased to think explicitly about its arguments, its effect began to show itself in my life. I began to have a desire to go to church—and a desire more sincere and mature and more deepseated than I had ever had before. After all, I had never before had so great a need. (p. 175)

Merton began to attend, though not regularly, the Zion Episcopal Church in Douglaston, where his father had once been organist. The influence of

Merton's initial church attendance on his life was perhaps slight, but it was a beginning.

> I cannot say I went to this church very often: but the measure of my zeal may be judged by the fact that I once went even in the middle of the week. I forget what was the occasion: Ash Wednesday or Holy Thursday. There were one or two women in the place, and myself lurking in one of the back benches. We said some prayers. It was soon over. By the time it was, I had worked up courage to take the train into New York and go to Columbia for the day. (p. 177)

The late winter and early spring in 1937 were months of growth and broadening of perspective, due very much to Merton's activities in and around Columbia. Columbia University was the instrument with which Merton ultimately fused the sacred and secular, where he "learned to live," and where, perhaps, he learned to "save his soul."

> . . . the function of a university is to help men save their souls, and in so doing to save their society: from what? From the hell of meaninglessness, of obsession, of complex artifice, of systematic lying, of criminal evasions and neglects, of self-destructive futilities.[4]

In *The Seven Storey Mountain*, Merton is more specific about his time at Columbia and its effect on his developing spiritual life.

> strangely enough, it was on this big factory of a campus that the Holy Ghost was waiting to show me the light, in His own light. And one of the chief means He used, and through which He operated, was human friendship. (p. 177)

Of the several important and nourishing friendships Merton formed while at Columbia, four stand out: those with Mark Van Doren, Daniel Walsh, and Indian monk Bramachari, and perhaps his closest friend during these years, Robert Lax.

> God brought me and a half dozen others together at Columbia, and made us friends, in such a way that our friendship would work powerfully to rescue us from the confusion and the misery in which we had come to find ourselves, partly through our own fault, and partly through a complex set of circumstances which might be grouped together under the heading of the "modern world," "modern society."

There were instrumental signs for Merton.

All our salvation begins on the level of common and natural and ordinary things. . . . And so it was with me. Books and music, buildings, cities, places, philosophies were to be the materials on which grace would work. The coming war, and all the uncertainties and confusions and fears that followed necessarily from that, and all the rest of the violence and injustice that were in the world, had a very important part to play.

All these things were bound together and fused and vitalized and prepared for the action of grace. (p. 178)

As Merton perceived it, everything, every person, place, and event was a sign, an instrument of God. Henri Nouwen perceptively summarizes this.

Books, people and events: we have described these as signs on the way to silence. They do not give an explanation of his call, but are only symptoms of it. Gilson, Huxley, John of the Cross, Therese of Lisieux, Ignatius of Loyola—he discovered them in literature and experimented with their ideas. Mark Van Doren, Daniel Walsh, Bramachari and Bob Lax—he met them in New York and experienced God's love in their friendship. The events of the second world war—they formed the context in which he read the books and met the people, supported his vague premonitions and quickened his personal decisions.

Nouwen contextualizes this period of Merton's life and provides some clues as to Merton's responses.

It is perhaps always a bit disappointing when we look for an answer to the question of God in our lives. We are left only with titles of books, names of people and a few old facts. It seems all a bit lean and superficial. God doesn't let Himself get caught in titles, names and facts. But He lets Himself be suspected. And therefore it is only the one who prays to God, quite possibly the one who searches for silence himself, who can recognize Him in the many little ideas, meetings and happenings on the way to silence.[5]

The Merton Nouwen describes here, the Merton of the spring of 1937, was already the monk, more than four years before his entrance into Gethsemani. True, Merton still had to reach the plateau of Catholicism, but he had definitely begun his journey to the "way to silence."

Merton normally would have graduated with his class in June 1937, but because he had some courses still left to complete, he decided to graduate in January 1938. He spent the summer of 1937 in Douglaston, writing another novel and "drawing cartoons for the paper-cup business" (p. 181). He returned to Columbia in the fall,

. . . with my mind a lot freer, since I was not burdened with any more of those ugly and useless jobs on the fourth floor. I could write and do the drawings I felt like doing for *The Jester*. (p. 182)

During the fall Merton had a more intense interaction with his Columbia friends, particularly Robert Lax, Ed Rice, Seymour Freedgood, Bob Gibney, and Bob Gerdy. These were individuals who, like Merton, were involved with a search for Truth, for God, and for a way to God. And Lax, Gerdy, and Gibney talked openly of becoming Catholics. For Merton, Lax was the most serious, "the one that had been born with the deepest sense of who God was." And there was Merton himself.

Having read *The Spirit of Medieval Philosophy* and having discovered that the Catholic conception of God was something tremendously solid, I had not progressed one step beyond this recognition, except that one day I had gone and looked up St. Bernard's *De Diligendo Deo* in the catalogue of the University library. (p. 184)

In November 1937, Robert Lax told Merton about a new book by Aldous Huxley, *Ends and Means*. Merton bought a copy, read it, and wrote an article about it for the March 1938 edition of *The Columbia Review*, "Huxley and the Ethics of Peace." Merton was impressed that Huxley would write such a book, one that affirmed Christian and Oriental mystical literature, and thought that the book marked a real conversion in Huxley. Merton could respond to such a conversion because at sixteen and seventeen he had read much of Huxley's fiction, so unlike *Ends and Means*.

As Merton had carefully studied Gilson as well as his book, so with Huxley and *Ends and Means*. The "big conclusion" of the book was, Merton said in his article, "that we must practice prayer and asceticism." But Merton's reactions were more specific.

. . . Out of it all I took these two big concepts of a supernatural, spiritual order, and the possibility of real, experimental contact with God. . . .
. . . My hatred of war and my own personal misery in my particular situation and the general crisis of the world made me accept with my whole heart this revelation of the need for a spiritual life, an interior life, including some kind of mortification. I was content to accept the latter truth purely as a matter of theory: or at least to apply it most vociferously to one passion which was not strong in myself, and did not need to be mortified: that of anger, hatred, while neglecting the ones that really needed to be checked, like gluttony and lust.

But the most important effect of the book on me was to make me start ransacking the university for books on Oriental mysticism. (pp. 186-87)

Though this passage, written almost ten years after the fact, is exemplary of Merton's rhetoric of guilt, it can still be taken as a sign of his retreat from "women and good scotch" and a search for (and movement toward) some modus operandi of greater substance and consistency. His reaction to the Huxley text is, I believe, related to this search.

Merton spent the next several weeks reading "hundreds of strange Oriental texts," which he had first read about in *Ends and Means*.

> . . . the strange great jumble of myths and theories and moral aphorisms and elaborate parables made little or no impression on my mind, except that I put the books down with the impression that mysticism was something very esoteric and complicated, and that we were all inside some huge Being in whom we were involved and out of whom we evolved, and the thing to do was to involve ourselves back in to him again by a system of elaborate disciplines subject more or less to the control of our own will. (p. 187)

In January 1938 Merton received his Bachelor of Arts degree from Columbia. On the same day he received his B.A., he registered for courses in the Graduate School of English.

> The experience of the last year, with the sudden collapse of all my physical energy and the diminution of the brash vigor of my worldly ambitions, had meant that I had turned in terror from the idea of anything so active and uncertain as the newspaper business. This registration in the graduate school represented the first remote step of a retreat from the fight for money and fame, from the active and worldly life of conflict and competition. If anything, I would now be a teacher, and live the rest of my life in the relative peace of a college campus, reading and writing books. (p. 188)

It was with some difficulty that Merton came to a decision about the subject for his M.A. thesis. His choice of William Blake was a significant one, with profound implications for Merton the future Catholic and future monk.

> Oh, what a thing it was to live in contact with the genius and the holiness of William Blake that year, that summer, writing the thesis. . . .
> . . . As Blake worked himself into my system, I became more and more conscious of the necessity of a vital faith, and the total unreality and unsubstantiality of the dead, selfish rationalism which had been freezing my mind and will for the last seven years. By the time the summer was over, I was

to become conscious of the fact that the only way to live was to live in a world that was charged with the presence and reality of God.

To say that is to say a great deal; and I don't want to say it in a way that conveys more than the truth. I will have to limit the statement by saying that it was still, for me, more an intellectual realization than anything else: and it had not yet struck down into the roots of my will. (pp. 189-91)

In early June 1938, while doing research on his thesis, Merton met a Hindu monk, Bramachari, who was a friend of Sy Freedgood. Bramachari spent several days with Freedgood and his wife, so Merton had an opportunity to talk with him and develop some kind of friendship.

I became very fond of Bramachari and he of me. We got along very well together, especially since he sensed that I was trying to reel my way into a settled religious conviction, and into some kind of life that was centered, as his was, on God. (p. 195)

Merton was quite impressed with the breadth of Bramachari's knowledge and wisdom, as well as the depth and consistency of his simplicity. And certainly that Bramachari was a Hindu monk made no small impression on the Merton, who at the time was reading Eastern and mystical texts, though not with a full understanding. But, oddly enough, the Hindu was to strengthen Merton's inclinations toward the Christian tradition and widen his approach to Catholicism.

He did not generally put his words in the form of advice: but the one counsel he did give me is something that I will not easily forget: "There are many beautiful mystical books written by the Christians. You should read St. Augustine's *Confessions* and *The Imitation of Christ*. . . . Yes, you must read these books."

It was not often that he spoke with this kind of emphasis. Now that I look back on those days, it seems to me very probable that one of the reasons God had brought him all the way from India, was that he might say just that. (p. 198)

Albeit presumptuous, Merton's last statement reflects the understanding he gleaned from the writing of his autobiography—that the important signposts of his journey to Catholicism and the monastic life were, in fact, people, books, places, and events.

After the end of the spring term at Columbia, in middle June 1938, Merton and Bob Lax went to Lax's home in Olean, New York, for a brief vacation.

Merton stayed only a week, "being impatient to get back to New York on account of being, as usual, in love" (p. 200). During that week, Merton and Lax visited Saint Bonaventure's, a Franciscan college in Olean. The father librarian there was a friend or Lax's, so he and Merton went up to the campus to visit him. When they arrived, Lax got out of the car but Merton would not.

> . . . when Lax tried to get me out of the car, I would not. "Let's get out of here," I said. "Why? It's a nice place." "It's O.K., but let's get out of here. Let's go to the Indian Reservation." "Don't you want to see the Library?" "I can see enough of it from here. Let's get going." (p. 68)

Merton's explanation reveals wariness and uncertainty.

> I don't know what was the matter. Perhaps I was scared at the thought of nuns and priests being all around me—the elemental fear of the citizen of hell, in the presence of anything that savors of the religious life, religious vows, official dedication to God through Christ. Too many crosses. Too many statues. Too much quiet and cheerfulness. Too much pious optimism. It made me very uncomfortable. I had to flee. (p. 201)

When Merton returned from Olean, he moved out of his grandparents' Douglaston house to a rooming house on 114th Street in New York City, just behind the Columbia library.

> Whatever else may have happened in that room, it was also there that I started to pray again more or less regularly, and it was there that I added, as Bramachari had suggested, *The Imitation of Christ* to my books, and it was from there that I was eventually to be driven out by an almost physical push, to go and look for a priest. (p. 201)

As the weeks progressed, Merton became more and more involved with his thesis research. He speaks of being "fairly happy and learning many things." The self-imposed discipline of the work seems to have had some good effect, for he was able to rid himself of the illusion of poor health. In the midst of all this preparatory reading and research, Merton discovered scholastic philosophy, or more specifically, scholastic philosophy as outlined in Jacques Maritain's *Art and Scholasticism*, an important text for Merton's thesis.

Merton had finally chosen to write a thesis entitled "Nature and Art in William Blake."

I did not realize how providential a subject it actually was! What it amounted to was a study of Blake's reaction against every kind of liberalism and naturalism and narrow, classical realism in art, because of his own ideal which was essentially mystical and supernatural. In other words, the topic, if I treated it at all sensibly, could not help but cure me of all the naturalism and materialism in my philosophy, besides resolving all the inconsistencies and self-contradictions that had persisted in my mind for years, without my being able to explain them.

Merton enlarges the discission to include his own views on art and his life at the moment and how his work with Blake and the Maritain text influenced them.

I had learned from my own father that it was almost blasphemy to regard the function of art as merely to reproduce some kind of sensible pleasure, or at best, to stir up the emotions to a transitory thrill. I had always understood that art was contemplation and that it involved the action of the highest faculties of man.

When I was once able to discover the key to Blake, in his rebellion against literalism and naturalism in art, I saw that his Prophetic Books and the rest of his verse at large represented a rebellion against naturalism in the moral order as well.

What a revelation that was! For at sixteen I had imagined that Blake, like the other romantics, was glorifying passion, natural energy, for their own sake. Far from it! What he was glorifying was the transfiguration of man's natural love, his natural powers, in the refining fires of mystical experience: and that, in itself implied an arduous and total purification, by faith and love and desire, from all the petty materialistic and commonplace and earthly ideals of his rationalistic friends. (pp. 202-3)

What Merton found in Blake and had reaffirmed by Maritain was the notion of Christian virtue. The section in *Art and Scholasticism* called "Art and Intellectual Virtue" received special attention from Merton.

When Maritain . . . in all simplicity went ahead to use the term [virtue] in its Scholastic sense, and was able to apply it to art, a "virtue of the practical intellect," the very newness of the context was enough to disinfect my mind of all the miasmas left in it by the ordinary prejudice against "virtue" which, if it was ever strong in anybody, was strong in me. I was never a lover of Puritanism. Now at last I came around to the same conception of virtue—without which there can be no happiness, because virtues are precisely the powers by which we can come to acquire happiness; without them, there can be no joy, because they are the habits which coordinate and canalize our natural energies and direct them to the harmony and perfection and balance, the unity of our nature with itself and with God, which must, in the end, constitute our everlasting peace. (p. 204)

In September 1938 Merton began to write his thesis. By this time, his conversion had already begun.

> . . . the groundwork of conversion was more or less complete. And how easily and sweetly it had all been done, with all the external graces that had been arranged, along my path, by the kind Providence of God! It had taken little more than a year and a half, counting from the time I read Gilson's *The Spirit of Medieval Philosophy* to bring me up from an "atheist"—as I considered myself—to one who accepted all the full range and possibilities of religious experience right up to the highest degree of glory. (p. 204)

The notion of conversion had become something much more than an intellectual conviction. Merton's conversion would take him beyond Catholicism as a religion to the greater demands and involvement of the religious life.

> I not only accepted all this [the notion of conversion] intellectually, but now I began to desire it. And not only did I begin to desire it, but I began to do so efficaciously: I began to want to take the necessary means to achieve this union, this peace. I began to desire to dedicate my life to God, to His Service. The notion was still vague and obscure, and it was ludicrously impractical in the sense that I was already dreaming of mystical union when I did not even keep the simplest rudiments of the moral law. But nevertheless I was convinced of the reality of the goal and confident that it could be achieved; and whatever element of presumption was in this confidence I am sure God excused, in His Mercy, because of my stupidity and helplessness, and because I was really beginning to be ready to do whatever I thought He wanted me to do to bring me to him. (p. 205)

This is powerful language for one not yet even a Catholic—at least in time. Thus, it is quite important to be aware that Merton is writing of his conversion after the fact, when he had already been a monk of Gethsemani for six years. And as he looks back at his process of conversion, Merton notes the conflict between theory and practice, between his genuine desire for God and the reality of his daily life.

> Oh, how blind and weak and sick I was, although I thought I saw where I was going, and half understood the way! How deluded we sometimes are by the clear notions we get out of books. They make us think that we really understand

things of which we have no practical knowledge at all. I remember how learnedly and enthusiastically I could talk for hours about mysticism and the experimental knowledge of God, and all the while I was stoking the fires of the argument with Scotch and soda. . . .

. . . My internal contradictions were resolving themselves out, indeed but still only on the plane of theory, not of practice: not for lack of goodwill, but because I was still so completely chained and fettered by my sins and my attachments. (p. 205)

One of Merton's attachments in this late summer of 1938 was a young woman on Long Island with whom he spent every Sunday. Merton relates that as each Sunday came, he experienced a desire to stay in New York City and attend some kind of church. One Sunday in September, Merton decided to attend a Catholic mass, due partially at least, to his thesis work with various texts of Catholics such as Joyce, Hopkins, and Waugh.

I called up my girl and told her that I was not coming out that weekend, and made up my mind to go to Mass for the first time in my life. . . .

I will not easily forget how I felt that day. First, there was this sweet, strong gentle clean urge in me which said: "Go to Mass! Go to Mass!" It was something quite new and strange, this voice that seemed to prompt me, this firm, growing interior conviction of what I needed to do. It had a suavity, a simplicity about it that I could not easily account for. And when I gave in to it, it did not exult over me, and trample me down its rasing haste to land on its prey, but it carried me forward serenely and with purposeful direction. (p. 206)

The church in which Merton attended his first mass was the Church of Corpus Christi, located behind Columbia Teachers College on 121st Street. The guiding light of Corpus Christi for twenty-one years was its second pastor, George B. Ford, who came to the parish in February 1935. He was a man at least a half-century ahead of his time, evident in his direction of the parish liturgy. An editorial in *Worship* from June 1964 (the year of Father Ford's fiftieth anniversary as a priest) aptly describes his liturgical sense and his liturgies themselves.

[George Ford was an early pioneer] in bringing Catholic worship to all members of the mystical body in a more vivid manner. . . . The now thirty-year-old custom of offertory processions, congregational participation in sung Mass with the use of sacred polyphony (rendered by one of the finest choirs in the country), excellent preaching, and use of as much vernacular as possible, place Corpus Christi far ahead of the times liturgically. All these practices were established by Fr. Ford as he carried out a conviction, one which permeates his whole priestly life, that nothing but the best is worthy of the Lord.[6]

The eleven o'clock mass Merton attended on that September Sunday was held in a church building of striking simplicity and subtle beauty.

It was a gay, clean church with big plain windows and white columns and pilasters and a well-lighted simple sanctuary. Its style was a trifle eclectic, but much less perverted with incongruities than the average Catholic church in America. It had a kind of seventeenth-century oratorian character about it, though with a sort of American colonial tinge of simplicity. The blend was effective and original. . . .

Merton was aware of the homogeneity of the congregation as he looked around from his place in the back of the church.

. . . The thing that impressed me most was the fact that the place was full, absolutely full. It was full not only of old ladies and broken-down gentlemen with one foot in the grave, but of men and women and children young and old—especially young: people of all classes, and all ranks on a solid foundation of workingmen and women and their families. (p. 207)

As he was kneeling Merton noticed a pretty young woman, "kneeling straight up and praying quite seriously." Merton was impressed by what he sensed to be the simplicity of her prayer and the fact that her prayer was "the real and serious and principal reason" for her going to church. But prayer was also a factor in Merton's reactions to the congregation at large.

What a revelation it was, to discover so many ordinary people in such a place together, more conscious of God than of one another: not there to show off their hats or their clothes, but to pray, or at least to fulfill religious obligation, not a human one. (p. 208)

Merton was stirred by the "vital tradition" of the homily on Jesus Christ, the God-Man. He found it neither "studied" nor "antique." He says it was just what he needed to hear on that day of his first mass.

When the canon of the mass came and the silence grew more intense, Merton left the church in fear. But not all was lost. Merton had reached another level by responding to one of the most important signs.

After he left the Church, Merton

walked leisurely down Broadway in the sun, and my eyes looked about me at a new world. I could not understand what it was that had happened to make me so happy, why I was so much at peace, so content with life for I was not yet used to the clean savor that comes with an actual grace—indeed, there was no impossibility in a person's hearing and believing such a sermon and being justified, that is, receiving sanctifying grace in his soul as a habit, and beginning, from that moment, to live the divine and supernatural life for good and all. But that is something I will not speculate about. All I know is that I walked in a new world. (pp. 210-11)

This first mass experience of Merton's was profound. Had he attended any other church, at any other time, the effect would have been markedly different. In fact Corpus Christi parish, and George Ford and his clerical staff, were responsible in no small way for Merton's conversion and monastic vocation. In an article in *The Critic* of January 1965, Merton wrote about that very relationship.

One reason why I am a Catholic, a monk, and a priest today, is that I first went to Mass in . . . Corpus Christi, in New York. It certainly would be ungrateful of me if I did not remember the atmosphere of joy, light, and at least relative openness and spontaneity that filled Corpus Christi at Solemn High Mass, indeed also at the private low Mass at which, immediately after my baptism, I received the body of Christ for the first time.[7]

Conversion and baptism, however, were to come only after the resolution of more conflict.

During the summer of 1938 Merton's reading had "become more and more Catholic." Through his reading of James Joyce's *Ulysses* for the second or third time and *Portrait of the Artist as a Young Man*, completely, for the first time, the life and poems of Richard Crashaw, the English metaphysical poet, and the poetry and notebooks of Gerard Manley Hopkins, Merton became interested in the Jesuits, particularly their priestly life. He became excited and enthused reading the article about them in the *Catholic Encyclopaedia*. As one reads Merton's description of his ideological and emotional involvement with the Jesuits, one senses a certain suppleness of imagination. Merton seemed to be functioning more on the level of fantasy. This is perhaps validated by his statement that he "came no nearer to the Church in practice, than adding 'a Hail Mary' to my night prayers. I did not even go to Mass again, at once" (p. 213).

But there were other more debilitating sources of conflict for Merton. In September 1938, Adolf Hitler brought the whole of Europe to the edge of war with his occupation of the Sudeten area of Czechoslovakia. Merton was profoundly troubled by this ominous sign. His thoughts clearly reflect the depth and sensitivity of his beliefs in the need for moral and ethical behavior, and his growing awareness that these beliefs would find solace and support in the Catholic tradition.

> I was very depressed. I was beyond thinking about the intricate and filthy political tangle that underlay the mess. I had given up politics as more or less hopeless, by this time. I was no longer interested in having any opinion about the movement and interplay of forces which were all more or less iniquitous and corrupt, and it was far too laborious and uncertain a business to try and find out some degree of truth and justice in all the loud, artificial claims that were put forward by the various sides.
>
> All I could see was a world in which everybody said they hated war, and in which we were all being rushed into a war with a momentum that was at last getting dizzy enough to affect my stomach. All the internal contradictions of the society in which I lived were at last beginning to converge upon its heart. There could not be much more of a delay in its dismembering. Where would it end?
>
> I knew that I myself hated war, and all the motives that led to war and were behind wars. But I could see that now my likes or dislikes, beliefs or disbeliefs meant absolutely nothing in the external, political order. I was just an individual, and the individual had ceased to count. I meant nothing, in this world, except that I would probably soon become a number on the list of those to be drafted. . . .
>
> The whole business was so completely unthinkable that my mind, like almost all the other minds that were in the same situation, simply stopped trying to cope with it and refixed its focus on the ordinary routine of life. (p. 214)

Merton's routine was typing his thesis and completing an article on Richard Crashaw. His ever-widening Catholic reading continued.

One rainy afternoon in the latter part of September, Merton sat in his room reading Leahy's biography of Gerard Manley Hopkins. As Merton began to read the section that deals with Hopkins's desire to become a Catholic, he became uncomfortable.

> All of a sudden, something began to stir within me, something began to push me, to prompt me. It was a movement which spoke like a voice.
>
> "What are you waiting for," it said. "Why are you sitting here? Why do you still hesitate? You know what you ought to do? Why don't you do it?"

Merton tried to quell the upheaval by dealing with it as a series of irrational impulses. But this technique did not seem to work.

> "What are you waiting for?" said the voice within me again. "Why are you sitting there? It is useless to hesitate any longer. Why don't you get up and go?" I got up and walked around the room. "It's absurd," I thought. "Anyway, Father Ford would not be there at this time of day. I would only be wasting time."

At this point Merton read of Hopkins's request to see Newman about his conversion to Catholicism and Newman's reply that Hopkins should come to see him at Birmingham.

> Suddenly I could bear it no longer. I put down the book, and got into my raincoat, and started down the stairs. I went out into the street. I crossed over, and walked along by the grey wooden fence, towards Broadway, in the light rain. (pp. 215-16)

As if to bring the matter to a perfect resolution, Merton spoke with Father Ford and told him that he wanted to become a Catholic and begin taking instructions immediately.

As Merton describes it, this incident conjures up images of Augustine's *tolle lege* experience of Book Eight in his *Confessions*.

> Eagerly then I returned to the place where Alypius was sitting; for there I had laid the volume of the Apostle when I arose thence. I seized, opened, and in silence read that section on which my eyes first fell: Not in rioting and drunkenness, not in chambering and wantonness, not in strife and envying; but put ye on the Lord Jesus Christ, and make not provision for the flesh, in concupiscence. No further would I read; nor needed I; for instantly at the end of this sentence, by a light as it were of serenity infused into my heart, all the darkness of doubt vanished away.[8]

Both Merton's experience and Augustine's involved actions were predicated on very serious thought and prayer as well as deep struggle and pain. The actions in both cases were symbolic of the end of one search and the beginning of another. Both men had reached the level of conversion and had responded in faith to what they thought to be God's call to a new life. The manner of conversion, the *tolle lege* in both is perhaps not as important as the responses themselves. Augustine and Merton had come to the painful process of decision. They chose and thus became part of an even more intense search, not only for greater intimacy with God but for an actual means to the intimacy.

Merton began his instructions with Father Moore, an assistant pastor of Corpus Christi (Father Ford was too busy to take him on), meeting two evenings a week.

> I was never bored. I never missed an instruction, even when it cost me the sacrifice of some of my old amusements and attractions, which had such a strong hold over me and, while I had been impatient of delay from the moment I had come to that first sudden decision, I now began to burn with desire for Baptism. (p. 217)

Toward the end of October 1938, Merton made a mission (day of recollection) with the men of Corpus Christi parish: hearing mass, attending benediction, and listening to homilies on the notion of living the Catholic life. Merton was especially moved by the homily on hell, which he compared to the sermon on hell in Joyce's *Portrait of the Artist as a Young Man*. His experience with the Joyce sermon may have made Merton more sensitive to what he heard during the parish mission.

> My reaction to the sermon on hell [the mission sermon] was, indeed, what spiritual writers call "confusion"—but it was not the hectic, emotional confusion that comes from passion and from self-love. It was a sense of quiet sorrow and patient grief at the thought of these tremendous and terrible sufferings which I deserved and into which I stood a very good chance of entering, in my present condition: but at the same time, the magnitude of the punishment gave me a special and particular understanding of the greatness of the evil of sin. But the final result was a great deepening and awakening of my soul, a real increase in spiritual profundity and an advance in faith and love and confidence in God, to whom alone I could look for salvation from these things. And therefore I all the more earnestly desired Baptism. (pp. 217-18)

It was during this period of instruction that Merton seriously entertained the thought of becoming a priest. This is perhaps the first time that he honestly confronted such a notion and dealt with it openly, allowing himself to see the many levels involved in making such a decision.

> Meanwhile, there had been another thought, half forming itself in the back of my mind—an obscure desire to become a priest. This was something which I tended to hold separate from the thought of my conversion, which I was doing my best to keep in the background. I did not mention it either to Father Ford

or Father Moore, for the chief reason that in my mind it constituted a kind of admission that I was toying the thought more seriously than I wanted to—it almost amounted to a first step towards application for admission to a seminary. (p. 218)

At this point, Merton was perhaps a bit impulsive. At the same time, however, the very fact that he thought about becoming a priest serves as some measure of the growing depth of his commitment to Catholicism and its principles. Even his thesis work and the attainment of his M.A. lost importance—in the light of his desire to become a Catholic.

The fall of 1938 was also the time when Merton formed his deep and lasting friendship with Daniel Walsh, a part-time professorial lecturer at Columbia. Merton took Walsh's course on Saint Thomas. Merton made friends quickly and easily with Walsh and was able to discuss with him his thesis work and his conversion.

His course and his friendship were most valuable in preparing me for the step I was about to take. But as time went on, I decided to leave the notion of becoming a priest out of the way for the time being. So I never mentioned it to Dan in those days. (p. 221)

In the beginning of November, Merton's "mind was taken up with this one thought: of getting baptized and entering at last into the supernatural life of the Church." And finally, the event was set.

Towards the end of the first week in November, Father Moore told me that I would be baptized on the sixteenth. I walked out of the rectory that evening happier and more contented than I had ever been in my whole life. (p. 221)

Merton speaks of a growing awareness of his own weakness and helplessness, "of what a poor and miserable thing [he] was," during the last days before his baptism. It is almost as if his deepest guilt feelings surfaced more frequently and intensely the closer he got to baptism. By the night before his baptism, Merton was extraordinarily sensitive toward his past, almost to the point of a kind of psychological/spiritual paralysis. His experience on this night was similar to the two psychological/physical epiphanies Merton had had in the infirmary at Oakham and in his hotel room in Rome.

I lay in my bed awake and timorous for fear that something might go wrong the next day. And to humiliate me still further, as I lay there, fear came over me that

I might not be able to keep the eucharistic fast. It only meant going from midnight to ten o'clock without drinking any water or taking any food, yet all of a sudden this little act of self-denial which amounts to no more, in reality than a sort of abstract token, a gesture of good-will, grew in my imagination until it seemed to be utterly beyond my strength—as if I were about to go without food and drink for ten days, instead of ten hours. I had enough sense to realize that this was one of those curious psychological reactions with which our nature, not without help from the devil, tries to confuse us and avoid what reason and our will demand of it, and so I forgot about it all and went to sleep. (pp. 221-22)

The next morning, Merton "went downstairs and out into the street to go to [his] happy education and birth" (p. 222).

With his friend Ed Rice as his godfather, and his friends Gerdy, Lax, and Seymour Freedgood in attendance, Merton was baptized by Father Moore.

What mountains were falling from my shoulders! What scales of dark night were peeling off my intellect, to let in the inward vision of God and His truth! But I was absorbed in the liturgy, and waiting for the next ceremony [the baptism]. It had been one of the things that had rather frightened me—or rather which frightened the legion that had been living in me for twenty-three years. . . .

And after Father Moore had symbolically exorcised Merton,

I did not see them leaving, but there must have been more than seven of them. I had never been able to count them. Would they ever come back? . . .

Merton made his first confession after the symbolic pouring of the water and reception of his baptismal name, Thomas.

I knelt in the shadows [of the confessional]. Through the dark, close-meshed wire of the grille between us, I saw Father McGough, his head bowed, and resting on his hand, inclining his ear towards me. "Poor man," I thought. He seemed very young and he had always looked so innocent to me that I wondered how he was going to identify and understand the things I was about to tell him.

But, one by one, that is, species by species, as best I could, I tore out all those sins by their roots, like teeth. Some of them were hard, but I did it quickly, doing the best to approximate the number of times all these things had happened—there was no counting them, only guessing. (pp. 223-24)

Father Moore said mass and Merton received his first communion. Merton's response was one of uncommon awe and love. It gives a vivid indication of where Merton had come from and where he had arrived and bespeaks the depth of his conversion.

> Heaven was entirely mine—that Heaven in which sharing makes no diminution. But this solitariness [Merton was the only one receiving communion] was a kind of reminder of the singleness with which this Christ, hidden in the small host, was giving himself to me, and with Himself, the entire Godhead and Trinity—a great new increase of the power and grasp of their indwelling that had begun only a few minutes before at the font.
>
> . . . In the Temple of God that I had just become, the One Eternal and Pure Sacrifice was offered up to the God dwelling in me: the sacrifice of God to God, and me sacrificed together with God, incorporated in His Incarnation. Christ born in me, a new Bethlehem, and sacrificed in me, His new Calvary, and risen in me: offering me to the Father in Himself, asking the Father, my Father and His, to receive me into His infinite and special love—not the love He has for all things that exist—for mere existence is a token of God's love, but the love of those creatures who are drawn to Him in and with the power of His own love for Himself.
>
> For now I had entered into the everlasting movement of that gravitation which is the very life and spirit of God: God's own gravitation toward the depths of His own infinite nature, His goodness without end. And God, that Center Who is everywhere, and whose circumference is nowhere, finding me, through incorporation with Christ, incorporated into this immense and tremendous gravitational movement which is love, which is the Holy Spirit, loved me.
>
> And he called out to me from His own immense depths. (pp. 224-25)

And so, Thomas Merton became a Catholic.

Beyond Merton's own words, how does one explain and understand this conversion? Karl Jaspers speaks of man's nothingness, his unfaith, his loss of selfhood, concepts useful in understanding Merton's condition of the time of his baptism. Pascal's "infinite abyss" or Kierkegaard's "dread" are also appropriate in describing Merton's pre-conversion state. Even Tillich's "holy void" is not an inappropriate description. But perhaps Augustine, one of Merton's autobiographical models, and his experience portrayed in the *Confessions* speaks most clearly and directly to Merton's conversion. Adolph Harnack writes most movingly of the *Confessions* and the sources of Augustine's conversion. The similarity to Merton's experience can hardly go unnoticed.

> . . . it is the work of a genius who has felt God, the God of the Spirit, to be the be-all and the end-all of his life; who thirsts after Him and desires nothing

beside Him. Further, all the sad and terrible experiences which he had had in his own person, all the rupture with himself, all the service of transient things, the "crumbling away into the world bit by bit," and the egoism for which he had to pay in loss of strength and freedom, he reduces to the one root, SIN; that is to say, lack of communion with God, godlessness. Again, what released him from the entanglements of the world, from selfishness and inner decay, and gave him strength, freedom, and a consciousness of the Eternal, he calls, with Paul, GRACE. With him he feels, too, that grace is wholly the work of God, but that it is obtained through and by Christ, and possessed as forgiveness of sins and as the spirit of love.[9]

At the point of his conversion, Merton was only incidentally interested in the communal, intellectual, liturgical life and tradition of the Catholic faith, though the experience with Corpus Christi parish strengthened his conviction that Catholicism was what he wanted. Rather, like Augustine, Merton's conversion to Catholicism was a deeply personal and individual engagement with the faith, an initial opening-up of himself to the love of God, in Christ and in the wisdom of the Spirit.

Indeed, Merton's conversion was a commitment to a new way of life, though in the first few months of his Catholicism he fell into a routine complacency in terms of incorporating the spirit of the religion into his daily life.

> . . . instead of becoming a strong and ardent and generous Catholic, I simply slipped into the ranks of the millions of tepid and dull and sluggish and indifferent Christians who live a life that is still half animal, and who barely put up a struggle to keep the breadth of grace alive in their souls. (p. 229)

As Merton writes of his postconversion life, one is led to believe that the change was not really very profound.

> The only thing that saved me was my ignorance. Because in actual fact, since my life after my Baptism was pretty much what it had been before Baptism, I was in the condition of those who despise God by loving the world and their own flesh rather than Him. And because that was where my heart lay, I was bound to fall into mortal sin, because almost everything that I did, tended by virtue of my habitual intention to please myself before all else, to obstruct and deaden the work of grace in my soul.

Merton's realization was that his conversion was one of intellect and not of will.

> But I did not clearly realize all this. Because of the profound and complete conversion of my intellect, I thought I was entirely converted. Because I believed in God, and in the teachings of the Church, and was prepared to sit up all night arguing about them with all comers, I imagined that I was even a zealous Christian.

Again, though the language is heavy with guilt, Merton's struggle is with the reconciliation of his love for the world with his intensifying desire for a truly spiritual life, with God.

> Where was my will? "Where your treasure is, there will your heart be also," and I had not laid up any treasures for myself in heaven. They were all on earth. I wanted to be a writer, a poet, a critic, a professor. I wanted to enjoy all kinds of pleasures of the intellect and of the senses and in order to have these pleasures I did not hesitate to place myself in situations which I knew would end in spiritual disaster—although generally I was so blinded by my own appetites that I never even clearly considered this fact until it was too late and the damage was done. (p. 231)

But Merton did attend mass occasionally on weekdays, in addition to his regular Sunday attendance. He went to confession every fortnight, and did spiritual reading and made occasional visits to church for prayer and the stations of the cross. Externally then, he was not inactive.

During this period after his baptism, Merton set the idea of the priesthood aside "for the time being." But his response to this setting aside is revealing.

> . . . when I ceased to think of myself explicitly as a possible candidate for a high and arduous and special vocation in the Church, I tended automatically to slacken my will and to relax my vigilance, to order my acts to nothing but an ordinary life. I needed a high ideal, a difficult aim, and the priesthood provided me with one. And there were many concrete factors in this. If I were going to enter a seminary or monastery some day, I would have to begin to acquire some of the habits of religious or seminarians—to live more quietly, to give up so many amusements and such worldliness, and to be very careful to avoid things that threatened to provoke my passions to their old riot. (pp. 228-29)

In a sense then, Merton used the ideal of the priesthood not only as a way of keeping his commitment to Catholicism active but also as a means of living a more-than-ordinary spiritual life. But as he sees it, he limped along those days due, in part, to his not seeking "constant and complete spiritual direction" from Father Moore and to his inability and/or unwillingness to "pray, really pray." But he hung on.

In the end of January 1939, Merton received his M.A. degree from Columbia. It had been a difficult month for Merton. Hangovers were almost as frequent as attendance at mass, as if to draw clear battle lines.

> What a strange thing that I did not see how much this meant and come at last to the realization that it was God alone that I was supposed to live for, God that was supposed to be the center of my life and all that I did.
>
> It was to take me nearly a year to untangle the truth from all my disorganized and futile desires: and sometimes it seems to me that the hangovers I had while I was finding it out had something to do with what was going on in the history of the world. For that was to be 1939, the year when the war that everybody had been fearing finally began to teach us with its inexorable logic that dread of war is not enough. (p. 233)

And as the battle lines were drawn, so the problem became all the clearer. The resolution, however, was another matter entirely.

Merton went to Bermuda for a week to "sit in the sun, and go swimming, and ride bicycles along the empty white roads, rediscovering the sights and smells that had belonged to a year of my early childhood" (p. 234). When he returned, he rented an apartment on Perry Street in Greenwich Village and began work on his Ph.D. in English at Columbia. He had already decided to do his dissertation on Gerard Manley Hopkins.

He spent a great deal of time in his apartment working on his courses, researching the letters and notebooks of Hopkins, and writing occasional reviews for the Sunday book sections of the *The New York Times* and the *New York Herald Tribune*. But something else was emerging.

> I sometimes managed to bring out, with labor and anguish, some kind of poem. I had never been able to write a verse before I became a Catholic. I had tried, but I never really succeeded, and it was impossible to keep alive enough ambition to go on trying. (p. 235)

Merton began writing the verses on November 19, 1938, and, in fact, won a poetry prize for "Fable for a War," which was reprinted in *The New York Times* as a result. It was important to Merton to publish his poems but, to his dismay, he received as many rejection slips as poems he sent out. His was a concern for some kind of reputation.

> My chief concern was how to see myself in print. It was as if I could not be quite satisfied that I was real until I could feed my ambition with these trivial glories, and my ancient selfishness was now matured and concentrated in this

> desire to see myself externalized in a public and printed and official self which I could admire at my ease. This was really what I believed in: reputation, success. I wanted to live in the eyes and mouths and the minds of men.

But there was another side, another more important dimension.

> . . . but when my mind was absorbed in all that, how could I lead a supernatural life, the life to which I was called? How could I love God, when everything I did was done not for Him but for myself, not trusting in His aid, but relying on my own wisdom and talents? (p. 236)

As was often the case, Merton discussed this conflict with his friend Bob Lax. As Lax saw things there was no conflict at all. For Lax, a true writer was one who functioned essentially in terms of the salvation of society, one who could tell people of God's love in a language of "authority and conviction: the conviction born of sanctity." This exchange reflected another conversation they had that spring of 1939. Lax had asked Merton what he wanted to be. "I don't know, I guess I want to be a good Catholic." "What do you mean, you want to be a good Catholic? What you should say is that you want to be a saint." Merton's response was telling: "I can't be a saint." Lax replied swiftly and directly. "All that is necessary to be a saint is to want to be one. . . . All you have to do is desire it" (p. 238).

Merton had great faith in and deep respect for Lax's thoughts and opinions.

> . . . certainly his was one of the voices through which the insistent spirit of God was determined to teach me the way I had to travel: [The talk about sainthood] was another one of those times that turned out to be historical, as far as my own soul was concerned. (p. 237)

Merton's sainthood discussion with Lax prompted him to talk over the same issue with his friend and confidant, Mark Van Doren. Van Doren agreed with Lax and Merton was led to the inevitable comparison.

> All these people were much better Christians than I. They understood God better than I. What was I doing? Why was I so slow, so mixed up, still so uncertain in my directions and so insecure? (p. 238)

But Merton thought deeply about sainthood and was convinced of its accessibility or at least its possibility of attainment. It was at this time that he purchased the first volume of the works of John of the Cross, hoping perhaps that a studied reading of the text would strengthen his Christianity, make him a saint.

> But it turned out that it would take more than that to make me a saint: because these words . . . although they amazed and dazzled me with their import, were all too simple for me to understand. They were too naked, too stripped of all duplicity and compromise for my complexity, perverted by many appetites. However, I am glad that I was at least able to recognize them, obscurely, as worthy of the greatest respect. (pp. 238-39)

In June 1939, Merton, Ed Rice, and Bob Lax went to Olean, New York, to spend most of the summer living in a cottage that belonged to Lax's brother-in-law. Shortly after they arrived, the three of them went to Saint Bonaventure's (Merton was unafraid this time because he was baptized). They met Father Irenaeus, the librarian and Lax's friend, who gave them complete access to all the books in the college library. The summer experience was to be the beginning of Merton's interest in and respect for the Franciscan friars, the men who ran Saint Bonaventure's.

Rice, Lax, and Merton all fancied themselves writers and so they spent their time in Olean writing novels. (Rice has called this period Merton's "Hemingway" phase.) Merton's was called *The Labyrinth*, an autobiographical novel, and its principal character was the infamous Terrence Metrotone.

> The mere pleasure of sitting on top of this wooded mountain, with miles of country and cloudless sky to look at, and birds to listen to all day, and the healthy activity of writing page after page of novel, out under a tree facing the garage, made those weeks happy ones, in a natural sort of way. (p. 241)

As Merton and his friends believed themselves writers, so there was the need to lead some kind of "serious" life, to play the part.

> I think we all had a sort of feeling that we could be hermits up on that hill: but the trouble was that none of us really knew how and I, who was in a way the most articulate, as well as the least sensible, whenever it came to matters of conduct and decisions concerning good and evil, still had the strongest urges to go down into the valleys and see what was on at the movies, or play the slot machines, or drink beer. . . .

As "hermits" who were living in a "hermitage," the three friends did not do well, though Merton did make an attempt to develop at least a sense of prayerful solitude.

> . . . The closest I got to using the solitude for meditation was when I spent a few afternoons under a little peach tree in the high grass of what might have been a lawn, and read, at last, St. Augustine's *Confessions* and part of St. Thomas' *Summa*. (pp. 241-42)

Merton returned to New York in the middle of August and immediately set about trying to have his novel published. The frustration of waiting and receiving rejection slips was agony. He genuinely wanted to be a writer, and to have his work so frequently rejected was uncommonly discouraging. And this time, for Merton, his reaction to the discouragement was as uncommon as the depth of the discouragement itself. He prayed. Though the book was never published, Merton's prayers did lead to a reawakening of his priestly vocation, at least to the point of awareness and desire, as well as to an intensification of his faith itself.

> God answered me by a favor which I had already refused and had practically ceased to desire. He gave me back the vocation that I had half-consciously given up, and He opened to me again the doors that had fallen shut when I had not known what to make of my Baptism and the grace of that First Communion. (p. 247)

But Merton's positive state of mind was disrupted by the monstrous dimensions of World War II. These were days of suffering for Merton, not only because of the anguish of war itself but also because of his sense of his own sinfulness.

> There was . . . in my own mind—the recognition: "I myself am responsible for this. My sins have done this. Hitler is not the only one who has started this war: I have my share in it too. . . ." It was a very sobering thought, and yet its deep and probing light by its very truth eased my soul a little. (p. 248)

September brought the invasion of Warsaw and the declaration of war on Germany by Britain and France. And it brought Merton through another epiphany of sorts, closer to his priestly vocation.

One night, Merton was out with Bob Gerdy and Ed Rice. The three of them ran into two friends, Bob Gibney and Peggy Wells. Eventually, Rice and Gerdy left and Merton, Wells, and Gibney remained at Nick's on Sheridan Square drinking and talking until 4:00 a.m. Rather than travel the long distance home, Gibney and Wells spent the night at Merton's apartment. Later in the morning, while they were eating breakfast, Merton had an idea.

While we were sitting there on the floor playing records and eating this breakfast the idea came to me: "I am going to be a priest." I cannot say what caused it: it was not a reaction of especially strong disgust at being so tired and so uninterested in this life I was still leading, in spite of its futility. It was not the music, not the fall air, for this conviction that had suddenly been planted in me full grown was not the sick and haunting sort of thing that an emotional urge always is. It was not a thing of passion or of fancy. It was a strong and sweet and deep and insistent attraction that suddenly made itself felt, but not as movement of appetite towards any sensible good. It was something in the order of conscience, a new and clear sense that this was really what I ought to do.

Eventually Merton mentioned his idea to his two friends.

"You know, I think I ought to go and enter a monastery and become a priest." . . . As we went out the door of the house I was thinking: "I am going to be a priest . . . Peggy, I mean it, I am going to enter a monastery and be a priest." (p. 253)

He took Peggy Wells to the subway. On his way back home, an instinct induced Merton to stop at the Church of Saint Francis Xavier on Sixteenth Street, though he was not sure why he stopped or what he was looking for. The main church doors were locked but the door to the lower church, the crypt, was open. When he entered the crypt, Merton saw that benediction of the blessed sacrament was going on, probably concluding a novena service of holy hour. He, like the liturgical service he was witnessing, had reached a point of resolution.

. . . it suddenly became clear to me that my whole life was at a crisis. Far more than I could imagine or understand or conceive was now hanging upon a word—a decision of mine.
I had not shaped my life to this situation: I had not been building up to this. Nothing had been further from my mind. There was, therefore, an added solemnity to the fact that I had been called in here abruptly to answer a question that had been preparing, not in my mind, but in the depths of an eternal Providence. . . .
It was a moment of crisis, yet of interrogation: a moment of searching, but it was a moment of joy. . . .
So now the question faced me:
"Do you really want to be a priest? If you do, say so. . . ."
. . . I looked straight at the Host, and I knew, now, Who it was that I was looking at, and I said:
"Yes, I want to be a priest, with all my heart I want it. If it is Your will, make me a priest—make me a priest."

> When I had said them, I realized in some measure what I had done with those
> last four words, what power I had put in motion on my behalf, and what a
> union had been sealed between me and that power by my decision. (p. 255)

Thus Merton had come to the point of decision, made the decision, and was
ready to act. But the actions themselves soon became confused, complicated,
and uncertain. As one might expect with a mind and heart as complex and
often contradictory as Merton's, no decisions were arrived at easily. And to
decide what to do and actually to do it are two very different matters. So
whereas Merton had made a monumental decision in his life, it was to take
him a bit longer than he anticipated to act on this decision.

September 1939 brought a return to some normalcy for Merton. He not
only continued his classes at Columbia but he also began teaching an English
composition section three nights a week in Columbia's Extension night school.
Merton liked teaching very much, as it gave him an opportunity to sort out
his own ideas about writing and the extent to which it can and should be
taught.

Merton returned to his conviction to talk with Daniel Walsh about the
priesthood and arranged to meet with him one September evening. The first
thing Walsh said to him was that he had thought from the time he met
Merton that he had a vocation to the priesthood.

> I was astonished and ashamed. Did I really give that impression? It made me feel
> like a whited sepulchre, considering what I knew was inside me. On the whole,
> perhaps it would have been more reassuring if he had been surprised. (p. 259)

But Daniel Walsh had great respect for him and was eager to help him
formulate and clarify the dimensions of his priestly vocation. They considered
several religious orders—Merton had at least determined his preference for the
religious life instead of the secular priesthood. The Jesuits were rejected
because they "were geared to a pitch of active intensity and military routine
which was alien" (p. 260) to Merton's needs. The Benedictines were rejected
because such a vocation "might just mean being nailed down to a desk in an
expensive prep school in New Hampshire" (p. 260). The Dominicans lost out
because Merton didn't want to sleep in a common dormitory. Strange
reasoning, but it satisfied Merton and helped him come to a clearer definition
of his vocation.

Walsh asked Merton what he thought of the Franciscans. He remembered
his visits to Saint Bonaventure's, the informality and simplicity of the friars'

lives, and the pleasant and peaceful atmosphere, the joy, of their community life. Merton was attracted to the Franciscans by their "sort of freedom from spiritual restraint, from systems and routine" (p. 261). Another attraction was what Merton called the Franciscans' "simple thirteenth-century lyricism." Merton was aware of Franciscan poverty, bodily and spiritual, but since he was looking for an easy religious rule he paid more attention and responded more positively to the lyricism.

> After all, I was really rather frightened of all religious rules as a whole, and this new step, into the monastery, was not something that presented itself to me, all at once, as something that I would just take in my stride. On the contrary, my mind was full of misgivings about fasting and enclosure and all the long prayers and community life and monastic obedience and poverty, and there were plenty of strange spectres dancing about in the doors of my imagination, all ready to come in, if I would let them in. And if I did, they would show me how I would go insane in a monastery, and how my health would crack up, and my heart would give out, and I would collapse and go to pieces and be cast back into the world a hopeless moral and physical wreck. (p. 262)

This passage is significant for its immaturity as well as its odd prophecy. Merton would indeed crack up as far as his Franciscan vocation was concerned, but only to embrace the more austere and demanding life of the Trappists.

Walsh spoke to Merton of the Order of the Cistercians of the Strict Observance, the Trappists, and the Abbey of Gethsemani in Kentucky where he had made a retreat. Merton recalls that he could "share Walsh's enthusiasm" but that he had absolutely no desire to join the Trappists when he learned of the monks' fasting and silence and physical labor.

> I sat in silence. In my heart, there was a kind of mixture of exhilaration and dejection, exhilaration at the thought of such generosity, and depression because it seemed such a drastic and cruel and excessive rejection of the rights of nature. (p. 264)

Walsh asked Merton if he would like such a life. "Oh, no," said Merton, "not a chance! That's not for me! I'd never be able to stand it. It would kill me in a week. Besides, I have to have meat. I can't get along without meat. I need it for my health" (p. 264). Walsh replied that it was good that Merton knew himself so well and the two of them decided that all the evidence seemed to suggest that Merton would be most content as a Franciscan. Thus, with a note from Daniel Walsh to his friend Father Edmund, a friar at the Monastery of Saint Francis of Assisi on Thirty-first Street, Merton began his journey.

Merton went to see Father Edmund and was most impressed by him. Their conversation was positive and Merton was encouraged to consider application to the order. Father Edmund further suggested that Merton plan to enter the Franciscan novitiate in August 1940 if his application was accepted.

> I walked down the steps of the monastery into the noisy street, with my heart full of happiness and peace.
>
> What a transformation this made in my life. Now, at last, God had become the center of my existence. (p. 266)

Merton now arranged his life in anticipation of life in the monastery. He began every day with mass and communion, made the stations of the cross every afternoon, went to confession frequently. Though he still was without any spiritual direction, Merton decided to go through the *Spiritual Exercises* of Ignatius Loyola. Every day for a month he spent an hour in his darkened Perry Street room, sitting on the floor, genuinely trying to comprehend and adhere to and pray over these demanding and often esoteric exercises. In spite of his apparent spiritual immaturity, Merton did profit from his experience with the *Spiritual Exercises*. Above all, he was able to attain more discipline in his prayer life. His lack of spiritual direction and personal experience made him push himself all the harder in order to achieve new awarenesses.

Merton may have been a novice in the spiritual life, but he was, in some fashion, naturally gifted in prayer and contemplation. He approached the *Spiritual Exercises* from his own position and thus was able to keep his gifts intact while at the same time progressing in basic discipline and methods of prayer. In a word, the *Exercises* strengthened Merton's individuality of spiritual life. And Merton's prayer life had begun to be "the consequence of God's existence" in him.[10]

During this fall and early winter of 1939, Merton brought a greater order to his life. After early morning mass and communion, he returned to his apartment and worked on the revision of *The Labyrinth*, which he was still trying to have published. Over lunch at a nearby drugstore he read the paper for news of the European conflict and then went to Columbia for classes. After his classes, he went to his desk in the graduate reading room of the Columbia library and read Aquinas's commentary on the *Metaphysics* of Aristotle. Merton was reading the *Metaphysics* as part of an informal "course" in philosophical readings with Daniel Walsh. Late in the afternoon he went either to Corpus Christi Church or to one a bit closer, Our Lady of Lourdes, and make the stations of the cross.

> . . . [The stations of the cross] did not come easily or spontaneously, and they very seldom brought with them any strong sensible satisfaction. Nevertheless the work of performing them ended in a profound and fortifying peace: a peace that was scarcely perceptible, but which deepened and which, as my passions subsided, became more and more real, more and more sure, and finally stayed with me permanently. (p. 268)

Merton also began to keep a journal, one volume of which was later published as his *Secular Journal* (this published volume covers October 1, 1939, to November 27, 1941). The journal was a means for Merton not only to express in writing his growing awareness of God's presence in the world and in his own life, but also to begin to create the important fusion between the sacred and secular, between the intellectual and spiritual; between Augustine's City of God and City of Man; between Loyola's Standard of Christ and Standard of Lucifer. The tension between the two elements in Merton was very powerful and thus his writing became a way of easing the tension and, in some cases, alleviating it altogether by eliminating one of its polarities. Increasingly, from the fall of 1939 on, Merton was saying no to the world either by rejecting it outright or by neutralizing it through what I call his spiritual viewpoint. Such a position made him restless and uncertain, but it allowed him to achieve his goal and thereby strengthen his commitment so that in the last years of his life he could come to embrace the world not from a position of weakness but from a position of depth and certainty and zealous love.

When the new semester began at Columbia in January 1940, Merton was asked to teach a grammar course. He decided against it since he wanted to have some vacation before he entered the Franciscan novitiate in August. He registered for two courses at Columbia, one of which was a tutorial with Daniel Walsh on Aquinas, and made plans for a lengthy vacation in Cuba after Lent. His plans were juggled a bit by an appendicitis attack. Armed with his toothbrush and a copy of Dante's *Paradiso*, Merton entered the hospital and underwent successful surgery.

> This lying in bed and being fed, so to speak, with a spoon was more than a luxury: it was also full of meaning. I could not realize it at the time—and I did not need to: but a couple of years later I saw that this all expressed my spiritual life as it was then. For I was now, at last, born: but I was still only new-born.

> I was living: I had an interior life, real, but feeble and precarious. And I was still nursed and fed with spiritual milk. (p. 277)

Merton spent ten days in the hospital, reading Dante and Maritain, and "surrounded with everything that could protect me against trouble, against savagery, against suffering" (p. 277) and two more weeks of recuperation at his aunt and uncle's in Douglaston.

During Easter week Merton was pronounced fit by his doctor and was on his way to Cuba. The almost two months that Merton spent in Cuba were formative. It was, in many ways, a retreat but a retreat on Merton's own terms, structured to his condition and taste.

> I think it was in that bright Island that the kindness and solicitude that surrounded me wherever I turned my weak steps reached their ultimate limit. It would be hard to believe that anyone was so well taken care of as I was: and no one has ever seen an earthly child guarded so closely and so efficiently and cherished and guided and watched and led with such attentive and prevenient care as surrounded me in those days. . . .
>
> Of course, with me there was no question of any real detachment. If I did not listen to my passions it was because, in the merciful dispensation of God, they had ceased to make any noise—for the time being. (p. 278)

Merton admits that the stay in Cuba was "nine-tenths vacation and one-tenth pilgrimage." This, I believe, is precisely why its effect was so profound. Merton deliberately set no standards for himself, nor did he have specific goals. Thus he had no expectations and could be open, "contemplatively" open, to the work of God's grace within him.

> Every step I took opened up a new world of joys, spiritual joys, and joys of the mind and imagination and senses in the natural order, but on the plane of innocence, and under the direction of grace.
>
> . . . I was living like a prince in that island, like a spiritual millionaire. (p. 279)

Even at this very early stage in his spiritual development, Merton had a deep devotion to the Blessed Mother. Consequently, one of his few specific intentions while in Cuba was to make a pilgrimage to the famous shrine of Our Lady of Cobre in Oriente and dedicate himself and his vocation to her.

> There you are in Caridad del Cobre! It is you that I have come to see; you will ask Christ to make me His priest, and I will give you my heart, Lady: and if you will obtain for me this priesthood, I will remember you at my first Mass

in such a way that the Mass will be for you and offered through your hands in gratitude to the Holy Trinity, Who has used your love to win me this great grace." (p. 282)

Merton wrote his "first real poem" while on this pilgrimage.

While I was sitting on the terrace of the hotel [in Santiago] eating lunch, La Caridad del Cobre had a word to say to me. She handed me an idea for a poem that was formed so easily and smoothly and spontaneously in my mind that all I had to do was finish eating and go up to my room and type it out, almost without a correction.

So the poem turned out to be both what she had to say to me and what I had to say to her. It was a song for La Caridad del Cobre, and it was, as far as I was concerned, something new, and the first real poem I had written, or anyway the one I liked best. It pointed the way to many other poems; it opened the gate and set me travelling on a certain and direct track that was to last me several years. (p. 283)

This event was a major step toward the elimination of the tension between his literary life and his faith, albeit an unconscious step. Indeed, the poem to La Caridad del Cobre was, for Merton, an instrument through which he strengthened not only his faith but also his priestly vocation. Francois Mauriac once said, in response to the question of whether his faith had hampered or enriched his literary life,

I would answer yes to both parts of the question. My Christian faith has enriched me. It has also hampered me, in that my books are not what they might have been had I let myself go. Today I know that God pays no attention to what we write; he uses it.[11]

Merton's faith was at once simple and profound, and I believe that it was this duality that allowed him to reconcile this writing with his literary ambitions and efforts. The reconciliation, however, would last, as Merton indicated, for only a few years. Then he would have to face the question once again.

It was during his last few days in Cuba that Merton had perhaps his most profound religious experience thus far, an experience uncommon for one so young spiritually. On one of the last Sundays in April he attended mass at the Church of Saint Francis at Havana after having been to communion in another church, El Cristo. Apparently this was a children's mass, for the whole front section of pews was full of young children. During the consecration of the mass, after the priest had elevated the chalice, the children began to sing, in Spanish, the creed, *Creo en Dios*, I believe in God. Merton was stirred.

> . . . that cry, "CREO EN DIOS!" It was loud and bright, and sudden and glad and triumphant; it was a good big shout, that came from all those Cuban children, a joyous affirmation of faith. . . . Then, as sudden as the shout and as definite, and a thousand times more bright, there formed in my mind an awareness, and understanding, a realization of what had just taken place on the altar, at the Consecration: a realization of God made present by the words of Consecration in a way that made Him belong to me.
>
> But what a thing it was, this awareness: it was so intangible, and yet it struck me like a thunderclap. It was a light that was so bright that it had no relation to any visible light and so profound and intimate that it seemed like a neutralization of every lesser experience. . . . It was as if I had been suddenly illuminated by being blinded by the manifestation of God's presence.

Merton's analysis of this experience is remarkable for its clarity, due largely perhaps to its after-the-factness of several years.

> . . . The reason why this light was blinding and neutralizing was that there was and could be simply nothing in it of sense or imagination. When I call it a light that is a metaphor which I am using, long after the fact. But at the moment, another overwhelming thing about this awareness was that it disarmed all images, all metaphors, and cut through the whole skein of species and phantasms with which we naturally do our thinking. It ignored all sense experience in order to strike directly at the heart of truth, as if a sudden and immediate contact had been established between my intellect and the Truth Who was now physically really and substantially before me on the altar. But this contact was not something speculative and abstract: it was concrete and experimental and belonged to the order of knowledge, yes, but more still to the order of love.
>
> Another thing about it was that this light was something far above and beyond the level of any desire or any appetite I had ever yet been aware of. It was purified of all emotion and cleansed of everything that savored of sensible yearnings. It was love as clear and direct as vision: and it flew straight to the possession of the Truth it loved.
>
> And the first articulate thought that came to my mind was: "Heaven is right here in front of me: Heaven, Heaven!"
>
> It lasted only a moment: but it left a breathless joy and a clean peace and happiness that stayed for hours and it was something I have never forgotten. . . .

Yet, in the uncommonality of this experience, Merton's insight was keen enough to show him that it was not all his own doing.

> . . . The strange thing about this light was that although it seemed so "ordinary" in the sense I have mentioned, and so accessible, there was no way of recapturing it. In fact, I did not even know how to start trying to reconstruct the experience or bring it back if I wanted to, except to make acts of faith and love. But it was easy to see that there was nothing I could do to give any act of faith that peculiar quality of sudden obviousness: that was gift and had to come from somewhere else, beyond and above myself. (pp. 284-85)

As before, it is tempting to compare Merton's experience with one of Augustine's first contemplative experiences, "his first purely contemplative glimpse of the One Reality," as Evelyn Underhill calls it.

> Which finding itself [Augustine's mind] also to be in me a thing variable, raised itself up to its own understanding, and drew away my thoughts from the power of habit, withdrawing itself from those troops of contradictory phantasms; that so it might find what this light was whereby it was bedewed, when, without all doubting, it cried out, "That the unchangeable was to be preferred to the changeable;" whence also it knew That Unchangeable, which, unless it has in some way known, it had had no sure ground to prefer it to the changeable. And thus with the flash of one trembling glance it arrived at THAT WHICH IS. And then I saw Thy invisible things understood by the things which are made. But I could not fix my gaze thereon; and my infirmity being struck back, I was thrown again on my wonted habits, carrying along with me only a loving memory thereof, and a longing for what I had, as it were, perceived the odour of, but was not yet able to feed on.[12]

Underhill discusses this passage of Augustine in the context of it being a "brief act" because of its awful brilliance. And she quotes Ruysbroeck, the fourteenth-century Rhenish mystic, who addresses himself to the "awful brilliance" of the contemplative act as well as to its "Otherness."

> "Contemplation . . . places us in a purity and a radiance which is far above our understanding . . . and none can attain to it by knowledge, by subtlety, or by any exercise whatsoever: but he whom God chooses to unite to Himself, and to illuminate by Himself, he and no other can contemplate God. . . . But few men attain to this divine contemplation, because of our incapacity and of the hiddenness of that light in which one sees. And this is why none by his own knowledge, or by subtle consideration, will ever really understand these things. For all words and all that one can learn or understand in a creaturely way, are

foreign to the truth that I mean and far below it. But he who is united to God, and illumined by this truth—he can understand Truth by Truth."[13]

Merton's experience at the mass in the Church of Saint Francis at Havana was a real contemplative act of prayer. The whole experience was a positive indication of the depth in prayer to which he had come.

But Merton cautions us not to think that this experience changed the condition of his prayer life.

> No, my prayer continued to be largely vocal. And the mental prayer I made was not systematic, but the more or less spontaneous meditating and affective prayer that came and went, according to my reading here and there. And most of the time my prayer was not so much prayer as a matter of anticipating, with hope and desire, my entrance into the Franciscan novitiate, and a certain amount of imagining what it was going to be like, so that often I was not praying at all, but only day dreaming. (p. 285)

Merton's harshness with himself disguises an uncertainty about his Franciscan vocation—perhaps even a wariness. But when he returned to New York in late May, he was not yet aware of the uncertainty.

His application to the Franciscans had been accepted and he was to enter the novitiate in August. Merton decided to go again to Olean to join his friends Lax, Rice, Gerdy, et al. On the way, he stopped at Ithaca to see his brother John Paul at Cornell. After a two-day stay he was on his way to Olean.

As Merton describes his several weeks in Olean,[14] it was a period of contemplation and self-examination. He spent a great deal of time alone in "a quiet sunny place." He also was able to arrange through a friend to go to Saint Bonaventure's for a couple of weeks. There he went on a schedule with the Franciscan clerics and spent a great deal of time praying and reading in the library.

> I don't think I had ever been so happy in my life as I now was in that silent library, turning over the pages of the first part of the *Summa Theologica*, and here and there making notes on the goodness, the all-presence, the wisdom, the power, the love of God. (p. 290)

In his other reading during this stay at Saint Bonaventure's, Merton had looked over Butler's *Lives of the Saints* to find some religious name to take as a Franciscan novice. Merton became very involved with finding a name and when he returned to the cottage in Olean, he told the people there his choice, Frater John Spaniard.

This concern with a name was a sign for Merton that perhaps his vocation to the Franciscan cloister was not as healthy as he once thought.

> All this fuss about choosing a fancy name may seem like nothing but harmless foolishness, and I suppose that is true. But nevertheless I now realize that it was a sign of a profound and radical defect in the vocation which so filled my heart and occupied my imagination in those summer days of 1940.
>
> It is true I was called to the cloister. That had been made abundantly clear. But the dispositions with which I was now preparing to enter the Franciscan novitiate were much more imperfect than I was able to realize. In choosing the Franciscans, I had followed what was apparently a perfectly legitimate attraction—an attraction which might very well have been a sign of God's will, even though it was not quite as supernatural as I thought. I had chosen this Order because I thought I would be able to keep its rule without difficulty, and because I was attracted by the life of teaching and writing which it would offer me, and much more by the surroundings in which I saw I would probably live. (p. 291)

Merton continued thinking and coming to realizations about the weakness of his Franciscan vocation, especially in relation to the slight personal sacrifice he would have to make. By this time, Merton had come to believe that if a vocation is to be fruitful it must "cost" the individual something and be a "real sacrifice." And he knew the Franciscan life would not be as costly as he would like it to be.

> . . . becoming a Franciscan at that precise moment of history, meant absolutely no sacrifice at all, as far as I was concerned.
>
> . . . All I would have to do would be to enter the novitiate and undergo one year of inconveniences so slight that they would hardly be noticeable, and after that everything would be full of fine and easy delights—plenty of freedom, plenty of time to read and study and meditate, and ample liberty to follow my own tastes and desires in all things of the mind and spirit. Indeed, I was entering upon a life of the highest possible pleasures: for even prayer, in a certain sense, can be a natural pleasure. (p. 292)

Merton was conscious of not having any problems with the impending draft (the Burke-Wadsworth bill was to be passed in September 1940, setting up the first peacetime selective service in American history) because of his entrance into the monastery, but he was sensitive to the plight of his friends Lax and Gibney. They would have to face the draft and the issue of whether to serve as combatants. This issue added some intensity to Merton's now-increasing questioning of his Franciscan vocation.

One evening at the cottage, Merton was reading the ninth chapter of the Book of Job and once again, as if to identify more closely with Augustine, he experienced a "stunning" epiphany.

> There was something in the words that seemed to threaten all the peace that I had been tasting for months past, a kind of forewarning of an accusation that would unveil forgotten realities. I had fallen asleep in my sweet security. I was living as if God only existed to do me temporal favors. . . .
>
> . . . The words struck deep. They were more than I would ever be able to understand. But the impression they made should have been a kind of warning that I was about to find out something about their meaning. (p. 294)

Chapter Nine of the Book of Job, especially verses 1-17 (particularly striking for Merton), deals with the power and the wisdom of God, against which no man can resist and survive; that the punishment for self-justification is severe and debilitating. This confrontation led Merton to question the very basis of his Franciscan vocation. He was a sinner and sinners do not make priests. How could he presume to enter a monastery? Did he really have a vocation after all, especially in view of his sinful past?

> An attraction to the cloister is not even the most important element in a religious vocation. You have to have the right moral and physical and intellectual aptitudes. And you have to be ACCEPTED and accepted on certain grounds.
>
> When I looked at myself in the light of this doubt, it began to appear utterly impossible that anyone in his right mind could consider me fit material for the priesthood. (p. 296)

So with the doubt came Merton's departure from Olean. He packed his bags and began the journey back to New York City. When he arrived he called Father Edmund at the Franciscan monastery but the priest could not see him that evening. Merton went out to Douglaston instead.

The next day Merton spoke to Father Edmund and told him of his past and all the troubles he had had. The priest asked Merton to come back after he (Father Edmund) had given the matter some serious thought.

> So the next day he told me kindly enough that I ought to write to the Provincial and tell him that I had reconsidered my application.

There was nothing I could say. I could only hang my head and look about me at the ruins of my vocation. . . .

There seemed to be no question that I was excluded from the priesthood forever. (pp. 297-98)

After seeing Father Edmund, Merton went over to the Church of the Capuchins on Seventh Avenue and went to confession. He said that he was confused and miserable and could not explain himself properly so that when he was relating all this to the priest, the priest got the story muddled. Apparently the priest thought that Merton had been thrown out of a novitiate and was having trouble accepting the decision.

The whole thing was so hopeless that finally, in spite of myself, I began to choke and sob and I couldn't talk anymore. So the priest, probably judging that I was some emotional and unstable and stupid character, began to tell my in very strong terms that I certainly did not belong in the monastery, still less in the priesthood, and, in fact, gave me to understand that I was simply wasting his time and insulting the Sacrament of Penance by indulging my self-pity in his confessional.

When I came out of that ordeal, I was completely broken in pieces. I could not keep back the tears, which ran down between the fingers of the hands in which I concealed my face. So I prayed before the Tabernacle and the big stone crucified Christ above the altar.

The only thing I knew, besides my own tremendous misery, was that I must no longer consider that I had a vocation to the cloister. (p. 298)

How does one comprehend the loss of Merton's Franciscan vocation? Was there actually a vocation to begin with, so that an essence was, in fact, lost? If one believes that a vocation is something that cannot be had for the asking, that it is a gift from God and that the will must be responsive both before and after God speaks to it and that God speaks to it through signs—people, places, events, books—then I believe there is some basis for Merton's Franciscan vocation. The uncertainty about the vocation emerges when one considers the degree of fabrication/rationalization involved. I do not think Merton ever really wanted to be a Franciscan, though he may have very well had a vocation to the priesthood.

I think the whole process of believing he had a Franciscan vocation was a way of testing himself to see how far he had come in his conversion; thus the choice of the "easier" Franciscan way of life as opposed to the Trappists or another contemplative order. In a sense, he created the Franciscan vocation not only to test himself but also to make some response to the intensity of his conversion experience. How easily he was defeated!

One wonders about the confrontation with the Book of Job: was it Merton's spiritual immaturity getting the best of him or was he truly engaged with and believing of the text? Did he see himself as a Job who had presumed a great deal of God, so much, in fact, that God "would rain blows on him"? Was his the often misleading literal reading of the Job text? Did Merton use the Job text to substantiate what was already an awareness that he did not genuinely desire to be a Franciscan, that in fact he had some kind of sense that it was not God's will for him? I am tempted to think that Merton was playing some kind of psychological game in order to prove to himself, once and for all, that he did not have a vocation to the priesthood because he did not have a vocation to the Franciscans. I do not doubt that Merton's sorrow at the "loss" of the Franciscan vocation was deep and, as far as possible within the context, genuine. Inasmuch as he could want something—and here I mean wanting more in terms of the emotions than anything else—he very likely desired the Franciscan life. But there was the other part of him that did not want this priestly life with its apparent ease but a priestly life more demanding and much more austere. And finally, I believe there was that part of Merton that was still fighting the whole notion of the priesthood; he wanted to go only so far and, at the moment, the limit was set at a committed Christian life. Anything beyond this was risky.

Thus for the moment, Merton had resolved the issue of a priestly vocation. But it is significant that Merton purchased a set of breviaries not long after his meeting with Father Edmund.

> The four books represented a decision. They said that if I could not live in the monastery, I should try to live in the world as if I were a monk in a monastery. They said that I was going to get as close as possible to the life I was not allowed to lead. . . .
> . . . "I am going to try to live like a religious." (p. 300)

Merton believed that though God had kept him out of the cloister, it was His will that he lead "something of the life of a priest or of a religious." Merton planned to live this life by praying the breviary daily, joining a third order (a secular spiritual organization) and teaching at a Catholic college where "he could live under the same roof as the Blessed Sacrament." So Merton was initially defeated only to return strengthened and with a sense of rededication to a religious life.

All I knew was that I wanted grace, and that I needed prayer, and that I was helpless without God, and that I wanted to do everything that people did to keep close to Him. . . .

But Merton was still reacting defensively, as if he was involved in some kind of internal warfare, no doubt intensified by his profound sense of guilt.

. . . All that occupied me now was the immediate practical problem of getting up my hill with this terrific burden I had on my shoulders, step by step, begging God to drag me along and get me away from my enemies and from those who were trying to destroy me. . . .

Buried within this rhetoric of guilt, however, were Merton's astonishing efforts to remain open to God's will, to what *really* God wanted, and to His grace.

. . . Buying these books [breviaries] . . . was one of the best thing I ever did in my life. The inspiration to do it was a very great grace. There are few things I can remember that gave me more joy. (p. 301)

After the troubling days in New York City in late summer 1940, Merton returned to the cottage in Olean because it was the "safest place" he could think of and because his chances for a teaching position at Saint Bonaventure were good. He was now praying the breviary daily.

Truly, He was sending forth His Spirit, uttering His divine Word and binding me to Himself through His Spirit preceding from the Word spoken within me. (p. 303)

Merton got the position at Saint Bonaventure and in the second week of September 1940 he moved to the campus, to a room on the second floor of the main monastery/dormitory building. He did "twice as much work in that room, in one year, as I had done in all the rest of my life put together" (p. 304). Merton's room afforded him an exquisite view of the natural beauty of the land around the campus: the gardens, fields, woods, Five Mile Valley, Martinny's Rocks (a view, in fact, not dissimilar to the view from the front of Merton's hermitage at Gethsemani). I believe that the impact of this "nature" of the Saint Bonaventure land was profound and that it had a great deal to do with what appeared to be tangible changes in Merton's life itself, not merely in the way he led his life.

> It amazed me how swiftly my life fell into a plan of fruitful and pleasant organization. . . . The answer to this was, of course, the God who lived under the same roof with me . . . the Office I recited every day was another answer. Finally there was the fact of my seclusion. . . .

Of the answers Merton provides, I believe seclusion is the most significant, for it bespeaks a removal from the ways and means of the world, a removal that Merton earnestly sought. This removal had much to do with Merton's Franciscan vocation in the first place. His position at Saint Bonaventure put him back in touch with this.

> By this time I had managed to get myself free from all the habits and luxuries that people in the world think they need for their comfort and amusement. My mouth was at last clean of the yellow, parching salt of nicotine, and I had rinsed my eyes of the grey slops of movies, so that now my taste and my vision were clean. And I had thrown away the books that soiled my heart. And my ears, too, had been cleansed of all wild and fierce noises and had poured into them, peace, peace . . .

But there was still the unresolved issue of Merton's guilt, that though his "will was in order" and "his soul in harmony with itself and with God," there was still the penetrating awareness of his sinfulness, that "crushing humiliation." *Peccatum meum contra me est semper.* Yet in spite of it all, there was peace.

> . . . there was in me the profound, sure certitude of liberty, the moral certitude of grace, of union with God, which bred peace that could not be shattered or overshadowed by any necessity to stand armed and ready for conflict. And this peace was all-rewarding. It was worth everything. (pp. 304-5)

Merton's contentment grew as he worked on a new novel and taught nine hours of English literature. The teaching was particularly satisfying as through it he was able to return to the Middle Ages that had so enraptured him as a child.

> . . . the serene and simple and humorous Middle Ages, not the lute and goblin and moth-ball Middle Ages of Tennyson, but the real Middle Ages, the twelfth and thirteenth and fourteenth centuries, full of fresh air and simplicity, as solid as wheat bread and grape wine and water-mills and ox-drawn wagons: the age of Cistercian monasteries and of the first Franciscans. (pp. 305-6)

By taking the position at Saint Bonaventure and redirecting, clarifying, and simplifying his life, Merton was not really resigning himself to his "lack of vocation" but in fact was confronting the vocation in an indirect way, thereby quietly strengthening it. In an entry from his *Secular Journal* dated November 29, 1940, Merton writes of reading Kierkegaard and his discussion of the "Dark Night of the Soul" in relation to the Old Testament story of Abraham and Isaac. What Merton really seems to be writing about is his own struggle to reach and comprehend the "terrible and anguishing paradox of the dark night of absolute faith in God."[15] For Merton, as for Kierkegaard and John of the Cross, this was the highest form of religious experience, though it was incommunicable. The apparently ordinary figures are those who reach it: Mary, Francis of Assisi, Abraham.

Thus Merton's attempts to become ordinary, to involve himself completely with the order and discipline of his life at Saint Bonaventure, to leave his lost vocation alone but at the same time to avoid burying its ashes. It is as if he wanted his own dark night because he knew this was the way to the real vocation, for there was no returning to the falsities of the Franciscan vocation.

Merton's apparent uncertainties and bursts of emotionalism belie his unusually acute sense of self. I believe that he knew he needed the period at Saint Bonaventure to clarify and enlarge his examination of self. It was a pulling back but a necessary one. Otherwise, the smouldering ashes of a vocation would have forever been extinguished and Merton's dark night never attained.

In November 1940, Merton gave his name to be drafted. His response was pessimistic and self-deprecating, but perhaps understandable given the circumstances. It bespeaks his still-intensifying sense of his own sinfulness.

> . . . it was enough to remind me that I was not going to enjoy this pleasant and safe and stable life forever. Indeed, perhaps now that I had just begun to taste my security, it would be taken away again, and I would be cast back into the midst of violence and uncertainty and blasphemy and the play of anger and hatred and passion, worse than ever before. It would be the wages of my own twenty-five years: this war was what I had earned for myself and the world. I could hardly complain that I was being drawn into it. (pp. 308-9)

Merton continued the pattern of his quasi-monastic life at Saint Bonaventure, particularly his engagement with the land. He walked, even in the now-bitter winter, and prayed his breviary, perhaps not fully knowing just how contemplative he was becoming; that his very well-being depended on the sustainment of the contemplative life.

As the months wore on, Merton began to think more about the need and the desire to make a Holy Week retreat, "in some monastery." In early March 1941, he wrote the Abbey of Gethsemani, the Trappist monastery that his friend Daniel Walsh had told him about.

> As soon as I thought about it, I saw that this was the only choice. That was where I needed to go. Something had opened out, inside me, in the last months, something that required, demanded at least a week in that silence, in that austerity, praying together with the monks in their cold choir.
> And my heart expanded with anticipation and happiness. (p. 310)

At this same time, Merton began to write poetry with regularity, almost daily, in fact. He writes that it might have had something to do with his reading the Spanish poet Garcia Lorca at the time, and with the fact that he was involved with the Lenten fast, which "instead of cramping my mind, freed it, and seemed to let loose the string of my tongue" (p. 310). The writing of the poetry is in direct proportion to his engagement with and openness to his spiritual contentment and very possibly his growing desire to intensify his commitment to a religious life, though not yet specifically to the Trappists. This increased involvement with writing was similar to Merton's experience in Cuba and the context of his poem to La Caridad del Cobre.

When he received a positive reply from Gethsemani, Merton also received a letter from the draft board that his number was up. Merton had carefully thought out his position on the war and he therefore applied for non-combatant objector status. He did not wish to have any direct part of the warfare. When he mailed his forms back to the draft board he said that he had an "ineffable sense of peace" in his heart.

> . . . For the first time in my life I realized that I no longer cared whether I preserved my place in all this or lost it, whether I stayed here or went to the army. All that no longer mattered. It was in the hands of the One Who loved me far better than I could ever love myself, and my heart was filled with peace . . . a peace that the world could not give. (pp. 313-14)

In March 1941, Merton was called for his military physical. He took it on March 19 and failed because of the poor condition of his teeth.

Three weeks prior to Easter, Merton went to the college library and looked up the Trappists in the *Catholic Encyclopaedia*. He also looked up the Cistercians and the Camaldolese. He was moved by what he read. The experience was not unlike many of the previous sudden insights and perceptions, those earlier epiphanies of self-discovery and resolution.

> The thought of those monasteries, those remote choirs, those cells, those hermitages, those cloisters, those men in their cowls, the poor monks, the men who have nothing shattered my heart.
>
> In an instant the desire of those solitudes was wide open within me like a wound.
>
> I had to slam the book shut . . . and I went out of the Library trying to stamp out the embers that had broken into flame, there, for an instant, within me.
>
> No, it was useless: I did not have a vocation, and I was not for the cloister, for the priesthood. Had I not been told that definitely enough? Did I have to have that beaten into my head all over again before I could believe it. (p. 318)

Merton had "enkindled the embers" of his elusive vocation. Admittedly, his reaction was precipitated somewhat by his enthusiasm for the approaching Gethsemani retreat, an almost uncontrollable sense of excitement and anticipation. But the fact remains that he knew what he was doing when he read the *Catholic Encyclopaedia* as he knew what his reaction would be.

When Merton came out of the library, he met one of the friars and told him enthusiastically that he was going to make a retreat at Gethsemani. The friar told him not to let the Trappists change him.

> I said: "It would be a good thing if they did change me." It was a safe, oblique way of admitting what was in my heart—the desire to go to that monastery and stay for good. (p. 318)

On the Saturday before Palm Sunday, Merton boarded the train for Gethsemani and one of the most important journeys he would ever make. The journey to Gethsemani is the first stage of Merton's final process of admitting, accepting, and embracing his monastic vocation. Again the vehicle for the journey was Merton's renunciation of the world, a juxtaposition of Gethsemani and the world.

> . . . I felt as if I owned the world. And yet that was not because of all these things [of the world], but because of Gethsemani, where I was going. It was the fact that I was passing through all this [Merton was referring to Cincinnati, where he spent the night], and did not desire it, and wanted no part in it, and did not seek to grasp or hold any of it, that I could not exult in it, and it all cried out to me: God! God! (p. 319)[16]

When Merton first saw the monastery from the road late Sunday evening he noticed the wooded hills and valley that surrounded it and called them "a barrier and defence against the world." And when he first entered the monastic enclosure:

> I felt the deep, deep silence of the night, and of peace, and of holiness enfold me like love, like safety.
> The embrace of it, the silence! I had entered into a solitude that was an impregnable fortress. And the silence that enfolded me, spoke to me, and spoke louder and more eloquently than any voice. (p. 321)

Merton's journal entry for Monday, April 8, reveals the initial impact of this experience. Not only does he say that this journal entry should really begin his journal—the earlier pages should be torn out—but he also contends that the monastery is really the center of America, its only real city; it is what holds the country together. He ends this entry with some astonishing—though genuine—self-deprecation.

> What RIGHT have I to be here?
> I feel like a thief and a murderer who has been put in jail and condemned and stealing and murdering all my life, murdering God's grace in myself and in others, murdering Him in His image. I have broken out of the jail in which I lay justly condemned and have rushed even into the place of the King Whose Son I murdered, and I implore the mercy of the Queen who sits here enthroned.[17]

By Tuesday, he has begun to appreciate the monastery.

> . . . behind the strictness of the Trappist discipline is this complete metaphysical freedom from physical necessity that makes the whole discipline, ontologically speaking, a kind of play. This making use of work, and penance as play, to save one's soul, results, indirectly, in the abbey being a kind of earthly paradise. . .

> The Cistercian monastery results from a combination of the Benedictine Rule, Christian spirituality, and the techniques of living an agricultural and feudal society. But this isn't merely medieval. There is no trace of any feudalism left, in this Abbey, except perhaps that it feeds the poor of the whole region. Otherwise, it is still a perfect combination of the Benedictine rule and agrarian culture. As long as Christian monasticism and agriculture exist, and they must always exist, this combination of them will be fruitful, and produce societies that are perfect in the same way as this. There is nothing out of date about this Abbey at all.[18]

But Merton cautions that the beauty and material excellence of the monastery are accidental, their importance and value secondary and trivial. Those who come to the monastery seeking only these things risk betrayal and ultimate disappointment. As Merton discovered, the "religious life exists and thrives . . . in the soul.'

> And there it exists not as a "good feeling" but as a constant purpose, an unending love that expresses itself now as patience, now as humility, now as courage, now as self-denial, now as Justice, but always in a strong knot of faith and hope, and all of these are nothing but aspects of one constant deep, desire, charity, love.
>
> Church windows and hymns cannot satisfy us all the time, or even seem to. If they seemed to, what a dangerous deception it would be, because then we would take them for God, who alone can end and fulfill all desire and all longing in peace![19]

With this awareness and context on which to build, Merton was able to experience the core of the monastic experience. His understanding was immediate and his reaction intensely personal.

> The silence, the solemnity, the dignity of these Masses and of the Church, and the overpowering atmosphere of prayers so fervent that they were almost tangible choked me with love and reverence that robbed me of the power to breathe. I could only get the air in gasps. (p. 323)

During the retreat, Merton had long talks with a Carmelite priest who was making his own retreat. He told Merton about the Carthusians, whose order was stricter than the Trappists: the Carthusians did everything alone.[20] As he heard more about the Carthusians, Merton began to think about them in relation to the Trappists. His words reveal the extent to which he still thought of his own "lost" monastic vocation.

> . . . what did it matter which one was the most perfect Order? Neither one of them was for me. Had I not been told definitely enough a year ago that I had no vocation to any religious Order? All these comparisons were nothing but fuel for the fire of that interior anguish, that hopeless desire for what I could not have, for what was out of reach. The only question was not which Order attracted me more, but which one tortured me the more with a solitude and silence and contemplation that could never be mine.
>
> Far from wondering whether I had a vocation to either one, or from instituting a comparison between them, I was not even allowed the luxury of speculation on such a subject. It was all out of the question. . . .

There was still this terrible tension within Merton. It was to become a matter of whether he could trust himself and what he believed to be God's will for himself or whether he would trust the word of the religious authorities who had told him his monastic vocation was dead, that in fact he never had a monastic vocation.

> But what was the matter with me? I suppose I had taken such a beating from my misunderstandings and misapprehensions that had arisen in my mind by the time that Capuchin got through with me, in his confessional, the year before, that I literally feared to reopen the subject at all. There was something in my bones that told me that I ought to find out whether my intense desire to lead this kind of a life in some monastery were an illusion: but the old scars were not yet healed, and my whole being shrank from another scourging. (p. 328)

Because he did not close off the possibility of his vocation, the retreat was a struggle for Merton, but a most important one.

> That was my Holy Week, that mute, hopeless, interior struggle. It was my share in the Passion of Christ which began, that year, in the middle of the night with the first strangled cries of the Vigils of Holy Thursday. (p. 328)

According to his journal, Holy Thursday was a significant day for Merton. He was in touch with the beautiful natural setting and spring colors of Gethsemani, which made him think of his time in Rome. In fact, he says he thought a lot about Rome during his stay at Gethsemani. Merton was most comfortable in a setting where nature's seasonal qualities are tangible.

> . . . the monks washed the feet of some poor men, put money in their hands, kissed their hands and feet, gave them a dinner. I had been afraid at first to see this, thinking it might prove false. Instead, I saw Christ washing the feet of Peter. The monks had heard Christ and were doing what He had told then to do—not a series of empty gestures but a living liturgical action. I never knew charity could be spelled out so simply, so innocently, without facade or complication. Christ spoke, in that act, and made me know Him better and love him more—and that is all I seek, in this place.[21]

Merton was also attracted to the monks' simplicity. It strengthened his own desire and determination to seek his lost monastic vocation.

> I was amazed at the way these monks, who were evidently just plain young Americans from the factories and colleges and farms and high-schools of the

various states, were nevertheless absorbed and transformed in the liturgy. The thing that was most impressive was their absolute simplicity. (p. 329)

Merton had followed the Holy Week liturgy intensely. In the afternoon of Good Friday, after ten hours of monastic office, he took a long walk to try to sort things out.

Out here I could think: and yet I could not get to any conclusions. But there was one thought running around and around my mind: "To be a monk . . . to be a monk." (p. 331)

Once again, Merton was overwhelmed by the trees, the woods, the fresh air. But the reaction was interpreted by him paradoxically: he needed nature but if he embraced the cloistered, contemplative life of Gethsemani he would not get enough of it. He returned to his room very troubled.

"I became the most humble and most abject of men, that thou mightest overcome thy pride by my humility," says the Lord in the words of *The Imitation of Christ* [by Thomas à Kempis].
It is not enough to study Christ's life with the intention of imitating Him. He must give Himself to us, He must live in us, He must be humble in us. Before we can understand the pattern of life that is given us in Him, we must receive Him, that He may be life in us. Hence the Cross—for by His death on the Cross and by the Sacrament of the Eucharist He gives Himself entirely to us to be our life.[22]

Merton continued to reflect and pray. His journal entry for Holy Saturday discloses some kind of resolve, though still incomplete and uncertain. Again, the vehicle is nature.

Now the sun is setting. Birds sing. Lent is over. I am tired. Tomorrow is Easter, and I go, for no good reason, to New York. Out there a couple of bluejays are fighting in a tree. I wonder if I have learned enough to pray for humility. I desire only one thing: to love God. Those who love Him, keep His commandments. I only desire to do one thing: to follow His will. I pray that I am at least beginning to know what that may mean. Could it ever possibly mean that I might some day become a monk in this monastery? My Lord, and my King, and my God![23]

In one of the last conferences Merton attended at Gethsemani, the retreat master told the retreatants that it was said that no petition one asks at the fourteenth station of the cross is ever refused. On Easter Sunday afternoon, in a practically empty abbey church, Merton made the stations of the cross and at the fourteenth station asked "for the grace of a vocation to the Trappists, if it were pleasing to God" (p. 332). And early Easter Monday morning, April 14, Merton left Gethsemani.

The train Merton took back to New York had its origin in Louisville, so he had some time in the city. Once again, he reacts—at least in *The Seven Storey Mountain*—to what he thought to be the meaninglessness of the world. Again Merton juxtaposed the city with the monastery and, as before, the monastic life prevailed.

> At a street corner, I happened to look up and caught sight of an electric sign, on top of a two-storey building. It read: "Clown Cigarettes."
>
> I turned and fled from the alien and lunatic street, and found my way into the nearby cathedral, and knelt, and prayed, and did the Stations of the Cross.
>
> Afraid of the spiritual pressures of the monastery? Was that what I had said the other day? How I longed to be back there now: everything here, in the world outside, was insipid and slightly insane. There was only one place I knew of where there was any true order.
>
> Yet, how could I go back? Did I not know that I really had no vocation? . . . It was the same old story again. (pp. 332-33)

The tension and conflict continued. Merton wanted to speak with someone at Saint Bonaventure about his struggle but was stopped by "a vague subconscious fear that I would once and for all be told that I definitely had no vocation" (p. 338). This perhaps bespeaks Merton's fear that he truly did have a vocation but was uncertain about admitting it.

To resolve his conflict Merton resorted to a technique he no doubt assimilated from his reading of Augustine's *Confessions*—opening the Scriptures and putting a finger down blindly on the page. He looked and found what he thought to be his answer from God: *Ecce eris tacens* (Behold you shall be silent) from Luke 1:20. With his tendency to complicate things, Merton found it difficult to interpret the passage.

> By the time I had got myself completely tied up in these perplexities, the information I had asked for was more of a nuisance, and a greater cause of uncertainty than my ignorance. . . .

But there was something more, however. On one level, Merton had found his answer.

> . . . Deep down, underneath all the complexity, I had a kind of conviction that this was a genuine answer, and that the problem was indeed some day going to end up that way: I was going to be a Trappist. (p. 334)

However, that insight made very little difference in his day-to-day life. It would take some time to reach Merton's innermost depths.

The monastery at Gethsemani was constantly on Merton's mind. He continued to walk around the woods and pastures of Saint Bonaventure, reflecting and "full of nostalgia for the Trappist monastery."

In early June 1941 Merton was absorbed with giving final examinations, preparing classes for the summer term, and writing a new book, the autobiographical novel published as *My Argument with the Gestapo*.[24] Thus, the issue of the Trappist vocation was pushed into the background, though certainly not out of mind altogether.

That summer, especially July, found Merton examining his obligations to other men, thus indirectly examining the validity of removing himself from any involved contact with mankind. As he was teaching nuns, clerics, and priests, his thoughts were intensified when he examined his students as students, as persons, and as religious. Many seemed "still children." Their lives were secure, "walled in by ramparts of order and decorum and stability, in the social as much as in the religious sphere" (p. 338).

Saint Bonaventure had a series of speakers on campus. One of them was Catherine de Hueck, founder and director of Friendship House.

> . . . someone sent from God for the special purpose of waking us up, and turning our eyes in that direction which we all tended so easily to forget, in the safety and isolation of our country stronghold, lost in the upstate hills. (p. 339)

Merton was deeply impressed by de Hueck's talk and by the woman herself. She was "so calm, so certain, peaceful in her absolute confidence in God" (p. 342). She was a woman in whom dwelled the Holy Spirit, and Merton responded to this. But one must also consider his powerful social conscience, so recently sharpened by the writing of the autobiographical novel and journal of fantasy that dealt so much with Merton's thoughts on war. It is not unusual then that Merton should ask de Hueck if he could come to Harlem and Friendship House and spend some time working, after the end of the summer term. So in the middle of August, Merton was on his way.

Merton stayed at Friendship House on 135th Street in Harlem for almost three weeks. He genuinely involved himself in the work there, not only because he believed in it and in his responsibilities to engage himself in such work but also because he was again putting the Trappist vocation to the test. How strong was it? How valid was it to shut himself away, in a monastery, from social responsibilities? As before, he was juxtaposing the Trappist vocation with the other side, in this case Friendship House.

But the juxtaposition did not work quite the same way because Merton saw and felt some of the same things about Friendship House that he had seen and felt about Gethsemani.

> I felt for Friendship House a little of the nostalgia I had felt for Gethsemani. Here I was, once again thrown back into the world, alone in the turmoil and futility of it, and robbed of my close and immediate and visible association with any group of those who had banded themselves together to form a small, secret colony of the Kingdom or Heaven in this earth of exile. . . .

Yet, from the juxtaposition of Friendship House and Gethsemani emerged a very important insight, the need for a supportive community.

> . . . it was all too evident: I needed this support, this nearness to those who really loved Christ so much that they seemed to see Him. I needed to be with people whose every action told me something of the country that was my home: expatriates in every alien land keep together, if only to remind themselves, by their very faces and clothes and gait and accents and expressions, of the land they came from. (pp. 349-50)

This need for community and community support is one of the most important factors in his ultimate decision to enter the Trappists. At the same time, however, I believe Merton knew that the community at Gethsemani would have a different kind of support from that of Friendship House, more subdued and detached, less direct and, to a certain degree, more demanding.

Merton left Friendship House Labor Day weekend of 1941. He then made a retreat at the monastery of Our Lady of the Valley near Providence, Rhode Island.

The retreat assumed great importance for Merton, though perhaps not in a completely conscious way. He now was giving serious thought to working permanently at Friendship House. Though he says very little about the retreat in *The Seven Storey Mountain*, there are several entries in the *Secular Journal* written while at the monastery.[25] The tenor of the rhetoric is social awareness and social involvement, but at the same time detachment from earthly things.

He was trying to determine the direction in which he should move, toward Gethsemani or toward Harlem.

> For I had come out of Harlem with what might well have been the problem of another vocation. Was it that? In these eight days [of the retreat] . . . the matter had made itself more or less clear. If I stayed in the world, I thought, my vocation would be first of all to write, second to teach. Work like that at Friendship House would only come after the other two. Until I got some more definite light, I should stay where I was, at Saint Bonaventure's. Had I been afraid, or perhaps subconsciously hoping, that the question of becoming a Trappist would once again become a burning issue here? It did not. That whole business remained in its neutral, indefinite state: relegated to the area which my mind could not quite perceive, because it was in darkness, and clouded with almost infinite uncertainties. (pp. 351-52)

But in hindsight, Merton felt the retreat more "serious and practical and successful" than he had realized. Though it was not as emotionally draining or subtly frantic as the retreat at Gethsemani, the time at Our Lady of the Valley was one of acquiring "nourishment and strength" and of developing "firmness and certitude and depth."

Merton took the train back to Saint Bonaventure on September 8. He had some more thoughts about the "emptiness and futility and nothingness" of the world. But he was not particularly disturbed by the thoughts, as in the past. He had come to the realization that though he might be in the world he did not have to be a part of it or belong to it, nor did he have to lead his life with the emptiness and complacency that he saw so much of.

When Merton began his teaching in the fall, he discovered that he had strictly organized his life in a kind of quasi-monastic fashion. He rose early to pray the office and prepare for mass and communion. He spent almost an hour each morning with mental prayer and throughout the day he did a great deal of spiritual reading, including the lives of the saints—Joan of Arc, Saint John Bosco, and Saint Benedict. He also went through again Saint John of the Cross's *Ascent of Mount Carmel* and *Dark Night of the Soul*.

Merton developed a deep devotion to Saint Thérèse of Lisieux, the Little Flower. She held for Merton an insight into his own dilemma.

> . . . here is what strikes me as the most phenomenal thing about her. She became a saint, not by running away from the middle class, not by abjuring and despising and cursing the middle class, or the environment in which she had

> grown-up: on the contrary, she clung to it insofar as one could cling to such a thing and be a good Carmelite. (p. 354)

Thérèse remained herself; she preserved her integrity while at the same time living a beautiful vocation.

During October, Merton continued to correspond with Catherine de Hueck of Friendship House. He found her forceful and encouraging. She urged him to consider "selling all," something Merton says had been in the back of his mind. Now, as a result of these letters, Merton began to come to serious terms with this most difficult of all Christian maxims. He decided to make a novena, "asking for the grace to know what to do next." Merton's journal entries for these novena days are reflective of his uncertainty with "selling all," not because he did not wish to embrace such a notion but because he was still hesitant about his motives for doing so.

During the novena, Merton was asked by one of the friars if he wanted to drive up to Buffalo to meet Catherine de Hueck and bring her back to Saint Bonaventure.

> . . . the following things come clear in my mind: that she will probably ask me to come to Friendship House. That if she does, it is not necessarily to be taken as a sign that I am supposed to go there—that it is God's will. I wouldn't decide anything before hand. Make no decisions until the time for making decisions. In general, I am tentatively on defense against going to Friendship House.[26]

Predictably, Catherine de Hueck did ask Merton when he was coming to Friendship House for good, and his response in *The Seven Storey Mountain* is one of surprise. At the same time he believed the question held his answer, that it was likely what he had been praying to find out. Merton answered that he would come if he could go on writing while he was there. That was the condition. De Hueck chided Merton about conditions and reservations and asked him whether he was thinking of becoming a priest; his letters had asked the questions of one who wants to become a priest. Merton answered that he did not have a vocation to the priesthood. But the discussion did convince Merton that he had outgrown Saint Bonaventure, that it was "too tame, too safe and too sheltered." He believed that it now demanded nothing of him and that as long as he remained there he would really have to give up very little. Merton decided that going permanently to Friendship House "was the most plausible thing" for him to do; if he sincerely wanted to write and teach, he could do more and better in each were he to make the move.

An entry from Merton's journal dated November 6, 1941, seems to contradict the certainty of *The Seven Storey Mountain*. At least it indicates that Merton was less inclined to make a firm decision about going to Friendship House than the autobiography would have us to believe.

> I do not say I will do this or I will do that. I pray God that in February [the end of the semester] I may do His will and that between now and then I will invent no arguments to sell myself one idea or the other. I will continue praying and writing exactly as I am doing now. . . .

This entry also reveals how strongly Merton was committed to a clear understanding of God's will in guiding him in his decision.

> . . . No need for anything new, or for any excitement whatever. If I pray, either I will change my mind or I will not. In any case, God will guide me. No need to be up in arms, no need to be anything other than what I am—but I will pray and fast harder. No more excitements, arguments, tearing of hair, trips to Cuba and grandiose "farewell world" gestures. No need for anything special—special joy or special sorrow, special excitement or special torment. Everything is indifferent, except prayer, fasting, meditation—and work. I thank God and all the saints that I am not running around in circles—not yet. Defend me later, O God, against all scruples![27]

Tongue-in-cheek rhetoric? Whatever, the journal entry does not fully prepare us for Merton's decision to go to Friendship House at the end of the fall semester.

Merton informed the head of the English Department that he would be leaving Saint Bonaventure in January 1942. Merton also told Father Thomas, the school's president, of his decision. Father Thomas, like Catherine de Hueck, asked Merton if he had ever thought of becoming a priest. Merton had great respect for Father Thomas, who previously had been both a professor of theology and a seminary rector. Thus he was caught off guard by the question.

Merton determined—perhaps by way of rationalization—that Father Thomas did not know the circumstances of his case. Additionally, Merton writes that he did not want to get mixed up in a discussion of his priestly vocation now that he had decided to go to Friendship House. However, he did admit to Father Thomas that he had thought about becoming a priest but in the same breath said that he did not believe he had a vocation. When Father Thomas said, "All right then. Go to Harlem if you must," Merton seemed to have sidestepped another confrontation with himself as to his *real* intentions.

This happened on or around November 7 or November 8. The narratives in both Merton's autobiography and his journal after the Father Thomas incident continue with an account of his Thanksgiving weekend in New York City. Thus we can only speculate on what occurred during the intervening three weeks. It is likely that Merton gave a great deal of thought to his Trappist vocation rather than to his pending departure for Friendship House since toward the end of November and the beginning of December, things happened too quickly and deliberately for one whose thoughts were poorly developed and not fully explored. Merton's conversation with Father Thomas was much more significant than he would have us believe, at least on the basis of his account in the autobiography (he makes no mention of it in the journal). Merton was still affected by those for whom he had respect, particularly individuals of an apparent deep spirituality. When someone like Father Thomas Flassman, a man of learning and of piety, suggested to Merton that he might have a priestly vocation, Merton could not help but be moved. Of course, he could resist, which seems to be what he did, but I do not believe the resistance was either powerful or lasting. In fact, because he did resist initially, Father Thomas's question could likely have had even greater impact as Merton began to open himself up to it during the two weeks prior to Thanksgiving.

Merton spent Thanksgiving weekend in New York City and on the Friday after Thanksgiving had lunch with Mark Van Doren to discuss the possibility of publishing *My Argument with the Gestapo*. As they were leaving lunch, Van Doren and Merton were discussing, in a detached sort of way, the Trappists and Van Doren asked Merton whether he had dropped the idea of becoming a priest, to which Merton responded with a neutral shrug. Van Doren went on to say that he had spoken to someone about Merton and his vocation and the person had indicated that the fact that Merton had given up the idea of a vocation when told he had none very likely was a sign that he actually had a vocation. Merton was aroused.

> This was the third time that shaft had been fired at me, unexpectedly, in these last days, and this time it really struck deep. For the reasoning that went with this statement forced my thoughts to take an entirely new line. If that were true, then it prescribed a new kind of attitude to the whole question of my vocation. (p. 362)

Merton began to see that Van Doren and the others were urging him to come to terms with this vocation because a vocation, as a gift from God, can be lost, as any gift, if it is refused. He even told Van Doren that "God's Providence" arranged that they should meet for lunch and that Van Doren should tell him what he did. He also said that if he "entered any monastery it would be to become a Trappist" (p. 362). But Merton also believed that this enlarged awareness of his vocation should have no bearing on his decision to begin work at Friendship House in January. If things did not work out there, he would then consider the monastery.

During this weekend, Merton, with Bob Lax, also made a day of recollection with the staff of Friendship House. The day, especially the conferences of the leader, Father Furfey, made a strong impression on both him and Lax.

> Father Furfey said in one of his talks: "You will have to be despised by the world, and if you are not despised and rejected by it there is something wrong! . . ." When he said that, I noticed the smile on the face of Betty S-. She smiled to herself like a kid that had been told something very pleasant, or invited out to a party. It was a nice, glad smile with more joy in it than I have seen anywhere else: a joy purified of merely earthly satisfaction![28]

On Sunday, Merton took the train back to Olean. Neither he nor Lax could talk after the day of recollection. A journal entry from Monday, November 24, may offer some explanation.

> I am not physically tired, just filled with a deep, vague undefined sense of spiritual distress, as if I had a deep wound running inside of me and it had to be staunched. . . . The wound is only another aspect of the fact that we are exiles on this earth.
>
> The sense of exile bleeds inside me like a hemorrhage. Always the same wound, whether a sense of sin or of holiness, or of one's own insufficiency, or of spiritual dryness. In the end as we experience these things, they all end up by being pretty much the same wound. In fact, spiritual dryness is an acute experience of longing—therefore of love.[29]

It is difficult to analyze these feelings because Merton provides so little background and context with which to work. In neither the autobiography nor the journal does he proffer any extensive treatment of the day of recollection with the Friendship House staff. Some insights do come with Merton's discussion of love as an "acute experience of longing." To say that he was looking for love is simplistic. But it is possible that, for Merton, the experience of love had much to do with giving God everything, the "perfect love" of the Fourth Gospel. In this sense, Friendship House may not have held as much certainty for Merton as he thought it did. Perhaps it was too easy, too illusionary, like the campus of Saint Bonaventure to which Merton returned that Sunday evening.

> . . . It is still and peaceful, but there is no place for me here.
> I am amazed at all this quietness which does not belong to me, and cannot. For a moment I get the illusion that the peace here is real, but it is not. It is merely the absence of trouble, not the peace of poverty and sacrifice. This "peace" cannot be enough for me anymore.[30]

Thursday, December 4, 1941, seems to be the day of resolution, when Merton came face-to-face with his vocation: "The time has come for me to go and be a Trappist" (p. 363).

That day's journal entry—the last, incidentally, of *The Secular Journal*—offers clues to how and why the resolution came about. Merton asks why the notion of the Trappists will not leave him. Should he do what he had wanted to do for several months and find out whether the Trappists would accept him in spite of those things for which he was rejected by the Franciscans?

> If you were to ask me what I thought they would answer, I would say I was almost certain they would let me in. But perhaps what I am afraid of is to write and be rejected, and have that last hope taken away—as if it were a hope.

With clarity and directness, Merton asks the crucial question and provides an equally direct response.

> Would I not be obliged to admit, now, that if there is a choice for me between Harlem and the Trappists, I would not hesitate to take the Trappists? Is that why I hesitate to find out if the choice exists? Is that my roundabout way of evading my vocation?

Merton would have to renounce everything in entering the Trappists, and therein lies the powerful attraction. Merton believed that by giving up everything he could do more for the church and its mystical body than if he were to work at Friendship House. He poses and answers another question.

> Perhaps I cling to my independence, to the chance to write, to go where I like in the world. . . . I must be prepared to give all these things up. It seems monstrous at the moment that I should consider my writing important enough ever to enter into the question. If God wants me to write, I can write anywhere.

Harlem would also not be anything special, though it would be a "good and reasonable way to follow Christ." Going to the Trappists, on the other hand, is "exciting, it fills me with awe and with desire, I return to the idea again and again: Give up EVERYTHING, give up EVERYTHING!" And the famous last words of Merton's journal: "I shall speak to one of the friars."[31]

I believe it is significant that in this last journal entry Merton, for one of the first times, addresses the issue of his writing and that he should be prepared to give even this up were he to enter the Trappists. Writing was the common denominator with Merton. He might turn out to be many things, but fundamentally—and by his own admission—he was a writer. It is therefore telling that he would be prepared to give up writing. His trust in God's wisdom and goodness was profound.

Merton devotes considerable space in his autobiography to the events of that Thursday. He writes with much more emotion and, occasionally, a kind of frantic rhetoric as he retells the story four or five years after the fact. One could almost see the calm and quiet perception of the journal as antecedent to the excitation and emotion of the autobiography.

In the autobiography, Merton writes that he was filled with a "vivid conviction" that he should go to the Trappists; the time had come. He needed to talk with someone about the "vivid conviction"—again, perhaps seeking the ultimate approval, the sanction and support for what he really wanted to do but was afraid to—and he thought of his old friend and confidant, Father Philotheus. But instead of going to Father Philotheus's room—it was evening and Merton had seen the light on—Merton went out to a grove of trees near the shrine of the Little Flower on campus and walked around, praying. Merton tried to go to Father Philotheus's room a second time but after getting within six feet of the door, went back to the shrine and the grove. Merton's description of the struggle is powerful.

> I don't think there was ever a moment in my life when my soul felt so urgent and so special an anguish. I had been praying all the time, so I cannot say that I began to pray when I arrived there where the shrine was: but things became more definite.

Into Merton's deeply emotional prayer to the Little Flower is interjected some insightful words of self-reproof.

> "Please help me. What am I going to do? I can't go on like this. You can see that! Look at the state I am in. What ought I to do? Show me the way." As if I needed more information or some kind of a sign! . . . "You show me what to do. . . . If I get into the monastery, I will be your monk. Now show me what to do."

It is strange to think of Merton making vocational deals in a fit of panic, not unlike Martin Luther's frightening experience in the thunderstorm. But Merton's is a more controlled situation and the terms seem to be different from those of Luther. Merton wanted to be a monk and his desire was intense; it is therefore not unusual that he wound be overcome with fear and doubt. Did he have a Trappist vocation? Could he really enter Gethsemani? We have seen that his greatest obstacle in this quest was he himself and his turning to the Little Flower seems to represent his continuing self-doubt.

I believe, however, that it was the *act* of prayer to the Little Flower—and not the prayer itself—that brought Merton through this quasipanic. This is reflected in his account of what happened after he made the prayer.

> Suddenly . . . I became aware of the wood, the trees, the dark hills, the wet night wind, and then, clearer than any of these obvious realities, in my imagination, I started to hear the great bell of Gethsemani rising in the night—the bell in the big grey tower, ringing and ringing, as if it were just behind the first hill. The impression made me breathless, and I had to think twice to realize that it was only in my imagination that I was hearing the bell of the Trappist Abbey ringing in the dark. Yet, as I afterwards calculated, it was just about that time that the bell is rung every night for the SALVE REGINA, towards the end of compline.
>
> The bell seemed to be telling me where I belonged—as if it were calling me home. (pp. 364-65)

Merton then finally went to Father Philotheus's room, asking his opinion. He replied that he did not see any reason why Merton should not desire to become a monk. The priest asked but one question: why Merton was sure he wanted to become a Trappist. Merton replied that he wanted to give God everything. It apparently was important to know what Father Philotheus thought and whether he accepted Merton's reply, for Merton writes, "I could see by the expression on his face that he was satisfied." And then, as if Merton had received the affirmation that he so desired and needed:

> I went upstairs like somebody who had been called back from the dead. Never had I experienced the calm, untroubled peace and certainty that now filled my heart. (p. 366)

It was during Merton's talk with Father Philotheus that everything became clear. He saw his worries and uncertainties as futile and meaningless instead of substantial and realistic, as they appeared to be. He believed, at that point, that he really did have a vocation to the monastic life and thus his doubts were now empty meanderings. He was full of peace and a newfound confidence, ready to begin the very final stages of his journey to Gethsemani.

The same evening as his decision—December 4, 1941—Merton wrote Gethsemani and cautiously asked to be admitted as a postulant. As soon as Merton had a favorable reply from Gethsemani, he received a letter from his draft board ordering him to appear for a second physical examination. Merton speculated that perhaps Providence was being deliberately cruel.

Merton wrote to his draft board immediately, informing them that he planned to enter a monastery and that he would need some time there to determine whether he would be formally admitted.

On Sunday, December 7, 1941—the next specific date given in the autobiography—Merton packed a lunch and went hiking in the valley near the campus, full of nostalgia.

> This was probably the last time I would see this place. Where would I be in a week from that day? It was in the hands of God. There was nothing I could do but leave myself to His mercy. (p. 367)

When he returned from his hike, Merton learned about Pearl Harbor. He didn't write about it in his journal, but in his autobiography he said that Pearl Harbor had little or no direct effect on his life at that time. Gethsemani was too important and too overpowering.

On Monday, Merton received a letter from his draft board telling him that his new medical examination would be postponed for a month. Consequently, he decided to leave immediately for Gethsemani. By the following afternoon, Merton had made all the necessary arrangements. His classes had been reassigned, much of his clothing given away—as also many of his books—his manuscripts were either destroyed or sent to friends for safekeeping,[32] the necessary letters written. "With an amazing and joyous sense of lightness, I was ready to go" (p. 369).

The train to Gethsemani left that evening. Merton arrived at the Olean station a few minutes early so he made a visit to Our Lady of the Angels church where he had often prayed.

> I knelt there for ten or twelve minutes in the silence without even attempting to grasp or comprehend the immense, deep sense of gratitude that filled my heart and sent out from there to Christ in His Tabernacle. (p. 369)

There is a certain ominousness about Merton's rhetoric as he describes boarding the train and his reactions to the trip itself. But there is also the now-familiar death-to-life theme through which Merton described so many of his steps to Gethsemani.

> . . . the train came in through the freezing, sleety rain, and I got on, and my last tie with the world I had known snapped and broke.
> It was nothing less than a civil, moral death.

And, most important, there is no longer any fantasy, any unreality.

> This journey, this transition from the world to a new life, was like flying through some strange new element—as if I were in the stratosphere. And yet I was on the familiar earth, and the cold winter rain streaked the windows of the train as we travelled through the dark hills. (p. 369)

Merton's reflections on his first and last journey to Gethsemani, the journey that would bring him to a life as a writer-monk, reveal the clarity of thought and intention that he had reached—keeping in mind, however, that this is all hindsight, as it must be in an autobiography.

> It was a strange thing. Mile after mile my desire to be in the monastery increased beyond belief. I was altogether absorbed in that one idea. And yet, paradoxically, mile after mile my indifference increased, and my interior peace. What if they did not receive me? Then I would go into the army. But surely that would be a disaster? Not at all. If, after all this, I was rejected by the monastery and had to be drafted, it would be quite clear that it was God's will. I had done everything in my power; the rest was in His hands. And for all the tremendous and increasing intensity of my desire to be in the cloister the thought that I might find myself, instead, in an army camp, no longer troubled me in the least.
> I was free. I had recovered my liberty. I belonged to God, not to myself: and to belong to Him is to be free, free of all anxieties and worries and sorrows that belong to this earth, and the love of things that are in it. (p. 370)

Merton's freedom was attained through the full realization of God's will for him. He believed, beyond any apparent doubt, that until it was proven otherwise, God wanted him to be at Gethsemani.

The months and months of struggle and redefinition, of posing questions and searching for answers, of stripping away, burning, and burying what he thought to be the contemptible ways and means of the world, of finally accepting the necessity, for himself, of the rebellion that he had gleaned from his study of Blake—"the rebellion of the lover of the living God, the rebellion of one whose desire of God was so intense and so irresistible that it condemned, with all its might, all the hypocrisy and petty sensuality and skepticism and materialism which cold and trivial minds set up as impassable barriers between God and the souls of men" (p. 87)—all this had brought Thomas Merton to the gate of Gethsemani that evening of December 10, 1941.

Toward the end of his life Merton wrote a passage that could very well describe him as he entered the gate of Gethsemani that cold winter evening.

> . . . My task is only to be what I am, a man seeking God in silence and solitude, with deep respect for the demands and realities of his own vocation, and fully aware that others too are seeking the truth in their own way.[33]

THREE

The Fusion of Writer and Monk: The Early Monastic Years

W hen Thomas Merton entered the Trappist community at Gethsemani, he had become by that time a writer, what Sherwood Anderson called a "word-fellow." Merton wrote at least forty-five pieces for the Columbia student publications with which he was connected, including his occasional column, "The Stroller," and his entries under the pseudonym F. Xavier Sheridan. There were his journals, one of which was to be published as his *Secular Journal* and his autobiographical novel, *My Argument With the Gestapo*, published posthumously. At least half of the poems in his first published book of poetry were written before his entrance into Gethsemani. In addition, Merton published at least eleven book reviews in *The New York Herald Tribune Book Review* and *The New York Times Book Review* and a short piece on Aldous Huxley for *The Catholic World*.[1]

Merton kept journals all his life and was well into this aspect of the writer's craft by the time he entered Gethsemani. John Howard Griffin, the American writer and Merton's first biographer, has written of the importance of journals, particularly in relationship to writing and the writer.

> . . . it allows the writer to create directly and without wending his way through all of the jungles of delusion and self-aggrandizement. The act of creation is far more profound in its sources than most of us consciously realize. It comes up mysteriously from the very depths of a being, and that SOUND BOX which is the spirit must be tempered and balanced as near as possible to the truth in

order to produce the truest work. This is . . . vital to all writers. The profoundest truth constitutes the greatest originality.[2]

The journal can bring the writer to a unique notion of himself, one that Griffin has called "wisdom and compassion."

Writing seems to have been that process which held Merton completely, without any significantly long periods of nonproduction and creative dryness. Perhaps Merton was aware of what Maxwell Geismar has called the writer's "slow form of poison."

> For the writer who does not write, all his life is a slow form of poison; and every good writer knows this, and every writer who is afraid of this spiritual corruption must, finally, come back to his writing.[3]

Merton had had the rich experience of life on which the writer must build and that must form his permanent learning process, and he had sought to come nearer to the heart of the truth, what Henry Miller has called "the ultimate aim of the writer." If one holds, as does Miller, that art teaches nothing but the significance of life, then it is possible to speculate that Merton's art was at least partially responsible for his entrance into Gethsemani, since it brought him to a keener awareness of the significance—and insignificance—of his own life and the extent to which this significance for him must ultimately rest in and with God.

So when Thomas Merton was formally admitted to Gethsemani, on December 13, 1941, he was admitted as he was, a writer who wanted to become a monk.

> I brought all the instincts of a writer with me into the monastery, and I knew that I was bringing them, too. It was not a case of smuggling them in. (p. 389)

If Merton's attitude about his writing was certain and unconflicted, so too was his attitude toward the monastic life, at least in the first few days. He sensed—again perhaps because of his extraordinary "natural" and very personal spirituality—that the contemplative life should be something beyond mere formality and practice. Already Merton had clarified for himself the core of the monastic vocation, God alone; and even without the historical and theoretical background of the Trappist life, he appeared to have the issues well sorted out.

> All that I needed to worry about was to do God's will, to enter the monastery if I was allowed to do so, and take things as I found them, and if God wanted

to do any of this "vouchsafing" he could go ahead and "vouchsafe." And all the other details would take care of themselves. (p. 375)

There was also that already profound nature of Merton's vocation itself, which he described in the context of his first evening in the monastic choir.

When we began to chant the *Magnificant* I almost wept, but that was because I was new in the monastery. And in fact it was precisely because of that that I had reason to weep with thanksgiving and happiness as I croaked the words in my dry, hoarse throat, in gratitude for my vocation, in gratitude that I was really there at last, really in the monastery, and chanting God's liturgy with his monks. (p. 380)

Of no little importance was Merton's awareness of community and the ramifications of community life.

By this time God had given me enough sense to realize at least obscurely that this is one of the most important aspects of any religious vocation: the first and most elementary test of one's call to the religious life—whether as a Jesuit, Franciscan, Cistercian or Carthusian—is the willingness to accept life in a community in which everybody is more or less imperfect. (p. 381)

By December 16, Merton had received his postulant's habit and his monastic name of Louis, and by February 1942 he had received his novice's habit, his first step toward the monastic vows. Though he suggests that his adjustment to the monastic life was neither easy nor automatic, Merton faced the difficulties directly and, as such, was able to progress naturally, as himself, rather than as the person his monastic superiors might want him to be.

What seems to be the essence of his progress was Merton's deep faith, his unquestioning trust in God.

I was hidden in the secrecy of His protection. He was surrounding me constantly with the work of His love, His wisdom and His mercy. And so it would be, day after day, year after year. Sometimes I would be preoccupied with problems that seemed to be difficult and seemed to be great, and yet when it was all over the answers that I worked out did not seem to matter much anyway, because all the while, beyond my range of vision and comprehension, God had silently and imperceptively worked the whole thing out for me, and had presented me with the solution. To say it better, He had worked the solution into the very tissue of my own life and substance and existence by the wise incomprehensible weaving of His Providence. (p. 385)

As the days and weeks wore on, Merton continued to explore what he thought the peculiar nature of the Trappist vocation to be. A short time after he received his habit as novice he entered the infirmary to be treated for a bad case of influenza. Merton initially looked on the period as a chance for greater solitude and deeper prayer but he soon realized that his true motives centered more on removing himself from the disciplines—he mentions chasing all over the monastery answering bells—a role essential to the Trappist life. On this recognition, Merton was able to structure his insights: what he called "the Cistercian formula" rested on two interrelated issues, the contemplative spirit itself and complete submission (obedience) to monastic superiors; the one could not be attained without the other.

Merton's reflections reveal his sincere yet still elementary level of understanding, a level that would lead him to oversimplification and to a kind of all-or-nothing mind-set.

> Doing things, suffering things, thinking things, making tangible and concrete sacrifices for the love of God—that is what contemplation seems to mean here—and I suppose the same attitude is universal in our Order. It goes by the name of "active contemplation." (p. 389)

He recognized also that from the time of Saint Bernard of Clairvaux, obedience has been "the Cistercian formula." And this brought Merton directly to his writing and its place in the monastic schema. Thus began his intensive struggle to reconcile the "personal Daemon" of his writing with what he believed to be the requirements of the monastic vocation.

Merton has said that writing was the one activity born in him and in his blood.

> It is possible to doubt whether I have become a monk (a doubt I have to live with), but it is not possible to doubt that I am a writer, that I was born one and will most probably die as one.[4]

One is reminded here of Edward Albee's comment that when he was six he decided not that he was *going* to be a writer but that he *was* a writer.

Recognizing both Merton's gift and his inclination/need to write, Father Master encouraged his young monk to write poems and keep his journal. (By the Christmas season Merton had already half filled an old notebook with his reflections.) Initially, Merton most frequently wrote after night office, usually between four and five-thirty in the morning, during what he called the "great silence." Eventually, however, the novice master told him that, as ordered by Saint Benedict's Rule, he must use this period for meditation and Scripture study, especially of the psalms. Merton's superiors did not tell him to stop writing, only to change the period when he wrote. But I suggest that Merton interpreted the order as an indication that he should stop writing. After receiving the directive from his novice master, Merton immersed himself more deeply in the monastic life, its prayers, disciplines, and labors (pp. 390-91).

When Merton entered Gethsemani he was prepared—even desirous—to give up his writing, but in deference to the wishes of his superiors continued to write. But the writing became a struggle because of Merton's either/or notion of monasticism.[5] To write would be to compromise the monastic life and lead to the dilution of the monastic ideals, something Merton's convictions would not tolerate. There is the further element of the limits to which Merton felt he could go spiritually. To try to reconcile his writing with his notion of the monastic ideals would be an almost impossible spiritual burden, one that Merton was not eager to take on.

So when Merton began to pull back from his writing in the spring of 1942, he was doing so in order to become a more perfect Trappist. As the spring moved into summer and the wicked Kentucky sun shone, Merton seemed positive about his vocation.

> [It is in the summer] when you really begin to feel the weight of our so-called active contemplation with all the accidental additions that it acquires at Gethsemani. You begin to understand the truth of the fact that the old Trappists saw in the "exercises of contemplation"—the choral office and mental prayer and so on—principally a means of penance and self-punishment. And so it is the season when novices give up and go back to the world—they give up at other times too, but summer is their hardest test. . . .
>
> But I had no desire to leave. I don't think I enjoyed the heat more than anybody else, but with my active temperament I could satisfy myself that all my work and all my sweat really meant something, because they made me feel as if I were doing something for God. . . .
>
> . . . I thought to myself: "Anybody who runs away from a place like this is crazy." But it was not as supernatural as I may have thought. It is not sufficient to love the place for its scenery, and because you feel satisfied that you are a spiritual athlete and a not inconsiderable servant of God. (pp. 391-92)

Merton was trying to strip away the extraneous dimensions of his life. He was as eager to give up the writing as he was to give up the memories of his

childhood in Douglaston. This past was on Merton's mind when his brother
came to visit him in late July.

John Paul Merton was in the Royal Air Force. He came to Gethsemani to
see his brother and to be baptized before he set sail for the war front. Merton
himself gave his brother instructions and it is at this point in his autobiography
that he reveals his desire to strip away his childhood.

> You might have expected two brothers, at such a time as this, to be talking
> about the "old days." In a sense, we were. Our own lives, our memories, our
> family, the house that had served as a home, the things we had done in order
> to have what we thought was a good time—all this indeed was the background
> of our conversation, and, in an indirect sort of way, entered very definitely into
> the subject matter.
>
> It was so clearly present that there was no necessity to allude to it, this sorry,
> complicated past, with all its confusions and misunderstandings and mistakes. It
> was as real and vivid and present as the memory of an automobile accident in
> the casualty ward where the victims are brought back to life. (p. 396)

One could suggest that the evidence of guilt was beginning to emerge, a guilt
Merton would struggle with all his monastic life. This is apparent in his
response to his brother's baptism.

> I realized, obscurely, that in those last four days [the days of John Paul's
> instructions] the work of eighteen or twenty years of my bad example had been
> washed away and made good by God's love. The evil that had been done by my
> boasting and showing off and exulting in my own stupidity had been atoned for
> in my own soul, at the time that it had been washed out of his, and I was full
> of peace and gratitude. (p. 398)

John Paul Merton was soon on his way to war—with Merton's premonition
that he would never see him alive again.

In the first six months of Merton's novitiate, he concentrated on what he
believed to be the proper modus operandi for the Trappist monk. Merton's
writing vocation—and his attempts to reconcile it with the Trappist
vocation—directly affected all aspects of his monastic life.

> God has brought me to the monastery to die to everything that I used to be.
> I used to love comfort and pleasure: therefore in the monastery I shall have
> much discomfort and no pleasure, although I aspire to close union with God
> and that will compensate for every pleasure by the joys it will bring. I used to
> love books and study, but God wants me to die to all that. Therefore I shall
> become a man of one book or of no books. I shall read nothing but Holy

Scripture and the Rule. I shall study nothing except what is necessary for the priesthood. When I read, I shall take no notes, but just read a line or two and then spend the rest of the interval deep in meditation and prayer.

I used to be a writer, but God wants me to die to all that. I shall give up all writing. Nothing more, not even a spiritual Journal. Poems I renounce forever: did I come to the monastery to be a poet? God forbid.[6]

So in the latter part of 1942 Merton did in fact give up writing. He tore up his journal. In addition, he stopped taking notes on the books and articles he read and, on the advice of his confessor, gave up reading books "to which [he] thought [he] was attached," particularly Saint John of the Cross. One is tempted to think that Merton may have manipulated his confessor in order to further his attempts at a kind of intellectual austerity.

Though Merton may have been able to withdraw for a period from his own writing, he could not withdraw from his considerable literary skills. In Lent 1943, at the request of his superiors, he began a series of translations—from French—of various Cistercian writings, all published anonymously. The first two translations, *The Kingdom of Jesus* and *The Soul of the Apostolate*, were published in 1946 and the last translations, *The Spirit of Simplicity* and translations of two texts from Saint Bernard, in 1948. Another project that Merton was asked to assume during his novitiate, this one more creative and original, was writing the lives of Cistercian saints, which eventually reached a length of over six hundred pages.

. . . in a monastery you work under strict obedience, you work by the bell, starting and stopping not when you get ideas or run out of them, but always at stated times. Then there are a thousand interruptions. You are half way through one book, when a more important job comes up and you drop what you are doing, in order to start that. Then when you get back to the other one, you have forgotten all the ideas you first had about it. As a matter of fact, when a big harvest comes along, or when there is a lot of corn to husk, it is a relief to be told to put your typewriter away for a month or so, and go out to the fields or the barnyard. . . . With all this, I was very content that I had given up writing poetry. It would only have been another job—another nuisance. The poems I wrote had become fewer and fewer, and the intervals between them got longer and longer, until finally it was about a year since I had written a line of verse, or felt the slightest desire to do so.[7]

Since when is writing a nuisance for one who was born a writer? This is difficult to understand except in the context of some kind of deep reaction *against* writing. One must then see Merton's attempts to withdraw from writing and his descriptions of the process—and his feelings involved—as part of the larger process of simplifying and purifying his monastic vocation by the excising of those personal values, interests, and gifts which he believed superfluous and contradictory to the Trappist life.

There is a certain irony in Merton's efforts to put aside his creative writing at this point in his life. Joseph Conrad said that a writer begins to live only after he begins to write. It is ironic that Merton would pull away from writing if he understood what Conrad was saying, which I suspect he did, that he was pulling away from that which could, at least on one level, bring him life.

Lent 1943 was soon over and at its conclusion, with the feast of the resurrection, Merton was left to face the death of John Paul, whose plane had crashed in the North Sea. Merton was moved to put aside his moratorium on writing and compose a striking poem, "For my Brother: reported Missing in Action, 1943."[8] He had expected his brother's death. In addition, he believed that God could—and should—take everything, including family. Merton was genuinely serious about giving all to God and sincerely believed that he should be willing to accept without question whatever God might do. This acceptance of God's will was an integral part of what Merton believed to be the monastic way, and in fact God's will was what Merton believed brought him to Gethsemani in the first place. It was personal faith in its most concrete and honest form.

Christmas 1943 held a surprise for Merton. Unannounced, his friend Robert Lax appeared at the last of the three Christmas masses, a pontifical high mass at which Merton was a minor minister. Merton received permission to visit with Lax and they talked of mutual friends and what they all were doing. Apparently, they talked also of Merton's writing, for when Lax returned to New York he took with him a manuscript of some of Merton's poems. Half of them he had written mostly at Saint Bonaventure and the other half after he entered Gethsemani.

Lax must have exerted some pressure on his friend, since Merton had to gather all his poems together and make some decision as to which ones he wanted to send back to New York.

> Getting these poems together and making a selection was like editing the work of a stranger, a dead poet, someone who had been forgotten. (p. 409)

Lax gave the manuscript to Mark Van Doren, who sent it to his friend James Laughlin, the publisher of New Directions, who decided to publish it. Merton learned of this just before Lent 1944. *Thirty Poems* was published on November 20, 1944. It is hard to know what to make of Merton's understated response. It may have been his true feeling.

> The exceedingly tidy little volume, *Thirty Poems*, reached me at the end of November, just before we began the annual retreat, in 1944.
> I went out under the grey sky, under the cedars at the edge of the cemetery, and stood in the wind that threatened snow and held the printed poems in my hand. (p. 410)

Merton's autobiography provides no information or background—no historical account—for the period from Christmas 1943 to November 1944. The only time reference is to January 21, 1944, the feast of Saint Agnes, when he wrote a poem to the saint.

> . . . when I had finished it my feeling was that I did not care if I never wrote another poem as long as I lived. (p. 412)

Some clues, however, can be gleaned from the structure of the text of the autobiography. Merton's reaction to *Thirty Poems* and his mention of the poem to Saint Agnes is a revealing discussion on his identity as a writer, the constant issue for Merton. During the period in question, Merton was more and more preoccupied with the issue of his identity as a writer.

> By this time [late fall 1944] I should have been delivered of any problems about my true identity. I had already made my simple profession [on March 19]. And my vows should have divested me of the last shred of any special identity.
> But then there was this shadow, this double, this writer who had followed me into the cloister.
> He is still on my track. He rides my shoulders, sometimes, like the old man of the sea. I cannot lose him. He still wears the name of Thomas Merton. Is it the name of an enemy?
> He is supposed to be dead.
> But he stands and meets me in the doorway of all my prayers, and follows me into church. He kneels with me behind the pillar, the Judas, and talks to me all the time in my ear.
> He is a business man. He is full of ideas. He breathes notions and new schemes. He generates books in the silence that ought to be sweet with the infinitely productive darkness of contemplation.
> And the worst of it is, he has my superiors on his side. They won't kick him out. I can't get rid of him.
> Maybe in the end he will kill me, he will drink my blood.

> Nobody seems to understand that one of us has got to die.
>
> Sometimes I am mortally afraid. There are days when there seems to be nothing left of my vocation—my contemplative vocation—but a few ashes. And everybody calmly tells me "writing is your vocation."
>
> And there he stands and bars my way to liberty. I am bound to the earth, in his Egyptian bondage of contracts, reviews, page proofs, and all the plans for books and articles that I am saddled with.
>
> When I first began to get ideas about writing, I told them to Father Master and Father Abbot with what I thought was "simplicity." I thought I was just "being open with my superiors." In a way I suppose I was.
>
> But it was not long before they got the idea that I ought to be put to work translating things, writing things. (pp. 410-11)

It is clear that Merton was not really facing the issue. His is a rhetoric of running, of fear that if he does not run he will be done in by the writer in him. But this is the internal context and I return to it in more detail later. There is also the external context within which the passage must be placed, a context that extends beyond the period during which the passage was written.

When Merton entered Gethsemani in 1941, the explosion of monasticism in America had not yet begun. Only two postulants entered with Merton, one of whom left after a few days. As the war drew to a close, however, more and more young men began to enter not only the Trappists but also other contemplative orders in America. At Gethsemani in 1947, there were only 170 monks at the abbey. By 1953, there were 270 monks and two daughter houses, one in Georgia and the other in Utah.[9]

> This material growth at Gethsemani is part of a vaster movement of spiritual vitality that is working throughout the Noble Order, all over the world. And one of the things it has produced has been a certain amount of Cistercian literature . . . all this means a demand for books in English about the Cistercian life and the spirituality of the Order and its history. (pp. 409-10)

There were additional circumstances at Gethsemani created by the Trappists' spiritual vitality: weekend retreats for laypeople and a larger number of pamphlets published by the monastery to inform the retreatants and others of the Trappist life and to help them with their spiritual struggles in the world.

> So it is not hard to see that this is a situation in which my double, my shadow, my enemy, Thomas Merton, the old man of the sea, has things in his favor. If he suggests books about the Order, his suggestions are heard. If he thinks up poems to be printed and published, his thoughts are listened to. There seems to be no reason why he should not write for magazines. (p. 412)

As each new year came, Merton took on more and more writing projects, so that by May 1947 he had as many as twelve projects going on at the same time, all in various stages of completion.[10] Externally, Merton was becoming deeply enmeshed in writing and would remain so for his entire monastic life. There were many things to be written, and Merton would write them. It was really a very simple matter, on one level. Merton was a man who could write. He was also a monk in a monastery that needed materials to be written. His superiors asked him to write and he wrote out of obedience.

Interiorly, however, the issues were complex. Though Merton wrote, he continued to resist the act, emotionally and spiritually. It is possible that his resistance was lessened by the nature of the writing and literary work he was occupied with: translations, biography, and a monastic history—writing not deeply personal and not as intensely creative as poetry, the autobiography, and journals. The writing of *The Seven Storey Mountain* in late 1944, its revision, and successful publication were a stage in Merton's process of coming to terms with his vocation as a writer and its fusion with his vocation as a monk.[11] There is no doubt about the value of the autobiography for Merton in this process of reconciliation. It is, however, significant that eventually the autobiography came to hold no interest for Merton; it came just one of the twelve books he published by 1953.[12]

Merton "suppressed the desire" to write, and even the "Joy of seeing another pretty book with my name on it" couldn't bring him any closer to the act of writing. When Robert Lax came to Gethsemani a second time, at Christmas 1944, he told Merton that he should be writing more poetry. In his heart Merton did not think it was God's will that he write, but he did not argue with Lax. Additionally, Merton's confessor Dom Vital felt as he did, that he should not write because it was not God's will.

Merton's abbot, however, apparently did not feel the same way, for on January 31, 1945, while in spiritual conference with Merton, he told him that he wanted him to go on writing poems and that when he had any idea for a poem he should write it down. As a result of this unexpected request, Merton put together another book of poems in the ensuing months, *A Man in the Divided Sea*, published on August 25, 1946.

This meeting with the abbot was one of the major signposts in the process of fusing the monastic with the literary, of bringing the "two Mertons" to a more satisfactory coexistence. Merton believed completely in obedience to his superiors and though he may have been disappointed by and uncertain about the abbot's request, he did not fail to implement it with the ultimate conviction that it was God's will for him to involve himself with his writing in a more holistic way. In *The Waters of Siloe* (1949), Merton writes about a late-nineteenth-century French Trappist, Father Joseph Cassant. Father Cassant was an active contemplative, possessing an intense faith through which he found Christ's love coming to him in all events of his life. The essence of Father Cassant's active contemplation was, as Merton saw it, contained in Cassant's French saying, *Il n'arrive que la volunté de Jésus semper* (with the Latin *semper*, "Only the will of Jesus is what happens, all the time"). Merton's description of Father Cassant's notion of obedience could well be applicable to himself.

> . . . he reached the point where his spiritual life could be summed up in an obedience which allowed God to work on him and guide him through his superiors.
>
> No matter what they did—and sometimes their decisions were very painful—it was God that acted on him, through them. Even when it seemed impossible to believe such a thing, he believed it. And his trust saved him from taking all the false roads he might have taken.[13]

Trust is the crucial word here. There was some unusual quality of purity in Merton's trust, in God and in his superiors, a purity seldom tainted, a consistency ever strong and profound. This was a trust like that of Father Cassant; one is led to believe that Merton's incorporation of the trust was also like Father Cassant's. And, like Father Cassant, Merton was able to avoid the false roads precisely because of the depth of his trust. He accepted the wishes of the abbot and believed that such acceptance would lead him to a richer and more fulfilling monastic life, even while he wrote.

But Merton would have to use some kind of instrument—a means—in order to come not only to the acceptance itself but also to the implementation of the acceptance. He had to have some way of knowing how and why successfully to incorporate the wishes of the abbot to return wholeheartedly to his writing. In a sense, his trust could take him only so far, for I believe it lacked sufficient intellectuality. Merton needed the intellectual, the rational, as part of him certainly functioned on this level. He turned then to monastic culture itself, to a study of its thought and its literature. Part of this study was a component of the usual monastic training every novice went through in preparation for the vows and especially ordination if it was to occur: the church fathers, scholastic philosophy, the major monastic fathers, traditional church theology, and, to some degree, Cistercian thinkers and writers. Much of this material dealt with contemplation and the contemplative life.

Merton's concern was with the meaning of contemplation both by itself and within the so-called contemplative life. He quoted Thomas Aquinas and made references to many of the more important Christian mystics, Bernard, Gregory, John of the Cross, John Ruysbroeck, Teresa, and Bonaventure, as he came to define contemplation and understand what it meant for himself, indeed, for all people.

> . . . in practice, there is only one vocation. Whether you teach or live in the cloister or nurse the sick, whether you are in religion or out of it, married or single, no matter who you are or what you are, you are called to the summit of perfection: you are called to a deep interior life perhaps even as mystical prayer, and to pass the fruits of your contemplation on to others. And if you cannot do so by word, then by example. (p. 419)

Merton seemed especially involved with Bonaventure's *Itinerarium*; he thought it one of the finest descriptions ever written of the contemplative vocation, especially the famous passage about Francis of Assisi's progression from the perfect example of the active life to the perfect example of contemplation. The *Itinerarium*'s perfect articulation of both the *process* of the vocation of contemplation as well as of the vocation itself is the embodiment of what Merton sought and what he was so definitely coming to.

> If you should ask how these things come about, question grace, not instruction; desire, not intellect; the cry of prayer, not pursuit of study; the spouse, not the teacher; God, not man; darkness, not clarity; not light, but the wholly flaming fire which will bear you aloft to God with fullest unction and burning affection. This fire is God, and the furnace of this fire leadeth to Jerusalem; and Christ the man kindles it in the fervor of His burning Passion, which he alone truly perceives who says, "My soul rather chooseth hanging and my bones death" (Job, 7, 15). He who chooses this death can see God because this is indubitably true: "Man shall not see me and live" (Exod., 33, 20). Let us then die and pass over into darkness; let us impose silence on cares, concupiscence, and phantasms; let us pass over with the crucified Christ from this world to the Father (John, 13, 1), so that when the Father is shown to us we may say with Philip, "It is enough for us" (John, 14, 8); let us hear with Paul, "My grace is sufficient for thee" (Cor., 12, 9); let us exult with David, saying, "For Thee my flesh and my heart hath fainted away; Thou art the God of my heart, and the God that is my portion forever (Ps. 72, 26). . . . Blessed be the Lord God of Israel from everlasting to everlasting; and let all the people say: So be it, so be it" (Ps., 105, 48). AMEN.[14]

Though there is a particular kind of anti-intellectualism, however slight, in the first few lines of the passage, it is nevertheless an unusual mixture of the rational and the mystical, a mixture to which Merton would be drawn. Bonaventure is not saying that the contemplative must not question, but that the questions should be directed to and answers sought from the mystical dimension, in God, rather than the rational dimension. Merton would respond to Bonaventure because he himself saw his own condition in much the same light. He was not going to find the answers to his questions about writing and its validity in the arena of rationality, for in fact they were not rational questions. Merton was beginning to see the significance of this deceivingly simple recognition and slowly and confidently set out to act on it. He went deeper and deeper into the monastic life and its culture, certainly a kind of Bonaventurian "darkness" as well as a kind of "passing over" process. He began to "impose silence" as Bonaventure would have him do, but he faced the profound questions head-on, quietly removing his fear of the darkness of the unknown and more positively facing the sufficiency of God's grace in the spirit of Paul's statemen, "My grace is sufficient for thee."

It is significant that *The Seven Storey Mountain* ends with a long prose prayer, the first part of which is Merton speaking to his God and the last part of which is Merton's God speaking to him. The prayer reflects Merton's frustration with his inability to reach a rational resolution of the problem of reconciling writing with the contemplative life. Merton—at least at this point in his monastic life, 1946-1947—still seems to be seeking both a rational explanation of the problem as well as a rational solution to it. His study of monastic culture and the writings of the monastic fathers in particular did, no doubt, provide greater insights into the dilemma and, to this extent, was of value to Merton, not only at the time but throughout his monastic life. The study of contemplation and Merton's attempts to make the notion something real and essential in his monastic life was not, however, an adequate means of dealing with the problem ultimately. Yet at the time, the rich tradition of monastic thought and culture strengthened Merton and gave him greater reason to continue to seek the reconciliation. The prayer reveals this.

. . . You have contradicted everything. You have left me in no-man's land.

You have got me walking up and down all day under those trees, saying to me over and over again: "Solitude, solitude." And You have turned around and thrown the whole world in my lap. You have told me, "Leave all things and follow me," and then You have tied half of New York to my foot like a ball and chain. You have got me kneeling behind that pillar with my mind making a noise like a bank. Is that contemplation? . . .

The months have gone by, and You have not lessened any of those desires, but You have given me peace, and I am beginning to see what it is all about. I am beginning to understand.

Because You have called me here not to wear a label by which I can recognize myself and place myself in some kind of category. You do not want me thinking about what I am, but about what You are. Or rather, You do not even want me to be thinking about anything much: for You would raise me above the level of thought. And if I am always trying to figure out what I am and where I am and why I am, how will that work be done?

I do not make a big drama out of this business. I do not say: "You have asked me for everything, and I have renounced all." Because I no longer desire to see anything that implies a distance between You and me: and if I stand back and consider myself and You as if something had passed between us, from me to You, I will inevitably see the gap between us, and remember the distance between us.

My God, it is that gap and that distance which kill me.

That is the only reason why I desire solitude—to be lost to all created things, to die to them and to the knowledge of them, for they remind me of my distance from You. They tell me something about You: that You are far from them, even though You are in them. You have made them and Your presence sustains their being, and they hide You from me. And I would live alone and out of them. O BEATA SOLITUDO!

. . . For I am beginning to understand. You have taught me, and have consoled me, and I have begun to hope and learn. . . . (pp. 420-22)

Perhaps to convince himself of the starkness and simplicity of the monastic vocation, of *his* monastic vocation and the way things were supposed to be, Merton closed his autobiography with God's charge to him and its terrifying last sentence: "That you may become the brother of God and learn to know the Christ of the burnt men." The entire prose prayer is as beautiful as it is revealing, but God's words, though beautiful and revealing of Merton, are hard and foreboding; they are fearsome words of warning. How does one explain this?

Merton himself offers substantial explanation. In one place he talks about his "crude theology" of his early monastic years and that he really did not understand the monastic life and its problems. His theology—"a clean-cut division between the natural and the supernatural, God and the world, sacred and secular"[15]—did not provide any interpretive flexibility. Yet one is not sure whether his theology emanated from his anger at the world he had left or whether it was a natural development from his conception of the monastic ideal. Whatever the source of the theological perspective, the rhetoric in the prayer is almost oppressive; it is a rhetoric of mortification and deep criticism of self. Merton had his God foretelling pain and suffering, rejection and frustration. It is difficult to think of the God of Job as more fearsome and terrible. But he put it all in the context of his quest for solitude.

> And when you have been praised a little and loved a little I will take away all your gifts and all your love and all your praise and you will be utterly forgotten and abandoned and you will be nothing, a dead thing, a rejection. And in that day you shall begin to possess the solitude you have so long desired. And your solitude will bear immense fruit in the souls of men you will never see on earth. (p. 422)

Merton is quite clear as to how he believed things will be and should be. Solitude comes only after severe self-denial and mortification; retribution must be made for those sins of the world, in the world. God is a just God, a God of fairness and righteousness; He is wise and all-knowing, so the actions of a young monk have meaning and substance even though they seem to make no earthly sense. The monastic ideal of solitude is elusive and the very tenor of the monastic life seems to make it even less attainable.

Merton sees clearly the evil he embraced in his life; he sees also the evil of the world in which he lived and worked. This recognition not only strengthens his will to stay in the monastery, apart from the world, but it also intensifies his need to make retribution, in the proper monastic way, for his past life. All those things of the world, even those pursuits which brought satisfaction and remuneration, must be carefully examined and put aside because they cannot be reconciled with the monastic life and ideal. Thus, Merton's autobiography becomes his apologia for renunciation. Absolutely every last worldly pursuit and earthly ecstasy was put aside, including his writing.

But Merton's superiors directed that he resume his writing and in the spirit of monastic obedience and trust in one's superiors, Merton complied. By March 1947, the month of his solemn vows, Merton seems to have begun to make something creative out of his abbot's order.

> My intention is to give myself entirely and without compromise to whatever work God wants to perform in me and through me. But this gift is not something absolutely blind and without definition. It is already defined by the fact that God has given me a CONTEMPLATIVE vocation. By so doing He has signified a certain path, a certain goal to be mine. That is what I am to keep in view because that is His will. It means renouncing the business, ambitions,

honors and pleasures and other activities of the world. It means only a minimum of concern with temporal things. Nevertheless, I have promised to do whatever a Superior may legitimately ask of me. That may, under certain circumstances, involve the sacrifice of contemplation. But it seems to me this sacrifice can only be a temporary thing. It can not mean the sacrifice of the whole contemplative vocation as such. (pp. 37-38)[16]

As mentioned, by May 1947 Merton had assumed twelve major writing projects. In July, Merton published his famous essay, "Poetry and the Contemplative Life." It is clear from *The Sign of Jonas,* specifically the May 20, 1947 entry, that he had given the matter of the relationship of contemplation and the aesthetic experience a great deal of thought. There also is the perhaps more basic issue of art and asceticism and their connectedness to which the entry addresses itself and which can be seen as a preliminary section of the essay, though it does not appear as part of the printed copy.

> Art and asceticism. The artist must be free, otherwise he will be dominated by his material instead of dominating it. Hence, art demands asceticism. Religious ascetics have something to learn from the natural asceticism of the artist: it is un-selfconscious, organic, integrated in his art. It does not run the risk of becoming an end in itself. But the artist also has something to gain from religious asceticism. It not only raises him above his subject and his material but above his art itself. He can now control everything, even his art, which usually controls him.
>
> Asceticism may involve a total sacrifice of art.
>
> The happiest consummation for the artist as such: his art may be integrated into an organic spiritual whole and become the most vital expression of a life of praise and worship. (p. 56)

In the essay itself, which not accidentally is autobiographical, Merton considers what poetry, artistic writing, and contemplation can offer one another, after calling for a more holistic approach to Christian artistry and literature. Merton contends that an artist has within his artistry the *means* to natural contemplation—if not natural contemplation itself—and that this natural contemplation can prepare the way for infused/mystical contemplation, the highest and truest form of contemplation. At the same time, however, mystical contemplation is not attainable by man alone. It is a gift of God given to whomever He chooses. And this is precisely where the major problem arises, as Merton understands it.

God wants "cooperation, peaceful cooperation and blind trust" from the mystic and necessarily from the artist who strives for mystical contemplation.

Through natural contemplation, however, which Merton also calls the aesthetic experience, the poet-writer can be led solely to the natural order of things and thus be led into himself "in order to reflect upon his inspiration and to clothe it with a special and splendid form and then return to DISPLAY IT TO THOSE OUTSIDE." And this, Merton concludes, is the crucial difference between the artist and the artist-mystic.

> The artist enters into himself in order to work. For him, the "superior" soul is a forge where inspiration kindles a fire of white heat, a crucible for the transformation of natural images into new, created forms. But the mystic enters into himself, not in order to work but to pass through the center of his own soul and lose himself in the mystery and secrecy and infinite, transcendent reality of God living and working within him.[17]

Merton is saying that the natural order of artistry is not good enough; that the artist who functions only on this level will be ever "cheated" of the superior union of the soul with God. It appears then that Merton would have the artist-writer leading an inferior life. I believe this is a valid interpretation, yet the title of the essay, "Poetry and the Contemplative Life," makes clear that Merton is really writing about himself. Unfortunately, however, as he was inclined to do in these early years, Merton is taking to task the whole artistic enterprise for its incomplete and inferior stance, for its naturalness and worldly-secular dimension. Consequently, everything comes down to this:

> . . . poetry can, indeed, help to bring us rapidly through that part of the journey to contemplation that is called active: but when we are entering the realm of true contemplation, where eternal happiness begins, it may turn around and bar our way.[18]

Merton has a response to this problem, the "only course" the poet-writer can take to protect his "own individual satisfaction: THE RUTHLESS AND COMPLETE SACRIFICE OF HIS ART." This sacrifice is the "simplest and the safest" way to deal with the problem; for him, the most obvious manner in which to face *and* solve a problem of this nature. It is a perception of absolutes: the natural and the supernatural, God and man, The City of God and The City of Man, worldly existence and eternity. For Merton, there really is no choice. God and the supernatural order are of highest priority and infinite value. In the context of his monastic life during these years, this facet of the essay reveals a great deal about Merton's own struggles and validates the autobiographical dimension of the writing.

Time and again, Merton attempted the "ruthless and complete sacrifice of his art," convinced that this would strengthen his contemplative life and make his vocation more pleasing to God and more reflective of the monastic ideal. As he notes in the essay, paraphrasing Paul, Christ not only preached that Godly wisdom makes man divine, but He Himself is both the model and the means for and through which this wisdom is attained. In comparison to the attainment of "this pearl of great price," the sacrifice of his art was a minor matter. In fact, there was no comparison. In this light then, it is easy to understand why Merton would be so eager to give up his writing, to renounce it forever.

The most significant and revealing part of the essay is its final paragraph. Merton raises again the question of monastic obedience, but in a specific context.

> . . . What if one is morally certain that God wills him to continue writing anyway? That is, what if one's religious superiors make it a matter of formal obedience to pursue one's art, for some special purpose like the good of souls? That will not take away distractions, or make God abrogate the laws of the spiritual life. But we can console ourselves with Saint Thomas Aquinas that it is more meritorious to share the fruits of contemplation with others than it is merely to enjoy them ourselves. And certainly, when it comes to communicating some idea of the delights of contemplation, the poet is, of all men, the one who is least at a loss for a means to express what is essentially inexpressible.[19]

There are many possible interpretations of this paragraph. But whatever interpretation one chooses, the outcome remains the same: Merton did not stop writing. This essay is indicative of the means by which Merton continued to write. There is a certain wisdom and experience both behind and within monastic obedience—Benedict's Rule attests to this—but its essence lies with the response of the individual monk. Merton believed in and deeply respected the traditions of Western monasticism, especially obedience. This is but one dimension, however. Another dimension is that he may have "used" this call to obedience to validate the writing that he felt to be in conflict with the monastic mores.

Nevertheless, he reacted to his abbot's order with integrity and positive acceptance.

> It was Dom Frederic [Merton's abbot, who died in August 1948] who had formed and shaped my whole monastic destiny. It was he, together with my novice master, Dom Robert, who decided that I should write books. It was he

137

who firmly and kindly encouraged me and indeed ordered me to continue, in spite of my own misgivings. At the same time, he continued patiently and wisely to show me, in every way that he could, that this writing was not supposed to interfere with my life of prayer: On the contrary, it DEMANDED a life of more intimate union with God on my part. And so, although I sometimes failed to see how this was possible, I now realize that Dom Frederic not only "made" me as a writer, but that he disposed my life, under the guidance of Divine Providence, in such a way that I had a greater opportunity to become a contemplative at Gethsemani. For Dom Frederic, though he was a very busy man, hated anything that savored of compromise. A monk, in his eyes, had to be a real monk—a man of prayer and a man of God. He could not abide activism and a secular spirit masking under a cowl. (p. 96)

Merton, like his abbot, rejected compromise at the same time that he was receptive to enriching traditions. Both the rejection and receptivity were part of the process through which he continued to write. Merton never hesitated to accept the help and encouragement of his abbot in the matter of his writing and never hesitated to express his gratitude for and reliance on the help.

"Poetry and the Contemplative Life" can be seen as another signpost in the process of reconciling Merton the writer with Merton the monk. Similarly, all the many conferences with his abbot and novice master in which he was told to continue to write can be seen as points of affirmation in Merton's process. Yet what is most interesting in all of this is that Merton not only continued to write but that he produced an astonishing amount of material, much of it very good.

The sheer volume of material produced by Merton in these early monastic years indicates the more functionalistic aspect of his writing. The monastery and the Trappist order needed translations, histories, pamphlets, biographies, readable volumes of spiritual direction, even poetry, to some extent. And, of course, the order and the monastery needed the revenue generated by the sales of these publications. Merton was assuming something like the journalist's role. Creativity and artistry are not necessarily absent, but they are secondary to the practical need of writing/producing the materials and publishing and distributing them.

Additionally, there is the question of Merton's compulsiveness in the context of this practical need for the production and distribution of materials, which in turn raises the problem of loss of self and loss of personal autonomy. *The Seven Storey Mountain*, especially, is full of references to the renunciation of self and of all gifts and abilities that the self possesses. This, of course, is part of the monastic ideal, as it is part of the Christian ideal. Merton's was not an empty giving up of self, a mindless abdication of the responsibilities of gifts and abilities. He was not a man taken in by pure means. For him, means were only part of the process, if not the process itself, to specific ends. Merton's end was articulated by Paul: "It is no longer I that lives but Christ lives in me."

The problems of Merton's means and ends were complicated by the zealousness with which he pursued his ends. But this zealousness was gradually tempered with the help of his own study of monastic spirituality and the guidance of his novice master and abbot. As the tension between ends and means was reduced, so too was the tension between writer and monk. And this was precisely Merton's gift, his ability to reconcile his artistry and love of learning with his desire and search for God. He recognized and accepted the notion of the monastery as a "school for the service of the Lord" and gradually came to understand that writing could be as much in the service of the Lord as could spreading fertilizer or painting a wall. His was the extraordinary sense of the richness of the monastic tradition, its motivating power and essential creativity. He came to know his intelligence and curiosity and to accept them and to make them part of his search for God and his service of the Lord. As he more clearly perceived his end, the means became less of a complication, less of a burden.

Yet the matter was not this simple and so perfectly analyzed. Indeed, it was extraordinarily complex. One thinks of the process of psychoanalysis (in which Merton had more than a casual interest) and the manner through which the patient comes to recognize, understand, and accept the tensions and conflicts of his or her life. Nothing is eliminated; it is uncovered and analyzed in order to be understood and dealt with in whatever way the patient chooses. Analysis is a process through which an individual comes to recognize that a problem (or problems) exists at the same time that he learns how to use his intellectual, spiritual, and psychological resources to deal with the problem. This is no simple or quick process.

So it was with Merton. The mid-1940s were perhaps the most important years of his process. "Poetry and the Contemplative Life" is an indication of his progress thus far, but it was by no means the last word just as it was surely not the end of the search and process of reconciliation. In a sense, Merton knew his problem and was coming to know and to use his resources in dealing with it. As his monastic life progressed, he would come to an awareness of even greater resources, richer means to his constant end of God alone.

Having said all this, one must face the events of the first few months of 1949 when Merton's "writing, which had once been a source of temporary problems, was now becoming a real problem and that problem was reaching a crisis" (p. 129). This problem led to a period of severe mental, physical, and spiritual suffering, which lasted from September 1949 until December 1950. Merton was trying to write a theological essay (finally published as *The Ascent to Truth* in 1951). This was his first attempt at writing theology and several times it became so difficult that he tore up whatever he had written. The paralysis Merton faced was one of the most intense of his monastic life, especially as it involved the complexities of the reconciliation of his artistic and monastic personages.

Merton offers several reasons for the paralysis. Primarily, he was concerned with his ordination to major orders and the priesthood. He had a great deal of anxiety about his ordination so it is not surprising that he would be uncertain, confused, and, to some degree, negative about his writing. Second, he was writing too much and he was "tired and stale." Also there was the matter of the success of *The Seven Storey Mountain* and the fan mail it generated. Any kind of public success for the Trappist monk, as he saw it, was a sign of failure and defeat. In this context especially, writing became the very indication that he had failed to renounce worldly success.

By March 19, 1949, the day of his ordination to the diaconate, the whole matter had intensified to an extent that Merton took significant action.

> . . . kneeling in the sanctuary after ordination and during the Canon of the Mass, I realized clearly that I ought to stop trying to be a poet and be definite about it too. I went to Reverend Father afterwards and he said, all right. And I have recovered a great deal of interior liberty by that one thing. In the afternoon I tore up all rough notes for a poem. They had been lying around for a few days.
>
> So after ordination, in this respect and in others, I felt for the first time in my life, like a more practical person. All of a sudden I seemed to know just what to do about everything that was on my mind at the moment. (p. 171)

Merton reflects on this decision. It is clear that there had already formed an unwillingness, even an opposition, to writing, especially poetry.

> It was a gesture that may or may not have had a profound meaning to me. I thought it had some meaning. What it meant, I am still not sure. But I decided to stop trying to be a poet any more. I did this first of all because I realized that I had never been a good poet anyway, and it seemed to me that by continuing to write poetry I would only be imposing an illusion on the people who thought my poetry was good. In so doing, I would run the risk of coming to

believe, myself, that it was good. What I was trying to do was, I think, all right. It was a movement toward integrity. If I could not write well, I would stop wasting words, time, paper, and get rid of this useless interference in my life of prayer. Since that day, in order to relax the element of pride that may have insinuated itself in this resolve, I have written verse where I thought charity demanded or permitted it. . . . To write thus is not, according to my vocabulary, an attempt to "be a poet." (p. 131)

There is something odd about this passage. Consider Merton's statement that he was not a good poet. Critics had praised Merton's first three volumes of poetry: *Thirty Poems* (1944), *A Man in the Divided Sea* (1946), and *Figures for an Apocalypse* (1948). A fourth volume, *The Tears of the Blind Lions*, was in press. (Two of the poems in this volume, "St. Malachy" and "From the Legend of St. Clement," originally published in *Poetry* magazine and *The Month*, received half of the Harriet Monroe Memorial Prize for 1949.) There is no *objective* justification for Merton's position.

Subjectively, however, there is ample reason for Merton's position. In all facets of his life a greater involvement was asked of him: the major orders and the priesthood, the demand for more written materials, and the success of *The Seven Storey Mountain*. These were enormous pressures, both from within and from without. As a result, Merton became frightened. He became wary of committing himself to any more writing for fear of intensifying the pressures and losing his contemplative life and spirit and the desire for solitude. In many respects, Merton saw his necessary position as one of survival, for at this stage of his life the writing had become the proverbial millstone. It was as if his 1947 essay, "Poetry and the Contemplative Life," and its reference to "the ruthless and complete sacrifice of his art" envisioned Merton's position in 1949.

Seeds of Contemplation, which Merton completed on July 1, 1948, and was published on March 2, 1949, provides additional explanation for Merton's aversion to writing.

> Many poets are not poets for the same reason that many religious men are not saints: they never succeed in being themselves. They never get around to being the particular poet or particular monk they are intended to be by God. They never become the man or the artist who is called for by all the circumstances of their individual lives.
> They waste their years in vain efforts to be some other poet, some other saint. For many absurd reasons, they are convinced that they are obliged to become

somebody else who died two hundred years ago and who lived in circumstances utterly alien to their own.

They wear out their minds and bodies in a hopeless endeavor to have somebody else's experiences or write somebody else's poems or possess somebody else's sanctity.

There can be an intense egoism in following everybody else. People are in a hurry to magnify themselves by imitating what is popular—and too lazy to think of anything better.

Hurry ruins saints as well as artists. They want quick success and they are in such haste to get it that they cannot take time to be true to themselves. And when the madness is upon them they argue that their very haste is a species of integrity.[20]

This is Merton speaking about himself, revealing his determination to be true to himself. The passage reveals, too, the dimension of Merton's struggles with writing and his increasing awareness of its potential artificiality if it becomes part of the quest for quick success and if it comes from one who has not succeeded in becoming himself. He speaks as one who is in the midst of an important search, the search for self. He speaks also as one who has come to know that his writing and its subjects must be his own as surely as they must be God's.

If you write for God you will reach many men and bring them joy.

If you write for men—you may make some money and you may give someone a little joy and you may make a noise in the world, for a little while.

If you write for yourself you can read what you yourself have written and after ten minutes you will be so disgusted you will wish that you were dead.[21]

This was written when Merton's skepticism about his spiritual life and its integrity was growing. He was also, again, becoming more impatient with the writing, almost disgusted, in fact, with the emerging awareness that he was writing more for himself. There is no accidental relationship between the spiritual life and its weakness, as Merton viewed it, and the writing for himself. The one is the source of the other.

What *Seeds of Contemplation* reveals, in addition, are the signs of the darkness that would face Merton in the latter part of 1949, after his ordination to the priesthood. Though he writes about this darkness/wilderness in the context of contemplation, it is valid to consider the passage as indicative of Merton's growing frustration with the conditions of his life.

The ordinary way to contemplation lies through a desert without trees and without beauty and without water. The spirit enters a wilderness and travels blindly in directions that seem to lead away from vision, away from God, away from all fulfillment and joy. It may become almost impossible to believe that this road goes anywhere at all except to a desolation full of dry bones—the ruin of all our hopes and good intentions.

The prospect of this wilderness is something that so appalls most men that they refuse to enter upon its burning sands and travel among its rocks. They cannot believe that contemplation and sanctity are to be found in a desolation where there is no food and no shelter and no rest and no refreshment for their imagination and intellect and for the desires of their nature.

. . . When God begins to infuse His light of knowledge and understanding into the spirit of a man drawn to contemplation, the experience is often not so much one of fulfillment as of defeat.[22]

Thus, with the writing and publication of *Seeds of Contemplation* came Merton's growing sense of what was to come—the "desert without beauty" and defeat instead of fulfillment.

Merton's path toward darkness was not so direct, however. As always, his character is elusive and he can exude such confidence and determination that one might assume every aspect of his life is in order and functioning well.

What do you think, you dope, after having been a Trappist for seven years? I think, Where did the time go? I caught myself wondering, Have I changed? Not that it matters. I have and I haven't. I'm balder. Somehow I have more of an interior life but I'd have a hard time trying to say how. But I know some of the things that account for it: solemn profession—theology—and minor forms of tribulation here and there concerning writing, singing, contemplation. What graces all these little crosses have been. They are the very best thing in our life here. It seems they are so small. They do their work. They are coming in greater abundance now. How God works on your soul by these obscure and unremarkable sufferings that cleanse and drain your wounds. I am glad of every kind of trouble I have had and thank God in advance for the trials that are to come. Other more pleasant graces—minor orders—the writing job, to some extent. All the reading, all the hours of prayer. God has taught me to find myself more in Him or lose myself more: it comes to the same thing. And I am tremendously glad of the prayers of the people who have read *The Seven Storey Mountain* and I am glad to pray for them. (p. 143)

This is an optimistic assessment. Merton seems content with and grateful for the life at Gethsemani. He views the monastic life positively, as a nourishing and essentially creative existence. This perspective is incomplete, however, because there was a great deal more behind Merton's gratitude and positivism.

> Can't I ever escape from being something comfortable and prosperous and smug? The world is terrible, people are starving to death and freezing and going to hell with despair and here I sit with a silver spoon in my mouth and write books and everybody sends me fan mail telling me how wonderful I am for giving up so MUCH. I'd like to ask them, what have I given up, anyway, except headaches and responsibilities? (p. 150)

This is more like the Merton of preconversion times—the elementary worldview of absolutes, the "how could I be so fortunate?" position. Was the only way Merton could accept his monastic life by rationalizing it as so much richer and fulfilling than life for so many in the world? Another more critical perspective on the passage is the suggestion that it represents Merton's attempts to convince himself that the monastic life at Gethsemani was rich and satisfying when in fact he was unhappy and dissatisfied. Perhaps Merton was trying to to convince himself of something he really did not believe or accept.

It is difficult to perceive Merton at this stage in his life as attempting to fool himself. He was much too genuine and aware for that. He was sincere and sensitive toward his monastic life, and felt responsible for living it honestly.

> For my own part this evening I was thinking, "Maybe I'm finished as a writer." Far from disturbing me, the thought made me glad. Nothing seems so foolish as to go on writing merely because people expect you to write. Not that I have anything to say, but fame makes me inarticulate. Anyway I certainly find it extremely difficult to believe in myself as a poet.
>
> On the other hand, I am haunted by beautiful thoughts—solitude, obscurity, emptiness, MUNDITA CORDIS, a virgin spirit. That my spirit, which has been raped by everything stupid, could again become a virginal spirit in the clean, simple darkness of pure faith, with no more half-lighted shadows between myself and God and no more desires biting my will like a bed of thorns! (p. 153)

Yet Merton was moving toward some kind of dark period. For every positive statement the journal includes during these last few months of 1948 and the first few months of 1949, there is an entry that reveals tangible signs of struggle. One is his difficulty with the theological text.

> My work has been tied up in knots for two months—more. I am trying to write *The Cloud and the Fire* [published as *The Ascent to Truth*] which is a book about contemplation and the theology of contemplation at that. The theology of contemplation does not mix well with fan mail. Also it is difficult. It is certainly impossible to write such a book with a lot of other concerns on your mind—for instance at the end of January the printers gave me the dummy for the

centenary book and I was busy for two weeks writing captions and finishing the copy for THAT.

It takes a tremendous effort of will to get back to *The Cloud and the Fire* and I am usually helpless when I try to move that typewriter and get something on paper. I have a huge mass of half-digested notes, all mixed up, and I can't find my way around in them. My ideas are not fixed and clear. I have been trusting more or less to see them work themselves out on paper as I type—and have in any case made up my mind to regard the whole first draft of this book simply as preliminary notes.

On the other hand, when I rewrite anything I entirely revolutionize it, sometimes with no improvement at all, because I only lose the freshness of the original and am just as prolix over again, but in a different and duller way. It is hopeless for me to write without the heat of some new ideas. (pp. 158-59)

During this period, Merton had been reading, with more than passing attention, *La Vie Intellectuelle* by the French Dominican A. D. Sertillanges. Merton's most revealing comment about the text is that its effect on him was similar to that which one of Dale Carnegie's books might have on a downhearted salesman. It cheered him up and helped him to organize his time and his work in a more effective manner. Sertillanges prompted Merton to reflect on his own writing chores and, as a result, he began to make some progress with *The Cloud and the Fire*.

> . . . with Our Lady's help—the book—now changed and called *The School of the Spirit*—goes quite smoothly. I have to simply sit down at the typewriter with what I want to say planned out. That is the SINE QUA NON—even if I write something completely different, as I did today. (p. 164)

Sometime between February 9, when he was lamenting his difficulties, and February 20, when his writing began to come more easily, Merton was able to collect his thoughts. Sertillanges must have had a much greater influence on him than he admits, since he read it during this period. Merton goes to some length to explain why the text was difficult for him to agree with, the most salient aspect being its dissimilarity with Saint John of the Cross, on whose theology *The Cloud and the Fire* was based. But at the same time, Merton seems to have been able to take from *La Vie Intellectuelle* some very practical direction. He had only two hours per day during which to do all his writing and it seems plausible that reading Sertillanges gave him some new perspective on how to use these two hours most efficiently. With major orders approaching, one wonders how Merton was able to marshal his resources to the extent he did, if not by means of something like the ideas suggested in *La Vie Intellectuelle*.

It is significant that Merton could bring himself to continue working on *The Cloud and the Fire* in the midst of all the distractions and obstacles, many of which were his own doing, and not the least of which was his self-deprecation and harshness.

> Every book that comes out under my name is a new problem. To begin with, each one brings with it a searching examination of conscience. Every book I write is a mirror of my own character and conscience. I always open the final, printed job, with a faint hope of finding myself agreeable, and I never do. (p. 166)

As noted, Merton's ordination to the diaconate brought with it his decision to "stop being a poet" and to pull back as far as possible from the writing. This decision appears symptomatic of a much deeper struggle.

> . . . since the diaconate I have a new attitude. Although it half kills me, I find myself accepting the idea that perhaps I do not have a purely contemplative vocation. I say "accept." I do not BELIEVE it. It is utterly impossible for me to believe any such thing: everything in me cries out for solitude and for God alone. And yet I find myself admitting that perhaps I don't know what that really means, and that I am too low in the spiritual scale of things to grasp it, and even that I am somehow excluded from it by God's love. The feeling is absolutely terrible—the power of attraction that seems to draw the whole life out of me, to tear out the roots of my soul—and then the blank wall against which I stop—dead.
>
> Yet in the middle of all this I find not unrest or rebellion but happiness and peace, and I rejoice in it, because blindly something in the middle of me clings to the one reality that remains accessible to me. This is the supreme reality of all—the love of God. (pp. 175-76)

In addition to an edge of darkness here, there is terror. Everything is beginning to come apart, most especially his spiritual life, which he finds superficial and false. But behind this coming apart and the stripping away of apparent nonessentials by Merton himself is a growing sense of abandonment and loneliness, a fear that a dreaded darkness is beginning to descend. The closer Merton came to his priestly ordination, the more intense and overpowering were his feelings of terror and abandonment. Increasing too was his sense of insignificance and unimportance. Merton was continuing to experience anxiety over the theological text he was still trying to write.

I wonder how many plans I have made for this book, *The School of the Spirit*? Perhaps six—including the ones I made for it when it was called *The Cloud and the Fire*. So I sit at the typewriter with my fingers all wound up in a cat's cradle of strings, overwhelmed with the sense of my own stupidity, and surrounded by not one but a multitude of literary dilemmas.

I am supposed now to be working on the book three afternoons a week and I try at all costs to get something down on paper, terrified that if I merely stop and read and organize notes I will go around in circles for ever and ever. This business of "getting my notes together" is something that can go on absolutely interminably, because there exists an almost unlimited number of combinations in which you can arrange the statements you have jotted down so carefully on some eight hundred pages of various notebooks.

All that undigested material is utterly terrifying, and fascinating at the same time. Sometimes I try to "meditate" on this monster which I call "my notes" (I should say "our" notes, but skip it)—but the statements standing out of context and in my own crazy handwriting do not have the meaning and unction they had in Migne or Saint John of the Cross or wherever I first discovered them. . . .

They seem to divide and slacken the mind and leave my spirit in a vague sense of anguish, at the thought that I have eaten the Fathers and produced nothing but this unhappy web.

But when I tell myself "I am no writer, I am finished," instead of being upset I am filled with a sense of peace and of relief—perhaps because I already taste, by anticipation, the joy of my deliverance. On the other hand, if I am not delivered from writing by failure, perhaps I may go on and even succeed at this thing, but by the power of the Holy Ghost—which would be a greater deliverance. But whatever happens, success or failure, I have given up worrying. I just wonder about the business on paper, on the assumption that it might mean something to me if I should ever re-read all this at another season. (p. 179)

It must have been agony for Merton to have to struggle with writing *The School of the Spirit* when his ordination was so near. He was forced as usual to try to bring the writing more in line with the condition and development of his interior life.

The problem is . . . my personality or if you like, the development of my interior life. I am not perplexed either by what I am or that I am not, but by the mode in which I am tending to become what I really will be. (p. 186)

In his preordination reflections, Merton focused on the quality of silence. He saw absolute poverty as an essential part of the contemplative life, perhaps its very core. Merton saw interior silence as the expression of absolute poverty. This recognition raised serious problems for his writing vocation.

> . . . in my prayer and all my interior life, such as it is, I am concerned with the need for a greater and more complete interior silence: an interior secrecy that amounts to not even thinking about myself. Silence about my prayer, about the development of my interior life, is becoming an absolute necessity, so that I am beginning to believe I should stop writing about contemplation altogether, except perhaps in the most general terms. It seems to me to be a great indecency for me to pass, in the opinion of men, as one who seems to have something to say about contemplation. The thought makes me feel as if I needed a bath and a change of clothing. (pp. 189-90)

For Merton to stop writing about contemplation would be tantamount to giving up all personal writing, since so much of it focused on his experiences with and reflections on contemplation. Merton seemed more and more humbled by the act of ordination, to the point, once again, of reflecting and acting in absolutes: absolute poverty, complete interior silence, no writing whatsoever, not even thinking about himself. It is not surprising therefore that *The Sign of Jonas* should hold such a rhetoric of unworthiness in the entries both preceding and following ordination. One might call it a rhetoric of nothingness.

> Now I know that I had the whole Church in America praying for me and I am scared and consoled by so much mercy and by the sense that I myself have contributed practically nothing to the whole business and that I have been worked on and worked in, carried upward on the tide of a huge love that had been released in people, somehow, in connection with a book printed over my name: and on this tide millions of us, a whole continent perhaps, is riding into heaven. It makes me truly the child of our Lady (MULIER, ECCE FILIUS TUUS!) to whom the greatest mercy was given. When she has produced in me something of her humility there will be no end to what God will pour out upon me, not for myself but for the whole world—even perhaps to make others very great while I remain in my nothingness: all this would be, to me, the greatest joy.

The spirit of this passage, written on May 29, three days after his ordination, derives from the presence of so many of Merton's friends at his ordination and the fact that he received a number of ordination gifts from all over the country. What is striking is Merton's attempt to detach himself from God's actions, through (Merton) himself, on the world. One could talk about responsibility, but this is not really the issue. It is more a question of Merton's efforts to reconcile himself to the contradiction that the three-day celebration of his ordination presented. He had decided on absolute poverty and complete interior silence—which meant not saying much of anything to anyone, either verbally or in writing—and the festivities brought a demand that he talk, open up, and celebrate.

> In a way the experience of these three days has been a reversal and contradiction of everything I was thinking about solitude, on retreat: or is it a fulfillment I do not understand? (pp. 192-93)

Once again, Merton's absolutes come under fire, but what is significant is his willingness to consider alternatives to his path of absolutes.

The weeks and months progressed. Occasionally Merton provides a clue to the state of his interior life.

> In the Chapter Room they are finishing *Seeds of Contemplation*, reading a couple of pages each evening before Compline. It began when I was on retreat for ordination. . . .
>
> I am glad the book has been written and read. Surely I have said enough about the business of darkness and about the "experimental contact with God in obscurity" to be able to shut up about it and go on to something else for a change. Otherwise it will just get to be mechanical—grinding out the same old song over and over again. But if it had not been read aloud at me I might have forgotten how often I had said those things, and gone on saying them again as if they were discoveries. For I am aware that this often happens in our life. Keeping a journal has taught me that there is not so much new in your life as you sometimes think. When you re-read your journal you find out that your latest discovery is something you already found out five years ago. Still, it is true that one penetrates deeper and deeper into the same ideas and the same experiences. (p. 201)

Merton seemed willing to continue probing his movement toward darkness and the ups and downs in his interior life produced by the movement. He recognized that rather than simply writing too much about darkness and obscurity, he was penetrating deeper into the two notions and the impact of each on his life. Once more, he reveals the intense scrutiny to which he subjected his every thought, prayer, and action. The degree to which Merton pushed this rigorous self-examination is astonishing—in addition to the demands of his monastic life, the growth of Gethsemani and the resultant community pressures, the burdens of literary and spiritual fame with the

149

newest success, *The Seeds of Contemplation*, his priesthood and its insistent awesomeness. If there was a limit here, Merton seemed not to have been aware of it. In fact, he appears to have benefited from it to some degree, particularly in terms of his struggle with the writing.

> I am finding myself forced to admit that my lamentations about my writing job have been foolish. At the moment, the writing is the one thing that gives me access to some real silence and solitude. Also I find that it helps me to pray, because when I pause at my work I find that the mirror inside me is surprisingly clean and deep and serene and God shines there and is immediately found, without hunting, as if He had come close to me while I was writing and I had not observed His coming. And this, I think, should be the cause of great joy, and to me it is. (pp. 204-5)

This passage was written on July 21, and it is curious that it followed by four days Merton's fainting at a pontifical high mass while reading the Gospel. He had begun to sing the Gospel, became dizzy, and passed out. He revived to some extent but was unable to continue the mass. There are myriad interpretations of such an incident, though two seem especially applicable. One, about which there can be little doubt, is that Merton was exhausted. He had been suffering from the flu on and off, had frequent colds, and had generally been worn down because of his many writing projects and other monastic duties. A second interpretation, and here there is perhaps less certainty, is that Merton was passing through some kind of extreme anxiety, of which the fainting was his initiation. Merton's biographer offers some help here, suggesting that Merton was experiencing "some of the classic movements of the passive purifications, sometimes called the dark night of the soul."[23] In a sense, then, the fainting spell can be seen as a classic sign of a profound anxiety and as a psychosomatic expression of a serious interior conflict.

What is notable, however, is the lack of any significant reaction from Merton to the incident. As he was wont to do, he reacted in a detached way, as if to suggest that such experiences were merely part of the monastic life and spirituality.

> I thought about a lot of things, lying on the straw mattress in the dormitory afterwards. One of the thoughts was that I am glad to be at Gethsemani and that the way to be a saint is to give yourself up entirely to your rule and the circumstances in which God has placed you and work out the secret which is His will. (pp. 203-4)

150

Merton also seemed to be saying that the experience was God's will. One cannot argue with this and yet, analytically, such an interpretation is limited.

Had Merton remembered Sertillanges's *La Vie Intellectuelle*, he would have found an intriguing explanation for his experience, one that would have given him some clearer notion of what might be going on in his life.

> When we want to awaken a thought in anyone, what are the means at our disposal? One only, to produce in him by word and sign states of sensibility and of imagination, emotion, and memory in which he will discover our idea and make it his own. Minds can only communicate through the body. Similarly, the mind of each one of us can only communicate with truth and with itself through the body. So much so, that the change by which we pass from ignorance to knowledge must be attributed, according to St. Thomas, directly to the body and only accidentally to the intellectual part of us.[24]

If Merton was passing from a kind of ignorance to a kind of knowledge, which I believe he was, then it seems apparent that he chose to interpret his fainting at mass as God's will and not as a sign of the passage and its strenuous demands. His journal entries for late July and all of August do not reveal any deep awareness of this passage, as do those entries preceding and immediately following his ordination. Occasionally, however, there is some revelation of anxiety and tension, but the revelations are scattered and, taken together, do not indicate in Merton a true sense of what is occurring.

When the summer was over and "the serious business of being a priest began," Merton's journal became a significantly different document. Its rhetoric became a rhetoric of revelation and insight instead of unworthiness, insensitivity, and elusiveness. Ordination to the priesthood was now seen as a beginning of a journey rather than an end. For Merton, it meant a purification by the fire of God, in solitude, rather than in the charity of the active ministry, as it was for the secular priest.

The fall brought Merton face to face with a dread of change, with a period of suffering and anguish, much of it mental and spiritual in nature. In fact, Merton was to experience a degree of spiritual death, though he was humble enough to see his way stubbornly through it and to emerge not only as a monk of greater integrity but as a writer more at peace with his vocation and one more willing to bear the consequences of his act.

> When the summer of my ordination ended, I found myself face to face with a mystery that was beginning to manifest itself in the depths of my soul and to move me with terror. . . . It was a sort of slow, submarine earthquake which

> produced strange commotions on the visible, psychological surface of my life.
> I was summoned to battle with joy and with fear, knowing in every case that the
> sense of battle was misleading, that my apparent antagonist was only an illusion,
> and that the whole commotion was simply the effect of something that had
> already erupted, without my knowing it, in the hidden volcano. (p. 226)

Everything seemed to be affected by this mysterious terror, including the monastic journal, *The Sign of Jonas*, which became sketchy at best after September-October, and which Merton attempted to give up completely in April 1950.

This whole experience, what Merton called the "abysmal testing and disintegration of my spirit," extended over a thirteen- to fourteen-month period, from September 1949 until about December 1950. It is important, I believe, to study this period carefully, since its process and resolution bear so much import on the reconciliation of Merton the writer with Merton the monk.

On September 1, Merton began to reread the Book of Job. His reflections on this reading led to some thoughts about his writing.

> I now know that all my own poems about the world's suffering have been
> inadequate: they have not solved anything, they have only camouflaged the
> problem. And it seems to me that the urge to write a real poem about suffering
> and sin is only another temptation because, after all, I do not really understand.

As he continues, he reveals a sense of resignation, which, however, seems to have led him to a more realistic view of his writing vocation.

> Sometimes I feel that I would like to stop writing, precisely as a gesture of
> defiance. In any case, I hope to stop publishing for a time, for I believe it has
> now become impossible for me to stop writing altogether. Perhaps I shall
> continue writing on my deathbed, and even take some asbestos paper with me
> in order to go on writing in purgatory. . . .
> And yet it seems to be that writing, far from being an obstacle to spiritual
> perfection in my own life, has become one of the conditions on which my
> perfection will depend. If I am to be a saint—and there is nothing else that I can
> think of desiring to be—it seems that I must get there by writing books in a
> Trappist monastery. If I am to be a saint, I have not only to be a monk, which
> is what all monks must do to become saints, but I must also put down on paper
> what I have become. It may sound simple, but it is not an easy vocation.

What follows, though certainly a kind of brow-beating process, is a most unusual perception and clarity of thought, albeit perhaps too perceptive and too clear. With such insight at the beginning of his trials, one wonders why Merton needed to experience fourteen months of anguish and confusion.

> To be as good a monk as I can, and to remain myself, and to write about it: to put myself down on paper, in such a situation, with the most complete simplicity and integrity, masking nothing, confusing no issues: this is very hard, because I am all mixed up in illusions and attachments. These, too, will have to be put down. But without exaggeration, repetition, useless emphasis. No need for breast-beating and lamentation before the eyes of anyone but You, O God, who see the depths of my fatuity. To be frank without being boring. It is a kind of crucifixion. Not a very dramatic or painful one. But it requires so much honesty that it is beyond my nature. It must come somehow from the Holy Ghost. (pp. 228-29)

Merton has questioned again for whom he is writing. This time, however, it is part of another question: How could Merton keep a journal and write about his monastic life, "put himself down on paper," with integrity and honesty when he knows the materials will be published? Merton's is a reasonably simple solution: he must lose himself in the Holy Spirit and the frankness and honesty will thus come from the Spirit. But at the same time, Merton is realistic enough to know that one just doesn't transcend oneself so that every thought, word, and deed is of the Holy Spirit. And so he writes at the end of the journal entry, ". . . after all, . . . nothing vital about myself can ever be public property!" (p. 229).

However, there was still the terrible pain of the "if I were a better person" mode of thought, and frequently Merton contextualized this mode within reflections on his writing. "If I were more immersed in the Rule of Saint Benedict, I would be a better writer. If I were more absorbed in the Presence of God, I would be a better writer and would write much less" (p. 233). But there is a larger context here, that of suffering and Merton's rational and psychological-spiritual conception of it. Merton notes that when he read the Book of Job before, he realized that he was both living and reading the text and that the same thing was happening as he read Job this time. And from Merton's perspective, the principal issue in Job is the question of suffering.

> . . . the problem of Job is not so much to find out who has the right answer to the question of suffering. All their answers are more or less correct. But what Job himself demands, and justly, is the DIVINE answer not to the problem of suffering in general but to his own personal suffering. In the end, the answer

that God gives to Job is simply a concrete statement of what Eliphaz (Job's friend) has said in the abstract: "Shall man be compared to God?"

Job wanted the answer and he got it. God himself was his answer. In the presence of God, Job acknowledged his sufferings to be just and God reproved all the arguments of Job's friends, because they were insufficient.

Thus, the Book of Job does not solve the problem of suffering, in the abstract. It shows us that one man, Job, received a concrete answer to the problem, and that answer was found in God Himself. (p. 230)

In an entry written ten days later, Merton quotes Job 13:15 and says that it is always with him: "Even though He kill me, yet I will trust in Him." In the Book of Job, one is inclined to think that Merton may have found the text for his rite of initiation into the genuine, Old Testament, fire-and-pestilence kind of suffering. It is almost as if he is revealing a preference for this more tangible suffering and a sense that if one does not experience the suffering of Job, one has not truly suffered. This analysis can lead, however, to a serious misconception, that through the Book of Job Merton was establishing an elaborate and contrived experience of suffering in order to test, again, his writing vocation and, for the first time, his priestly vocation.

For instance, one can wonder why on September 1 Merton began reading the Book of Job or why it was necessary, or at least *seemed* necessary, to describe his own experience with suffering in such Old Testament terms. But these are ultimately fruitless questions as is the pursuit of the conception that Merton's was a contrived spirituality. Merton was ever a sensitive artist and if one pursues his suffering within this context alone, there is ample evidence that the suffering was as real as it was frequently overpowering.

> It is not much fun to live the spiritual life with the spiritual equipment of an artist.
>
> Yesterday afternoon, in the cornfield, I began to feel rather savage about the whole business. I suppose this irritation was the sign that the dry period was reaching its climax and was about to go over again into the awful battle with joy. My soul was cringing and doubling up and subconsciously getting ready for the next tidal wave. At the moment all I had left in my heart was an abyss of self-hatred—waiting for the next appalling sea. . . .

Merton's suffering as he reflects on his experience is apparent. There is honesty and sincerity in his rhetoric, qualities that bring the reader to a point of acceptance and, to some degree, real empathy. The very quality of Merton's writing is oftentimes sufficient evidence of the validity of his experiences.

. . . The word "poignant" is taking a very prominent place in my vocabulary these days! That is because there is some power that keeps seizing my heart in its fist and wringing cries out of me (I mean the quiet kind that make themselves heard by twisting within you) and beating me this way and that until I am scarcely able to reel. Day and night I am bullied by the most suspicious of joys. I spend my time wrestling with emotions that seem to be now passion, now anguish, and now the highest religious exaltation. . . .

But occasionally I get a little rest. Yesterday, for instance, I was able to relax practically all day in a blessed aridity in which things were, once again, mercifully insipid and distasteful. What a relief to be indifferent to things, after having been pushed around by a crowd of different intoxications, some of which seem to be intensely holy and some of which do not even bother to wear a disguise. (p. 235)

The preceding journal entry was from September 21. From then on, the journal becomes sketchy. The next two entries, for instance, are for October 7 and November 16. Were the intervening days exceedingly difficult for Merton, days on which he "wrote page after page and then tore everything up," days that added up to weeks, during which he was unable to write anything at all? As if to burden himself even more, on November 16, Merton began to give a regular series of introductory theology conferences to the novices and scholastics in the community.

It seems a real lack of wisdom on the part of Merton's superiors to request him to assume such a responsibility at this particular stage in his life; he was already overextended and in some kind of state of anxiety. On the other hand, perhaps Merton did not let his superiors know the extent of his upheaval, either because he did not know himself or because his view of monastic obedience did not allow him to decline a superior's wish and did not include revealing the potential seriousness of his emotional or physical condition.

The journal includes two more entries for November, before picking up on December 3. The last entry for November, the 25th, includes a reference to "sacred exhaustion," which Merton suggests that he experienced from head to foot. The entries for December reveal the amount of preparation Merton gave to his conferences, especially on mystical theology and Saint John of the Cross.

Not only did Merton give the conferences but he also held extra seminars on Sundays and feast days to discuss specific points raised in the conferences. Invariably, his conferences (and later his course) were prepared with extraordinary diligence. This would, for instance, include going through John of the Cross in the original Spanish. Though not necessarily a meticulous scholar, Merton was conscientious about his teaching responsibilities and about what he believed to be the necessary scholarship that went with such responsibilities.

In early December, most likely the second week, Merton began to read and write about Rilke's *The Notebooks of Malte Laurids Brigge*, and for the first time in any consistent fashion, began to speak of solitude in reference to himself.

> I am abashed by the real solitude of Rilke which I admire, knowing however that it is not for me because I am not like that. But his is a solitude I understand objectively, perhaps not by connaturality at all but it moves me tremendously. . . . He did not WANT it or go looking for it. It found him. . . .
>
> Anyway, here is something Rilke himself wrote down. It will make one page of mine look good.
>
>> For a while yet I can write all this down and express it. But there will come a day when my hand will be far from me and when I bid it write it will write words I do not mean. The time of that other interpretation will dawn when not one word will remain upon another and all meaning will dissolve like clouds and fall down like rain. Despite my fear I am yet like one standing before something great. . . . This time I shall be written. I am the impression that will change.
>
> No, one does not envy the fear that is another man's private vocation. But I am abashed by that fear and by Rilke and Kafka [Merton had apparently been reading Kafka at this time, also] who are solitaries without, for all that, being my brothers—not my close brothers like the calm and patient and long-suffering men in cowls who live and pray with me here in this busy family.
>
> I guess it is the right fictional element that makes this solitude in Rilke's book just intangible: real, but not quite my own. Same too with Kafka. (pp. 241-42)

There is not only an awareness here of solitude; there is also Merton's growing sense that solitude is something he must define and experience for himself, in his own context. There is, too, Merton's capacity to juxtapose whatever he reads and contemplates, in this case Rilke, with the reality of his monastic existence. His is the eye of an artist, a writer, with which he sees essences instead of ornamentations and superficialities. His applications are precise and direct and they often serve as a motif through which the richness of a character or the fullness of an insight is revealed.

> Rilke's Notebooks have so much power in them that they make me wonder why no one writes like that in monasteries. Not that there have not been better books written in monasteries, and books more serene. But monks do not seem

to be able to write so well—and it is as if our professional spirituality sometimes veiled our contact with the naked realities inside us. It is a common failing of monks to lose themselves in a collective, professional personality—to let themselves be cast in a mold. Yet this mold does not seem to do away with what is useless or even unpleasant about some personalities. We cling to our eccentricities and our selfishness, but we do so in a way that is no longer interesting because it is after all mechanical and vulgar. (p. 245)

Merton's writer's eye reveals what the common eye misses and thus is Merton left to face what his eye has revealed. He is talking about his own selfishness and eccentricity here, qualities that were made even clearer by his reading and understanding of Rilke. It is difficult enough truly to face oneself and even more so when one is essentially an artist. One can speak of the courage of the artistic sensibility most especially when it discloses to the artist what that artist wants most not to recognize. This was partly the case with Merton but he, unlike many others, seems to have been much more open to the revelation, in fact eager to have it. In a very real sense, Merton sought out the recognition and when he found it, faced it directly. Thus we begin to see the breadth of the struggle when one's artistry becomes both an ally and an enemy in the process of self-illumination.

Joined with the awareness of and quest for solitude (a solitude of the heart more than a physical solitude) was Merton's intensifying fear and its impact on his life. Merton seemed almost more afraid of the fear itself than of the darkness that he believed was the source of the fear. Nevertheless, he was beginning to make some important relationship between his darkness and his fear, his loneliness, and his growing sense of solitude.

. . . feeling of fear, dejection, non-existence. Yet it gives me a kind of satisfaction to realize that it is not by contact with any other creature that I can recover the sense that I am real. Solitude means being lonely not in a way that pleases you but in a way that frightens and empties you to the extent that it means being exiled even from yourself. (p. 243)

When this journal entry was written, December 15, Merton was again serving as deacon and experiencing the almost irrational fear that such an activity provoked. (Remember that Merton passed out at the pontifical high mass in July while serving as deacon.) In addition to experiencing many physical signs of anxiety the first day of his week-long role, he began to wake up in the middle of the night worrying about whether he could get through the week without passing out again. The whole thing became so overwhelming he asked to be relieved of his service for the rest of the week.

The middle two weeks of December 1949 were difficult for Merton. The abbot was concerned enough about him to make him sleep an hour or so later every morning. Merton himself wrote that he was involving himself far too much in his preparations for the conferences and that the preparation was wearing him down. He was still more concerned with making an impression on the novices and with showing them "all his treasures" than with sharing with them the riches of the material. On December 17, Merton quotes from John of the Cross's Spiritual Canticle: "*Vacio, hambriento, solo, llagado y doliente de amor, suspense en el aire*" ("Empty, famished, alone, wounded and suffering with love, suspended in the air!"). And, as if to add a spirit of comic relief, Merton was "elevated" to a position in the monastery fire department.

His journal makes reference, again, to the enormous amount of time and energy he was expending in the preparation and teaching of his classes.

> The terrible thing is the indignity of thinking such an endeavor is really important. The other day while the new high altar was being consecrated I found myself being stripped of one illusion after another. There I stood and sat with my eyes closed and wondered why I read so much, why I write so much, why I talk so much, and why I get so excited about the things that only affect the surface of my life—I came here eight years ago and already knew better when I arrived. But for eight years I have obeyed the other law in my members and so I am worn out with activity—exhausting myself with proclaiming that the thing to do is rest. (pp. 245-46)

Merton has accurately described the tension between the self who seeks physical solitude and a state of nondoing and the self who is fulfilled and excited by community activity and engagement with others. But this description pales when it is compared to Merton's journal entry of December 22.

Merton is reflecting on the events of the day before. He experienced on that day a "wordless decision, a giving of the depths and substance of myself . . . a conversion of the deep will to God." He says too that this decision-conversion is not something that can be written down but then proceeds to describe the very experience. Merton's rhetoric is of death and speaks directly to the writer-monk conflict. Its progression is from death to rebirth, but one is uncertain to what or to whom Merton is reborn, as Merton himself may have been uncertain. Still, it reveals a richness of language and a relatively non-defensive stance, qualities not seen in other journal entries of this same period.

> The reality of the present and of solitude divorced from past and future. To be collected and gathered up in clarity and silence and to belong to God and be nobody else's business. I wish I could recover the liberty of that interior decision which was very simple and which seems to me to have been a kind of blank check and a promise.
>
> To belong to God I have to belong to myself. I have to be alone—at least interiorly alone. This means the constant renewal of a decision. I cannot belong to people. None of me belongs to anybody but God. Absolute loneliness of the imagination, the memory, the will. My love for everybody is equal, neutral and clean. No exclusiveness. Simple and free as the sky because I love everybody and am possessed by nobody, not held, not bound. In order to be not remembered or even wanted I have to be a person that nobody knows. They can have Thomas Merton. He's dead. Father Louis—he's half dead too. For my part my name is that sky, those fence-posts, and those cedar trees. I shall not even reflect on who I am and I shall not say my identity is nobody's business because that implies a truculence I don't intend. It has no meaning.
>
> Now my whole life is this—to keep unencumbered. The wind owns the fields where I walk and I own nothing and am owned by nothing and shall never be forgotten because no one will ever discover me. This is to me a source of immense confidence. (pp. 246-47)

Merton is saying no to a great many aspects of his life, historically and prophetically, in the process of dissolving his personage. Thomas Merton is dead and all that he was, is, and might be—the writer, the man in and of the world, the teacher, the guide for so many souls. But Father Louis, the monk and priest, is only half dead, perhaps to suggest that the identity that is no identity must be reached at least partially through the dimensions of the monastic life. Merton is giving everything up in order to have nothing; he is dying; he is disappearing and wants to leave no trace of where he has been and no indication of where he might go. Yet he *is*, just the same; he exists, though his existence is without a past and without a future. He affirms only God, as God becomes the here and the now.

The next paragraph describes tearing down the old monastic horse barn. He uses words like *ruins* and *wreckage* and includes the ominous sentence, "And house upon house shall fall." Predictably, however, Merton does not mention what will replace the barn, only that it was torn down by a Traxcavator and left in wreckage.

But Merton himself seems intent on not only tearing down his Thomas Merton personage but also doing away with that wreckage. There must be no trace of anything. There is no intent to have something else. The snake sheds its skin and moves to another part of the land, to live its life until it sheds its skin again the next spring. Yet the essence of snakeness never changes; still the snake is a snake. So with Merton. Persona after persona is shed and he is still Merton. Merton must shed his personages in order to remain himself.

There is more in this journal entry. Merton includes five lines from Psalm 55, lines "truer of my life than anything I have ever written."

> My heart is troubled within me: and the fear of death is fallen upon me.
> Fear and trembling are come upon me: and darkness has covered me.
> And I said: who will give me wings like a dove, and I will fly and be at rest?
> Lo, I have gone far off, flying away; and I abode in the wilderness.
> I waited for Him that has saved me from pusillanimity of spirit and a storm.

Once more it is fear that motivates Merton, but now the motivation is strong and positive, for it brings him closer to the solitude he seeks.

> It is fear that is driving me into solitude, Love has put drops of terror in my veins and they grow cold in me, suddenly, and make me feel faint with fear because my heart and my imagination wander away from God into their own private idolatry. It is my infinity that makes me physically faint and turn to jelly because of the contradiction between my nature and my God. I am exhausted by fear. (pp. 246-48)

As December comes to an end and he begins to move into the first few months of 1950, Merton's journal reveals a more intense concern with solitude, a movement toward solitude that begins to take shape during the Christmas season. In reflecting on the virginity of the Mother of God, on Christmas Eve Merton exhibited how far he had already progressed.

> She comes bringing solitude and society, life and death, war and peace, that peace may come out of war and that my solitude may place me somewhat in the history of my society. It is clear to me that solitude is my vocation, not as a flight from the world but as my place in the world, because for me to find solitude is only to separate myself from all the forces that destroy me and destroy history, in order to be united with the Life and Peace that build the City of God in history and rescue the children of God from hell. . . .

Merton has provided a significant clue to the structure and process of his rebirth, the reconciliation of writer and monk. He drops his guard and says that he is no longer bent on fleeing the world. He determines that he has a place in the world, in and through solitude. Admittedly, there is still evident the rhetoric of detachment, the apartness of his position, but nevertheless he has extended the boundaries to the extent of recognizing his place in the world. Solitude thus becomes a means of reconciliation as well as a way of living. With solitude comes a conscious need for silence, but now a nondefensive silence, a silence that is part of the movement toward an end, not a silence of guilt, iniquity, and mindless renunciation.

> . . . The best thing for me is a lucid silence that does not even imagine it speaks to anybody. A silence in which I see no interlocutor, frame no message for anyone, formulate no word either for man or paper. There will still be plenty to say when the time comes to write, and what is written will be simpler and more fruitful. (pp. 251-52)

Lest one think Merton has turned the corner, there is his journal entry for December 30, his reflections on the year.

> . . . another year is over. I wish I knew what I had done to justify my existence this year—besides collecting royalties with which the monastery supports General Motors by buying new trucks. There is only one thing—and that is better than anything else I have done in my life. For six months I have been saying Mass. That one fact is teaching me to live in such a way that I do not care whether I live or die.
>
> Yet there is a sinful way of being prepared to die; to live in the midst of life, at the source of life, and to feel in your heart that cold taste for death that is almost ready to refuse life—the dead rot of acedia that eats out your substance with discouragement and fear!
>
> I wonder if there are not hundreds of people in monasteries with that most pitiable of sicknesses. It makes you wish you could get something respectable, with a real pain attached to it, like cancer, or a tumor on the brain. (p. 253)

Once more Merton reveals that his is not the deathlike way of life of so many others, the refusal of life, though it is this very quality that he has been struggling with. Merton recognized its seductiveness, especially for a monk, and how terrifying it was to have to face it; rather something tangible, like cancer or heart disease.

Merton's truly was a concern with and a quest for tangibles. This concern was a method of maintaining his reality, of keeping as many dimensions of this

161

reality as he could within both comprehension and grasp. He vowed to "clean up" his prose style during 1950, as well as bring more discipline to his work. (As a catalyst for the former, he received an English Grammar and Rhetoric text for study through the kindness of his friend Evelyn Waugh.) Merton gave more and more of his attention to the woods and forests around the monastery. They became part of his search for solitude.

> Solitude is not found so much by looking outside the boundaries of your dwelling, as by staying within. Solitude is not something you must hope for in the future. Rather, it is a deepening of the present, and unless you look for it in the present you will never find it. (p. 256)

And with solitude is silence. Again the role of the tangible, in this case, language.

> For the first time in my life I am finding you, O solitude. . . . Now I know I am coming to the day in which I will be free of words: their master rather than their servant, able to live without them if need be. For I still need to go out into this no-man's land of language that does not quite join me to other men and which throws a veil over my own solitude. By words I mean all the merely human expressions that bind men to one another. I also mean the half helpless and half wise looks by which they seek one another's thoughts. But I do not abdicate all language. For there is the word of God. . . . The speech of God is silence. His Word is solitude. Him will I never deny, by His grace! We are travelers from the half-world of language into solitude and infinity. We are strangers. Paper, I have not in you a lasting city. Yet there is a return from solitude, to make manifest His Name to them who have known it. Then to re-enter solitude and dwell in silence. (pp. 260-61)

Merton's use of tangibles is further demonstrated by his reaction to a novel of Brice Parain, *La Mort de Jean Madec*, only the second novel he had read since his entrance into Gethsemani eight years before. The core of the book was what Merton called purity of heart and Madec's rediscovery of the silence that had always been in him. From this comes the realization that purity of heart—solitude—does not mean the absence of people, but only a withdrawal from a superficial level of interaction with people.

> It is in deep solitude that I find the gentleness with which I can truly love my brothers. The more solitary I am, the more affection I have for them. It is pure affection, and filled with reverence for the solitude of others. Solitude and silence teach me to love my brothers for what they are, not for what they say. (p. 261)[25]

Solitude and silence seem also to have brought Merton to an acceptance of himself for what he is, a writer and a monk. On January 14, 1950, he signed a long-term contract with Harcourt, Brace for four books, one of them the theological text he was having so much difficulty writing. This event was perhaps the clearest sign thus far, the most significant tangible, of the reconciliation of writer and monk.

> I did not expect this legal act to have the effects it did. I put the thing in the mail, completely reconciled to my position and determined to waste no more time turning around and around like a dog before lying down in the corner that has been prepared for me by Providence. That probably means the final renouncement forever of any dream of a hermitage. God will prepare for me His own hermitage for my last days, and meanwhile my work is my hermitage because it is WRITING that helps me most of all to be a solitary and a contemplative here at Gethsemani.
>
> But the real reason why the signing of this contract left me in peace, with no more desire to rationalize my fate, was the fact that all my days are now completely ordered to God's work in prayer and teaching and writing. I have no time to be anything but a contemplative or a teacher of the contemplative life. And because I still know so little of my subject I can no longer afford to waste time dramatizing my approach to it in mental movies or interior controversies. There is nothing left for me but to live fully and completely in the present, praying when I pray, and writing and praying when I write, and worrying about nothing but the will and the glory of God, finding these as best I can in the sacrament of the present moment. (pp. 262-63)

The Sign of Jonas from this point on, January 18, 1950, reflects the ordering of his days of which Merton speaks. Much of his reflection was on theological materials, particularly Saint Bernard and the Cistercian fathers, materials he was teaching in his conferences; on Scripture, especially Genesis and other Old Testament books, and the letters of Saint Paul; on the liturgy and the mass; on nature and its frozen beauty; on Eliot's *Four Quartets* and Gregorian chant. In the midst of all this reflection, all this activity, is Merton's growing conviction that the contemplative life is a discovery of Christ in "new and unexpected places," in the essence of his ordered days. Merton's reflections are quiet and assured.

> Two and three and four years ago when I complained bitterly that there was no time in my life for contemplation, all these demands on our time and energy would probably have upset me considerably. For now it is actually a fact, and not a fancy, that we get very little time to ourselves. But it no longer upsets me, and I find that I am not tempted to waste time in complaining. That shows that

I must have learned something since ordination. So now, the time I would have lost in complaining is spent in something more like union with God. (pp. 276-77)

In the spring, the community at Gethsemani was hit by a serious epidemic of flu. Merton, working as hard as he was, was not spared any misery. He was especially ill from March 25 until April 5. It is intriguing that Merton's first day out of bed was a day on which he served as deacon at high mass, the liturgy of Good Friday in fact. Merton had obviously come some distance to have overcome the powerful anxiety involved with service as deacon and the memory of his fainting spell and his week of terror. No, this anxiety seemed no longer to have concerned Merton. Solitude and silence were in his heart and mind and on the pages of his journal.

The Easter season of 1950 seemed an especially rich period for Merton. Once more, it was the liturgy that precipitated fullness of thought and expression.

> The mystery of speech and silence is resolved in the Acts of the Apostles. Pentecost is the solution. The problem of language is the problem of sin. The problem of silence is also a problem of love. How can a man really know whether to write or not, whether to speak or not, whether his words and his silence are for good or for evil, for life or for death, unless he understands the two divisions of tongues—the division of Babel, when men were scattered because of pride, and the division of Pentecost when the Holy Ghost sent out men of one dialect to speak all the languages of the earth and bring all men to unity: that they may be one, Father, Thou in Me and I in Them that they may be one in us! The apostles . . . the more they loved one another and loved God, the more they declared His word. And He manifested Himself through them. That is the only possible reason for speaking—but it justifies speaking without end, as long as the speech grows up from silence and brings your soul to silence once again. (pp. 291-92)

This journal entry was the second to last for April and the second to last until October 9. In his prologue (written after the fact) to the part of the journal from which the entry is taken, Merton states that he gave up the journal in April 1950, as he thought, for good. This decision would be easier to understand had it come in the last two or three months of 1949, when everything was so terribly dark and bleak. I have suggested, however—based on the journal of the period—that things began to change significantly in late January 1950, and by April Merton had reached some level of contentment, some level of acceptance of who and what he is. The prologue may clear up some of the confusion.

> Before becoming a priest I had made a great fuss about solitude and had been rather a nuisance to my superiors and directors in my aspirations for a solitary life. Now, after my ordination, I discovered that the essence of a solitary vocation is that it is a vocation to fear, to helplessness, to isolation in the invisible God. Having found this, I now began for the first time in my life to taste a happiness that was so complete and so profound that I no longer needed to reflect on it. There was no longer any need to remind myself that I was happy—a vain expedient to prolong a transient joy—for this happiness was real and permanent and even in a sense eternal. It penetrated to the depths below consciousness, and in all storms, in all fears, in the deepest darkness, it was always unchangeably there. (p. 227)

Merton gave up the journal because he no longer felt the need to keep it: "There was no longer any need to remind myself that I was happy," nor was there any need to remind himself that he was troubled or confused or beleaguered with doubt and uncertainty. One senses that Merton saw the keeping of the journal, and perhaps all of his writing at this time, as a function of need. Additionally, Merton was growing into a kind of silence and as a consequence found language and the use of the written word more and more frustrating and more and more inadequate and incomplete. Words were a way of distancing himself from himself and as he uncovered the character of his need to write and its relationship to the exiling effect of language, Merton said no. As far as he was concerned, need alone was not a healthy basis on which to write; the forming of words was not going to be his pursuit.

It is important, in this context, to understand the nature of Merton's decision to discontinue the journal. On previous occasions Merton had decided to stop writing and in most cases followed through with the decision, for example the decision to stop being a poet. However, the discontinuance of the journal is unlike the other incidents in that it appears to be a more substantive decision.

Merton was not running aimlessly from writing. In fact, two books on which he spent a great deal of time were published during this period. *The Waters of Siloe*, his history of the Trappists, was published on September 5, 1949, and *What Are These Wounds?*, a biography of a Cistercian mystic, Saint Luygarde of Aywieres, was published February 28, 1950. He was giving up only the personal and introspective writing in his journal; it had become an unnecessary burden and he was positively putting it aside. There does not appear to have been any conflict with this decision; it was clear, forthright, and simple.

The journal was important to Merton as a means to greater self-knowledge and integrity. But as he gained a greater awareness of himself and reached a certain wholeness of being, the journal became almost unnecessary, and certainly not a pleasant task to maintain. In addition, Merton had less time to write in the summer and fall of 1950, as his teaching duties grew and he tried to fulfill his contract with Harcourt, Brace. There is also the most important issue of Merton's priesthood, which he took extremely seriously. He was consistently awed by the priesthood, not an insignificant consequence of the careful and rigorous manner in which he exercised his priestly functions. By now, it is obvious that Merton was absolutely serious about everything he did, about every responsibility he accepted and, most of all, about the painstaking maintenance of his spiritual life. And though he put aside his most intense writing project, his journal, the exactitude with which he functioned began to take its toll. In September, Merton was sent to the hospital for a series of tests and examinations as well as for general recupation.

The spring flu epidemic in the monastery was very hard on Merton and he did not fully recover from this virus. In addition, there was mounting concern about Merton's persistent gastric problems. Eventually, these problems were traced to a serious allergy to milk and milk products, for which Merton received regular treatment.[26]

The four journal entries from October 1950 (Merton resumed the journal on October 9) provide little detail about Merton's stay in the hospital in Louisville. However, in early November, he returned to the hospital to have some minor surgery to clear up a blockage in his nose. While there he also had more tests to determine the nature of the stomach disorder, and a series of chest X-rays. It appears that Merton had suffered tuberculosis as a child and there was concern that he might have suffered a recurrence. The X-rays were not altogether negative and Merton was treated with penicillin and told to rest and abstain from all of his monastic duties. There was indication too that Merton may have contracted colitis, which would explain some aspects of his stomach trouble.[27] Though the journal's six entries for November provide some background on Merton's assorted illnesses, there is little discussion of the origin of these disorders or the implications they might hold for the future.

I believe that there is an important relationship between Merton's year-long spiritual anguish and the physical illness that was diagnosed and treated at the end of that time.[28] It is precisely the holistic quality of Merton's being that makes one suspect there was for Merton more than an incidental relationship among mind, soul, and body. Merton himself was certainly aware of this relationship, but he did not discuss it in his journal.

Of course, Merton knew the journal would be published and it is in this context that we come to understand more perfectly his earlier comment that nothing "vital" about himself could ever be public property. Thus we are left to try to determine the significance of the periods during which Merton did not keep the journal.

Silence becomes an extremely helpful element here, the silence that is part of the solitude of the heart, the interior quietude. Merton reflects on this in a journal entry for November 19, 1950, just six days before he returned from the hospital after his nose surgery. This entry is unusual—Merton has given his reflections a title, "The Necessity of Silence."

> When you gain this interior silence you can carry it around with you in the world, and pray everywhere. But just as interior asceticism cannot be acquired without concrete and exterior mortification, so it is absurd to talk about interior silence when there is no exterior silence. (p. 302)

Interior silence comes only after the establishment of an exterior silence, a calmness of daily life, and a kind of wordless communication with oneself and with others. There emerges a decisive relationship between interior silence and prayer, an inseparability, in fact. And prayer, unlike the introspective private journal, is a dialogue. Paul Tournier has made a useful distinction between introspection and dialogue.

> In introspection we become buried in ourselves, in a solitude in which . . . the person vanishes. In a dialogue, on the other hand, . . . in the dialogue with God, the person is asserted and made more definite through the personal relationship that is established.

As Tournier continues his reflection, we see how it could apply to Merton as well as to the possibility that Merton had reached an awareness that his journal may have become an intrusion into his prayer life and a burdensome process of introspection.

> It does sometimes happen that my prayers degenerate into introspection. I can soon sense the difference: I begin, in fact, to listen to myself more than to God, to concentrate on myself instead of on him. It is then that the human dialogue can help to revitalize the dialogue with God. Contact with other Christians, their

167

witness, what they have to say about their own experience of the activity of the Holy Spirit, renews the quality of my own prayer.

So prayer is far from being the "disorderly" monologue of introspection . . . in which everything gets more and more muddled. On the contrary, apart from awakening and developing our love towards God, it is a sure road to the setting in order of our lives and the discovery of the person. For it is before God, who knows us and loves and forgives us, that we dare to see ourselves as we are.[29]

Tournier closes his discussion with a quote from the journal of François Mauriac, that no man can look at himself except in the sight of God. This is the point to which Merton had come in these last weeks of 1950. He had come to view the keeping of the publishable journal as an intrusion into and an impediment to his life of prayer. Though he had begun to see himself as he was, before God and before his monastic brothers, the demands of this journal came to form a hindrance to Merton's life and prayer and its link with his being himself, especially in that it became an obstacle to interior silence.

It is significant, I believe, that Merton added twenty-five pages to the manuscript of *Bread in the Wilderness* (which had to be sent back from the publisher) while he was in the hospital in November. His journal reveals, even with its small number of entries, that these three weeks were a period of silence and prayer and "do-nothingness," this last medically enforced. (The journal entry "The Necessity of Silence" also was written while in the hospital.) Merton always did well with these periods of quietude and enforced lack of activity.

As he continued to reflect on the Psalms, the subject matter of *Bread in the Wilderness*, even after the manuscript had been sent to his publisher, Merton's insights grew and his immediate experience began to show him a more fulfilling dimension of interior silence. This is reflected in the added pages themselves, especially in a section entitled "The Silence of the Psalms."

Much of this section focuses on verse 21 of Psalm 31. Merton writes that the "wrangling of tongues" was the symbol of the confusion in the city of Babel as the citizens attempted to reach heaven with their makeshift structure and were set upon by God. Merton contrasts this hopeless confusion with the union and peace of the City of God. And thus he comes to his notion of interior silence.

> . . . there is only one language spoken in the City of God. That language is charity. Those who speak it best, speak it in silence. For the eternal Word of Truth is uttered in silence. If He is uttered in silence, He must be heard in

deepest silence. And His Spirit, the Spirit of Love, is also poured out into our hearts, proceeding from the Father and the Son, in an everlasting silence.

Merton continues his reflection with a more specific application to the Psalms.

> The Psalms are more than language. They contain within themselves the silence of high mountains and the silence of heaven. It is only when we stand at the bottom of the mountain that it is hard for us to distinguish the language of the Psalter from the tongues of this earth: for Christ must still perforce travel among us as a pilgrim disguised in our own tattered garments. The Psalter only truly begins to speak and sing within us when we have been led by God and lifted up by Him, and have ascended into its silences. When this is done, The Psalms themselves become the Tabernacle of God in which we are protected forever from the rage of the city business, from the racket of human opinions, from the wild carnival we carry in our hearts and which the ancient saints called "Babylon."[30]

It is apparent from this added section and, in fact, from the whole of *Bread in the Wilderness* that as he prayed and wrote about the Psalms, Merton came to know and to experience interior silence more intimately and to pursue it more deliberately. At the same time, Merton himself brought to his study and prayer of the Psalms a great sensitivity toward interior silence and a firmer conviction that it was an essential part of his spiritual and mental being.

Sometime just before Christmas 1950, and after completing six entries for December, Merton once again "discontinued" *The Sign of Jonas*.[31] He resumed the entries on February 21, 1951, though with a certain detachment.

> Today is the ninth anniversary of my reception of the habit of novice, and it occurred to me that I should go on writing this notebook which I had deliberately stopped again. There is nothing against it, since it is not a "Spiritual Journal."
>
> This morning at Prime—at once I write something professionally and tediously spiritual—this morning at Prime I was struck by the title the Trappist printer invented for Psalm 14, DE VIA DUCENTE AD BEATITUDINEM. . . .
>
> The line that struck me most was "QUI LOQUITOR VERITATEM IN CORDE SUO." It could mean—the man who is completely true to the Word God utters within him, who is, by his simplicity, in perfect harmony with truth. That is our vocation—mine. I have to think about it more, but not on paper. (pp. 309-10)

In light of the last sentence of this entry, Merton's detachment seems understandable, or at least explainable. One begins to wonder why he continued the journal at all and whether he was under any kind of pressure to do so, either externally or from himself. As discussed, Merton did not believe need or compulsion was a legitimate basis on which to write. But perhaps he was not fully convinced of this and was unwilling to put this writing project aside. Whatever the case, Merton was uncomfortable with the journal and, as a result, began, once again, to question and react to his writing vocation.

The entry for March 3, 1951, reveals this questioning and reaction and suggests that Merton, as he had done so many times before, was questioning the whole notion of what it meant for him to be a writer *and* a monk instead of just a monk.

> How weary I am of being a writer. How necessary it is for monks to work in the fields, in the rain, in the sun, in the mud, in the clay, in the wind: these are our spiritual directors and our novice-masters. They form our contemplation. They instill us with virtue. They make us as stable as the land we live in. You do not get that out of a typewriter.

Merton then quotes a passage from Saint Benedict's Rule, that those who are truly monks are so when they live by the "labor of their hands" as did the apostles and the monastic fathers. Merton, of course, never writes that his is an inferior monastic life, but the implication is there.

What follows in the entry is Merton's reflection on his autobiographical novel, published posthumously as *My Argument with the Gestapo*. The context of the reflection is Merton's preoccupation with his becoming an American citizen, which he did on June 22, 1951.

He viewed this youthful novel as inhibited, void of action, and peculiarly immobile. Its principal concern was Merton's relationship to the world and to World War II. Merton had a "very supernatural solution" to this relationship when he wrote his novel. But now this solution is to be rejected.

> . . . After nine years in a monastery I see that it was no solution at all. The false solution went like this: the whole world, of which the war is a characteristic expression, is evil. It has therefore to be first ridiculed, then spat upon, and at last formally rejected with a curse.
>
> Actually I have come to the monastery to find my place in the world, and if I fail to find this place in the world I will be wasting my time in the monastery. . . .

Merton realized that his was a "psychological withdrawal" from the world and from mankind and expressed his preparedness to change.

. . . Coming to the monastery has been for me exactly the right kind of withdrawal. It has given me perspective. It has taught me how to live. And now I owe everyone else in the world a share in that life. My first duty is to start, for the first time, to live as a member of a human race which is no more (and no less) ridiculous than I am myself. And my first human act is the recognition of how much I owe everybody else. (pp. 311-12)

There is movement forward here, a reaching out, a process of coming to embrace the world, as it is, and the admission that Merton himself is capable of distinguishing the positive from the negative qualities of the world. It is no longer the "all or nothing" position; it is now a position of reconciliation and openness, no longer a fearful defensiveness. Merton had grown more comfortable with himself.

By April 22, Merton was writing about an end to his journal at the same time that he sensed he was not quite ready to end his reflections. There is silence for the rest of April and all of May with the exception of an entry for May 7. Silence again until June 13, when Merton writes of his death and rebirth and the fact that he has become very different from what he used to be.

The man who began this journal is dead, Just as the man who finished *The Seven Storey Mountain* when this journal began was also dead, and what is more the man who was the central figure in *The Seven Storey Mountain* was dead over and over. And now that all these men are dead, it is sufficient for me to say so on paper and I think I will have ended up by forgetting them. Because writing down what *The Seven Storey Mountain* was about was sufficient to get it off my mind for good. Last week I corrected the proofs of the French translation of the book and it seemed completely alien. I might as well have been a proofreader working for a publisher and going over the galleys of somebody else's book. Consequently, *The Seven Storey Mountain* is the work of a man I never even heard of. And this journal is getting to be the production of somebody to whom I have never had the dishonor of an introduction. (pp. 317-18)

One could conclude that Merton was, once again, trying to run from himself, even though it was now the self that "had been." One could speak of a process of disownnent-of-self; Merton had written of his past self and through the commitment of this self to paper and to publication had forever put it aside, to be forgotten. But I believe there is a deeper significance. Rather than running from his past, I suggest that Merton was acknowledging it and by that very acknowledgment leaving it and being reborn in the present *and* the presence of the monastery and his monastic life. One must understand the context in which Merton is writing.

On May 20, Trinity Sunday, Merton was appointed master of scholastics. The scholastics are the youngest monks in terms of profession of vows and in many monasteries the size of Gethsemani, their number was often large, sometimes twenty or thirty. Therefore it was essential to the life of the monastery to establish a scholastic family. Merton was appointed spiritual director, teacher, friend, father figure, and head of the family, and part of the monastery was set aside to house the scholastics and their master. So Merton was embarking on a new journey, a new way of life.

> Thus I stand on the threshold of a new existence. The one who is going to be most fully formed by the new scholasticate is the Master of the Scholastics. It is as if I were beginning all over again to be a Cistercian: but this time I am doing it without asking myself the abstract questions which are the luxury and the torment of one's monastic adolescence. For now I am a grown-up monk and have no time for anything but the essentials. The only essential is not an idea or an ideal: it is God Himself, who cannot be found by weighing the present against the future or the past but only by sinking into the heart of the present as it is. (p. 319)

The last sentence gives a sense of what I believe Merton was trying to say in the journal entry from June 13. "Sinking into the heart of the present as it is" meant accepting himself as he was but at the same time not denying the past or the future. In saying that the man who wrote *The Seven Storey Mountain* and who began *The Sign of Jonas* was dead, I believe Merton was saying that he was not going to live in that past, that part of himself, any longer. He had evolved into the present—the master of scholastics and mature monk of Gethsemani, who was also a writer who continued to write. He truly was the author of *The Seven Storey Mountain* and the journal but he is not now what he was at the time he wrote the autobiography and began the journal. The "what" has changed while the "who" remains constant.[32]

And what of Merton the writer? More by circumstance than by intent, his time for writing was severely limited by his new position as master of scholastics. But Merton also had a growing sense of work as prayer and work as allowing and often creating prayer. So the time spent in the fields and the forests with his young monks, digging, planting, and trimming, though time away from his writing, was ultimately helpful to this vocation because it gave him a new sense of what it meant to pray and to worship God through one's work responsibilities and talents. It is not that Merton wrote less, but that he began to write more out of who he was when he wrote, to write freely and willfully rather than under monastic obedience or a mindless commitment to "the writer in his blood."

Merton's beloved silence and solitude were important cogs in his wheel, for they brought him closer to the reconciliation and creative tension of writer and monk. In late November 1951, after having been master for almost half a year, Merton wrote of his silence and solitude in his new context.

> I do not know if they [his scholastics] have discovered anything new, or if they are able to love God more, or if I have helped them in any way to find themselves, which is to say: to lose themselves. But I know what I have discovered: that the kind of work I once feared because I thought it would interfere with "solitude" is, in fact, the only true path to solitude. One must be in some sense a hermit before the care of souls can serve to lead one further into the desert. But once God has called you to solitude, everything you touch leads you further into solitude. Everything that affects you builds you into a hermit, as long as you do not insist on doing the work yourself and building your own kind of hermitage.
>
> What is my new desert? The name of it is COMPASSION. There is no wilderness so terrible, so beautiful, so arid and so fruitful as the wilderness of compassion. It is the only desert that shall truly flourish like the lily. It shall become a pool, it shall bud forth and blossom and rejoice with joy. It is in the desert of compassion that the thirsty land turns into springs of water, that the poor possess all things. There are no bounds to contain the inhabitants of this solitude in which I live alone, as isolated as the Host on the altar, the food of all men, belonging to all and belonging to none, for God is with me, and He sits in the ruins of my heart, preaching His Gospel to the poor. (p. 323)

At the beginning of this chapter, John Howard Griffin was quoted on the writer's movement toward wisdom and compassion through the discipline and process of the art itself. I believe that this is precisely what Merton had come to in the last months of 1951. His writing, especially *The Sign of Jonas*, had brought him to wisdom and compassion, wisdom and compassion with which he could "care for his souls," the young scholastics. His writing had brought him to a richer monastic life as master and purveyor of the monastic tradition and sensibility.

It was out of this context that Merton could move to embrace the world and to care for its souls, not merely as a writer but as a writer who had truly become a monk, a monkish word-fellow for the souls of mankind.

173

Conclusion

Thomas Merton's story is significant because his life was one of integrity and wholeness, as artist, as monk, as religious figure, and as teacher. What Henry Miller has written of himself is equally applicable to Merton.

> . . . when my writing becomes absolutely truthful there will be no discrepancy between the man and the writer, between what I am and what I do or say. This, I say it without hesitation, is the highest goal a man can set himself; it is the goal of all religious teachers.[1]

It is impossible to know whether any individual actually reaches the highest goal, be it as artist or athlete, monk or preacher, doctor or academician. But the importance is the *awareness* of the highest goal and of the *need* to reach it and the *process* through which to strive for it. It is this awareness and need that Miller speaks of, not the achievement.

I have argued that Merton's highest goal was the reconciliation of his vocation as a writer with his vocation as a Trappist monk and, on this premise, discussed the process through which Merton came to the awareness of this goal, the need to reach it, and the extent to which he did reach it. He became himself through the merging of writer and monk.

There is significance, too, in the way Merton chose to live his life. Why would Thomas Merton the artist and writer become Thomas Merton the monk and spend twenty-seven years secluded in a Trappist monastery? The choices themselves are important, for when one thing is chosen many other things are put aside.

In one of his more objective statements on the condition of this civilization, Merton wrote about "man's present state of alienation in a world that seems to be without meaning because of the moral, cultural, and economic crises of society."[2] Merton not only attempted to understand and write about the condition of civilization but he also, in his own way and in his own context, prescribed ways of changing the condition to something more fulfilling and creative. Merton's writings and prescriptions are only a part of his import. The other and greater part comes with who he was and what in this century of alienation and turmoil he would do and stay committed to until his death.

Thomas Merton, primarily, was an artist. It is helpful to consider the "whatness" of an artist and how this "whatness" might be part of Merton's import.

Merton wrote about man's innocence and also man's inherent dignity and ultimate worthiness as a creature of God. Contemporary civilization and our technological culture have brought mankind to a new anxiety and meaninglessness. Merton the artist saw this condition, faced it directly in order to understand it, and adjusted the condition of his own life to deal with it. Paul Tillich has described this last dimension as living creatively, "expressing the predicament of the most sensitive people of our time in cultural production."[3]

Merton warred against the "stagnation, crystallization, immobility" of contemporary civilization because he understood its destructiveness. As an artist, he tried to articulate this destructiveness, creatively urging man to face the condition at the same time that he provided him with a certain strength with which to face it. And inasmuch as Merton was against this death, this cultural dissolution, he was against the civilization that produced it.

It was primarily as an artist that Merton came to Gethsemani to become a Trappist monk. On one level, this journey was to bear witness to his artistic sensibility. This was perhaps a partially negative level, as Merton came to the monastery to escape the destructiveness of the civilization and to keep intact his artistic sensibility and integrity. Yet Merton himself recognized this negative dimension and was able to work with it and turn it into something creative and nourishing to his artistic and monastic life.

There is an important vehicle, common to both his artistry and his life as a monk, that Merton incorporated to bring the two vocations closer together. This common element is language, what Tillich has called "the expression of man's freedom from the given situation and its concrete demands." Tillich makes a distinction between "human" language and "religious" language, which is helpful in understanding Merton's incorporation of the two types.

> . . . there is human language, based on man's encounter with reality, changing through the millennia, used for the needs of daily life, for expression and communication, for literature and poetry, and used also for the expression and communication of our ultimate concern. . . . Religious language is ordinary language, changed under the power of what it expresses, the ultimate of being and meaning. The expression of it can be narrative (mythological, legendary,

historical), or it can be prophetic, poetic, liturgical. It becomes holy for those to whom it expresses their ultimate concern from generation to generation.[4]

There is no better description of Merton's witness than Tillich's. As an artist, Merton honed and refined his language, essentially "human" language, to the extent that it could become "religious" language, human language utilized by one who is part of monastic culture and tradition.

There is, of course, a process involved here, one that precludes the incorporation of language. Merton himself provides an excellent description of this process.

> In an aesthetic experience, in the creation or the contemplation of a work of art, the psychological conscience is able to attain some of its highest and most perfect fulfillments. Art enables us to find ourselves and lose ourselves at the same time. The mind responds to the intellectual and spiritual values that lie hidden in a poem, a painting, or a piece of music, discovers a spiritual vitality that lifts it above itself, takes it out of itself, and makes it present to itself on a level of being that it did not know it could ever achieve.[5]

The uniqueness of Merton is found not only in his artistic sensibility—indeed, that is the uniqueness of any artist—but more importantly in his choice of the monastic vocation from and within which to experience and express this sensibility. It is not so much that the aesthetic experience is, in itself, incomplete and imperfect, though Merton had suggested this in "Poetry and The Contemplative Life." Rather, it is that Merton chose to merge the aesthetic experience and his artistic sensibility with his monastic sensibility, to merge the two spiritualities, in order to reach a higher level of awareness and experience. For Merton, this higher level was the profound awareness and experience of man's relationship with the Ultimate Being.

The uniqueness comes also in Merton's ultimate acceptance of his artistry rather than its rejection. Through a long and painful struggle, Merton came to accept, completely, his artistry and all that is part of it. This acceptance is, I believe, Merton's ultimate yes. Once again, Henry Miller has described this yes of the artist and, in so doing, of Merton.

> The first word any man writes when he has found himself, his own rhythm, which is the life rhythm, is Yes! Everything he writes thereafter is Yes, Yes, Yes,—Yes in a thousand million ways. No dynamo, no matter how huge—not even a dynamo of a hundred million dead souls—can combat one man saying Yes![6]

There is another dimension of Merton's yes which, though touched on earlier, needs to be further analyzed, and that is the relationship between literature and the man of letters on the one hand and monastic culture and the mystical life on the other. It is this relationship and Merton's understanding of it that contributes in large part to the uniqueness of his person. As an aid to the analysis of this relationship and its application to Merton, it is advantageous to consider Jean Leclercq's provocative essay, "Literature and the Mystical Life."

Leclercq believes that monastic culture is "primarily literary and traditional or, more precisely, literary because it is traditional" and is marked by its embracing of "the literary tradition of antiquity." The Roman writers, the authors of Scripture, the early church fathers used the language of literature, artistic and technical, and cultivated an "elegant style." They used language and literary techniques, however, not as ends in themselves but as means with and through which to worship God. As an example, Leclercq considers St. Jerome, whom he considers a "professional writer."

> He [Jerome] knows that the efficacy of his teaching depends in part upon the quality of his language. Consequently, he takes great pains not only with his style but also with his reputation . . . for he is a man of letters and his culture is so much a part of him that he cannot express himself without consciously reverting to it. He wishes to be respected as the discipline of the Word that has become writing.[7]

It is this tradition that Western monastic culture maintained and developed, from Gregory and Benedict to Bernard especially. Leclercq describes the process as "the continuous expansion of monastic literature whose form derived from classical tradition but whose inspiration was exclusively Christian."

However, the essence of monastic culture is not merely the "learned Christians." The monk possesses a "mystical orientation" and, as such, has a "constant inner urge to transcend belles-lettres in order to safeguard the primacy of the spiritual domain." In other words, literature and its techniques and skills are never an end in itself for the monk. The monk's "grammar is Christ." Leclercq describes the condition this way:

> Faith and literature, instead of satiating the Christian [the monk] stimulate his thirst for God, his eschatological desire. Grammar's role is to create an urgent need for total beauty; eschatology's role is to indicate the direction in which to look for its fulfillment.[8]

He is speaking here of a mergence of the spiritual life and cultural values, precisely the polarities of Thomas Merton's struggle. It is a conflict between "learning" and "conscience," but not a conflict beyond resolution. In a beautiful and penetrating description of this conflict and its attainable resolution, Leclercq also characterizes Merton and his process of reconciliation.

> To combine a patiently acquired culture with a simplicity won through the power of fervent love, to keep simplicity of soul in the midst of the diverse attractions of the intellectual life and, in order to accomplish this, to place oneself and remain firmly on the plane of the conscience, to raise knowledge to its level and never let it fall below: this is what the cultivated monk succeeds in doing. He is a scholar, he is versed in letters but he is not merely a man of science nor a man of letters nor an intellectual, he is a spiritual man.[9]

By way of exemplifying this description of the cultivated monk, Leclercq refers to Bernard of Clairvaux and calls him "indissolubly and simultaneously, a learned man and a man of God, a thinker and a saint, a humanist and a mystic." Once more, we are offered a description of Merton's uniqueness, and in the final pages of the essay, as Leclercq enlarges his discussion of Bernard, we begin to see more of Merton and how he worked out the relationship between the man of letters and the man of God.

The signs of a true mystic—in Leclercq's context, St. Bernard, and in our context, Thomas Merton, the contemplative monk—are found in the detachment from self with which he writes, the simplicity of artistry and expression and the ultimate concern with what is said rather than how it was said. The true mystic, and the contemplative monk, realizes fully that spiritual experience produces spiritual literature and that experience itself produces as well as transforms literature.

> Neither a mystic without literary ability nor a man of letters without spiritual experience will ever, even in collaboration, write a great spiritual work. Literary genius without holiness, holiness without literary genius will never adequately explain the writings which result from the union of these two gifts of God. Literature alone could not give these texts their religious intensity; holiness would not be sufficient to give them the beauty which is one of the reasons for their permanent value.[10]

The true mystic, the contemplative monk who is also the man of letters, is one who writes with sincerity and purity of heart, which allows him to recognize that whereas literature and writing imitate, mysticism and the monastic way create and renew.

> Literature makes the beauty of a written work, mysticism gives it its grandeur. Literature's portion is the literary genre and style which have been adopted; sincerity contributes the experience these devices are to express: it finds them essential and they do it no injury. Amid genres and literary conventions, the mystic can be recognized by the extreme simplicity of the means he uses. His style becomes as limpid as his soul is pure. And the more elevated his thought, the less contrived his expression.[11]

In freeing himself from the concern with worldly success and reputation, the true mystic, the contemplative monk and man of letters, achieves a freedom of spirit. Because his "grammar is God," he is freed to a large extent of the burden of writing and literature as ends in themselves, and to that same extent has achieved a self-detachment. In the ultimate, the mystic's freedom of spirit allows him to use his literary gifts as he chooses. By virtue of his mysticism, the mystic would thus be silent because the experience of God and the exchange of love are beyond verbal and written language, beyond rhetoric.

But the mystic, the writer-monk, is a man of charity and it is this charity that urges him to forgo his beloved silence and instead to communicate, with his literary gifts, his knowledge and love of God. Thus we have Merton's understanding of the unique relationship of the man of letters with the man of God, of the writer with the monk. And yet, Merton's singularity was not only his ability to resolve the conflict between the two vocations and to achieve a reconciliation, but also his ability to write about the experience and the outcome.

> If the Christian poet is truly a Christian poet, if he has a vocation to make known to other men the unsearchable mystery of the love of Christ, then he must do so in the Spirit of Christ. And his "manifestation of the Spirit" not only springs from a kind of contemplative intuition of the mystery of Christ, but is "given to him for his profit" and will therefore deepen and perfect his union with Christ. The Christian poet and artist is one who grows not only by his contemplation but also by his open declaration of the mercy of God.[12]

We are brought once more, and finally, face-to-face with the man of compassion, the man of compassion who understands and who loves, who knows the wisdom and purity of the heart and who gives of this knowledge because he believes he has the responsibility to do so. In the end, it is simply that Thomas Merton, in his life and his legacy, has the awesome burden of being a contemporary man of the spirit. Time and history will reveal the uniqueness of his achievement and the extraordinary richness of his life.

Notes

INTRODUCTION

1. Marquita E. Breit and Robert E. Daggy, eds. and comps., *Thomas Merton: A Comprehensive Bibliography. New Edition* (New York, N.Y.: Garland Publishing, Inc., 1986).
2. Thomas Merton, *My Argument with the Gestapo/A Macaronic Journal.* (Garden City, N.Y.: Doubleday and Co., 1969), p. 6.
3. For further discussion see Peter Kountz, "On John Howard Griffin on Thomas Merton," *Kairos* (Vol. 2, No. 2, 1988): pp. 80-97.
4. See Merton's *The Way of Chuang Tzu* (New York: New Directions, 1965), "Three in the Morning," a fable on following two courses at once, p. 44.

CHAPTER ONE

1. Unless otherwise stated, all quotations are from Thomas Merton, *The Seven Storey Mountain* (New York: Harcourt, Brace and Company, 1948).
7. John Dewey, *Experience and Education* (New York: Collier Books, 1963), pp. 19-20.
3. Will Lissner, "Toast of the Avant-Garde: A Trappist Poet," *Catholic World* 166 (February 1948): 427.
4. George Mowry, *The Urban Nation* (New York: Hill and Wang, 1965), pp. 2-3.
5. Ibid., pp. 5-6.
6. Dewey, *Experience and Education*, p. 61.
7. Karl Weintraub, *Visions of Culture* (Chicago: University of Chicago Press, 1966), p. 119.
8. Ibid., p. 158.
9. See Merton, *Seven Storey Mountain*, pp. 44-48, and *My Argument with the Gestapo, A Macaronic Journal* (Garden City: Doubleday and Company, Inc., 1969), pp. 238-42.
10. Merton, *My Argument with the Gestapo*, pp. 193-95, 205.

11. Thomas Merton, "The White Pebble," *Where I Found Christ*, ed. John A. O'Brien (New York: Doubleday and Company, 1950), p. 241.
12. Struthers Burt, "The Unreality of Realism," *The Writer and His Craft*, ed. Roy Cowden (Ann Arbor: University of Michigan Press, 1954), p. 194.
13. Ibid., p. 196.
14. Ibid., p. 199.
15. Paul Tillich, *On the Boundary, An Autobiographical Sketch* (New York: Charles Scribner's Sons, 1966), pp. 24-26.
16. Stephen Spender, "The Young Writer," *To the Young Writer*, ed. A. L. Bader (Ann Arbor: University of Michigan Press, 1965), p. 7.
17. Quoted in Malcolm Cowley, "The Beginning Writer," in ibid., p. 83.
18. It is interesting to note that *My Argument with the Gestapo*, Merton's autobiographical novel, had as its principal character, Merton the journalist, in London to write about the war for his American paper.
19. Merton, *My Argument with the Gestapo*, p. 60.
20. Ibid., pp. 62-63.
21. Ibid., pp. 63-64.
22. Ibid., pp. 131-33.
23. Ibid., pp. 143-44.
24. Cf. Burt, "The Unreality of Realism," p. 199.
25. Merton, *My Argument with the Gestapo*, p. 142.
26. Ibid., pp. 80-87.
27. Ibid, pp. 142-43.
28. See Elena Malits, "Journey into the Unknown: Thomas Merton's Continuing Conversion" (Ph.D. dissertation, Fordham University, 1974), pp. 361-92.
29. Edward Rice, *The Man in the Sycamore Tree* (New York: Doubleday and Company, 1970), p. 29.
30. Douglas Day, *Malcolm Lowry, A Biography* (New York: Oxford University Press, 1973), p. 471.
31. Merton, *My Argument with the Gestapo*, pp. 107-9.
32. Ibid., pp. 27-28.
33. Ibid., p. 35.
34. Thomas Merton, *Contemplation in a World of Action* (New York: Doubleday and Company, Inc., 1971), pp. 205-17.
35. Merton, *My Argument with the Gestapo*, p. 146.
36. Edward Rice, in *The Man in the Sycamore Tree*, suggests that Merton had a very intense relationship with a woman while in London during those months. Elaine, the woman Merton mentions in the text at this point, may have been the woman Rice had in mind.
37. Merton, *My Argument with the Gestapo*, pp. 147-49.
38. Frank Freidel, *America in the Twentieth Century*, 3d ed. (New York: Alfred A. Knopf, 1970), p. 328.
39. Thomas Merton, "Learning to Live," *University on the Heights*, ed. Wesley First (New York: Doubleday and Company, Inc., 1969), pp. 196-98.

40. See Mark Van Doren, "Thomas Merton," *America* 120 (January 4, 1969): 21-22.
41. See Frank Dell'Isola, *Thomas Merton: A Bibliography* (New York: Farrar, Straus and Cudahy, 1956), pp. 91-93.
42. "At the Corner," *The Columbia Review* 17, no. 1 (November 1935): 8.

CHAPTER TWO

1. Etienne Gilson, *The Spirit of Medieval Philosophy* (New York: Charles Scribner's Sons, 1940), p. 54.
2. Ibid, pp. vii-viii.
3. Merton had a similar attraction to and respect and emulation of Jacques Maritain, which he maintained his entire life.
4. Merton, "Learning to Live," p. 188.
5. Henry J. M. Nouwen, *Pray to Live* (Notre Dame: Fides Publishers, Inc., 1972), p. 37.
6. Quoted in George Barry Ford, *A Degree of Difference* (New York: Farrar, Straus and Giroux, 1969), pp. 228-29.
7. Quoted in Ford, *A Degree of Difference*, p. 80.
8. Augustine, *The Confessions*, trans. Edward B. Pusey (New York: Washington Square Press, Inc., 1960), pp. 147-48.
9. Adolph Harnack, *What is Christianity?* trans. Thomas B. Saunders (New York: Harper & Row, Publishers, 1957), pp. 258-59.
10. See James Carroll, "Living a Prayerful Life," *The National Catholic Reporter*, July 1974, p. 7.
11. Interview with François Mauriac, *Writers at Work*, The Paris Review Interviews, ed. Malcolm Cowley (New York: The Viking Press, 1959), p. 49.
12. Augustine, *Confessions*, pp. 121-22.
13. Evelyn Underhill, *Mysticism* (New York: E. P. Dutton and Company, Inc., 1961), pp. 331, 333-34.
14. Merton offers no description of this experience in his *Secular Journal* which is odd because the journal was kept during that summer. Since this journal was published in 1959, long after Merton's entrance into Gethsemani, it is possible that Merton may have edited out those entries.
15. Thomas Merton, *The Secular Journal* (New York: Farrar, Straus and Cudahy, 1959), p. 135.
16. Compare Merton's reflections on the trip in *The Secular Journal*, pp. 170-71. Not only does this description belie Merton's concern in the autobiography with renunciation, it strikes one as a description of greater immediacy and a more accurate account of Merton's true feelings.
17. Merton, *The Secular Journal*, p. 184.
18. Ibid., p. 188-89.

19. Ibid., pp. 189-90.
20. It is at this point in text of the autobiography that Merton begins to use the phrase *O beata solitudo*, a phrase that reappears with frequency until the end of the text.
21. Merton, *The Secular Journal*, p. 199.
22. Ibid., pp. 200-201.
23. Ibid., p. 203.
24. *My Argument with the Gestapo* reflects the state of Merton's mind that summer. One could suggest that even then Merton was using his writing as a means of understanding and accepting his past.
25. Merton, *The Secular Journal*, pp, 239-53.
26. Ibid., pp. 259-60.
27. Ibid., pp. 262-63.
28. Ibid., p. 265.
29. Ibid., p. 264.
30. Ibid., p. 265.
31. Ibid., pp. 269-70.
32. Once again, Merton seems to use his writing as a means of controlling history. One senses that as Merton burned his manuscripts he thought he was burning—and wiping out—the past that he was so burdened with.
33. Merton, *Contemplation in a World of Action*, p. 231.

CHAPTER THREE

1. Dell'Isola, *Thomas Merton: A Bibliography*, pp. 91-93.
2. Bradford Daniel, ed., *The John Howard Griffin Reader* (Boston: Houghton Mifflin Company, 1968), p. 29.
3. Ibid., p. 21.
4. Thomas P. McDonnell, ed., *A Thomas Merton Reader* (New York: Harcourt, Brace and World, Inc., 1962), p. x.
5. Peter Kountz, "The Seven Storey Mountain of Thomas Merton," *Thought* 49, no. 194 (September 1974): 250-67.
6. Thomas Merton, "Todo y Nada," *Renascence* 2 (Spring 1950); 89 (unpublished section from the original manuscript of *The Seven Storey Mountain*).
7. Ibid., pp. 92-93.
8. Thomas Merton, *Thirty Poems* (Norfolk: New Directions, 1944).
9. John Tracy Ellis, *American Catholicism*, 2d ed. rev. (Chicago: University of Chicago Press, 1969), pp. 135-36, suggests that Merton's autobiography had something to do with the unusual increase in the number of scholastics and novices.
10. Thomas Merton, *The Sign of Jonas* (New York: Doubleday, 1953), p. 53.
11. See Kountz, "The Seven Story Mountain of Thomas Merton."

12. See Merton, *The Sign of Jonas*, pp. 246-47, 317-18.
13. Thomas Merton, *The Waters of Siloe* (New York: Harcourt, Brace and Company, 1949), p. 321.
14. Saint Bonaventure, *The Mind's Road to God* (Indianapolis: The Bobbs-Merrill Company, Inc., 1953), pp. 45-46.
15. Thomas P. McDonnell, "An Interview with Thomas Merton," *Motive* 28 (October 1967): 32.
16. Unless otherwise stated, all quotations are from Merton *The Sign of Jonas*.
17. Thomas Merton, "Poetry and the Contemplative Life," *The Commonweal* 46 (July 4, 1947): 284.
18. Ibid., p. 285.
19. Ibid., pp. 285-86.
20. Thomas Merton, *Seeds of Contemplation* (New York: The Dell Publishing Company, Inc., 1949), pp. 59-60.
21. Ibid., p. 65.
22. Ibid., pp. 146-47.
23. Letter from John Howard Griffin to author, May 31, 1975.
24. A. D. Sertillanges, O. P., *The Intellectual Life* (Cork: The Mercier Press, 1946), pp. 34-35.
25. See also Thomas Merton, *The Silent Life* (New York: Farrar, Straus and Cudahy, 1957), pp. vii-xiv, 1-20, 71-72, on purity of heart.
26. Letter from John Howard Griffin to author, May 31, 1975.
27. Letter from John Eudes Bamberger, O.C.S.O., to author, June 14, 1975.
28. See David Bakan, *The Duality of Human Existence* (Boston: Beacon Press, 1966), pp. 154-236; Paul Tournier, *The Meaning of Persons* (London: SCM Press Ltd., 1957), pp. 67-119.
29. Tournier, *The Meaning of Persons*, pp. 168-69.
30. Thomas Merton, *The Bread in the Wilderness* (New York: New Directions, 1953), p. 129.
31. It is significant, I believe, that Merton began anew *The Ascent to Truth* in December 1950 and finished the text by the end of February 1951. This effort followed immediately his November hospital stay.
32. See McDonnell, "An Interview with Thomas Merton."

CONCLUSION

1. Thomas H. Moore, ed., *Henry Miller on Writing* (New York: New Directions, 1964), p. 116.
2. Thomas Merton, "The Catholic and Creativity: Theology of Creativity," *The American Benedictine Review* 11 (December 1960): 198.
3. Paul Tillich, *Theology of Culture* (New York: Oxford University Press, 1959), p. 46.
4. Ibid., pp. 47-48.

5. Thomas Merton, *No Man is an Island* (New York: Dell Publishing Company, 1957), p. 53.
6. Moore, *Henry Miller on Writing*, pp. 10-11.
7. Jean Leclercq, O.S.B., *The Love of Learning and the Desire for God* (New York: The New American Library, 1961), pp. 253-54.
8. Ibid., p. 255.
9. Ibid., p. 256.
10. Ibid., p. 262.
11. Ibid., p. 264.
12 Thomas Merton, "Poetry and Contemplation: A Reappraisal," *The Commonweal* 69 (October 24, 1958): 87-92, quoted in *A Thomas Merton Reader*, pp. 449-50.

Bibliography

PRIMARY WORKS

Because of the nature of this book, not all of Merton's more than forty books and his many articles were used as primary source material. I have not included the unused materials in the bibliography. Frederick Kelly's *Man before God: Thomas Merton on Social Responsibility* is the most carefully researched and complete Merton bibliography available. I also refer the reader to both editions of *Thomas Merton: A Bibliography* by Frank Dell'Isola.

Books

The Ascent to Truth. New York: Harcourt, Brace and World, 1951.

The Asian Journal of Thomas Merton. New York: New Directions Publishing Corporation, 1973.

Bread in the Wilderness. New York: New Directions, 1953.

The Climate of Monastic Prayer. Spencer, Mass.: Cistercian Publications, 1969.

Conjectures of a Guilty Bystander. Garden City: Doubleday and Company, Inc., 1966.

Contemplation in a World of Action. Edited by Naomi Burton. New York: Doubleday and Company, Inc., 1971.

Contemplative Prayer. New York: Herder and Herder, 1969.

The Last of the Fathers. New York: Harcourt, Brace, 1954.

My Argument with the Gestapo: A Macaronic Journal. Garden City: Doubleday and Company, Inc., 1969.

New Seeds of Contemplation. New York: New Directions, 1961.

No Man is an Island. New York: Dell Publishing Company, 1957.

The Secular Journal of Thomas Merton. New York: Farrar, Straus and Cudahy, 1959.

Seeds of Contemplation. New York: Dell, 1949.

The Seven Storey Mountain. New York: Harcourt, Brace and World, 1948.

The Sign of Jonas. New York: Harcourt, Brace and World, 1953.

The Silent Life. New York: Farrar, Straus and Cudahy, 1957.

A Thomas Merton Reader. Edited by Thomas P. McDonnell. New York: Harcourt, 1962.

The Waters of Siloe. New York: Harcourt, Brace and World, 1949.

What are These Wounds? The Life of a Cistercian Mystic, Saint Lutgarde of Aywieres. Milwaukee: Bruce, 1950.

Articles

"As Man to Man." *Cistercian Studies* 4 (1969): 90-94.

"Blake and the New Theology." *The Sewanee Review* 86 (Autumn 1968): 673-82.

"The Catholic and Creativity: Theology of Creativity." *The American Benedictine Review* 11 (December 1960): 197-213.

"Conversatio Morum." *Cistercian Studies* 1 (1966): 130-40.

"Day of a Stranger." *Hudson Review* 20 (Summer 1967): 211-18.

"Learning to Live." *University on the Heights*. Edited by Wesley First. New York: Doubleday and Company, 1969, pp. 187-99.

"Poetry and Contemplation: A Reappraisal." *The Commonweal* 69 (October 24, 1958): 87-92.

"Poetry and the Contemplative Life." *The Commonweal* 46 (July 4, 1947): 280-86.

"The Solitary Life." *Cistercian Studies* 10 (1969): 213-17.

"Todo y Nada." *Renascence* 2 (Spring 1950): 87-101. Unpublished material of writing and contemplation from the original manuscript of *The Seven Storey Mountain*.

"The White Pebble." *Where I Found Christ*. Edited by John A. O'Brien. New York: Doubleday and Company, 1950. pp. 235-50.

"Writing as Temperature." *The Sewanee Review* 77 (Summer 1969): 535-42.

SECONDARY SOURCES

Published and Unpublished Materials on Thomas Merton

Books and Dissertations

Bailey, Raymond H. "The Evolution of the Mystical Thought of Thomas Merton." Ph.D. dissertation, Southern Baptist Seminary, 1973.

_____. *Thomas Merton on Mysticism.* Garden City: Doubleday and Company, Inc., 1975.

Baker, James T. *Thomas Merton: Social Critic.* Lexington: The University Press of Kentucky, 1971.

Breit, Marquita. *Thomas Merton: A Bibliography.* Metuchen, N.J.: The Scarecrow Press, 1974.

Dell'Isola, Frank. *Thomas Merton: A Bibliography.* New York: Farrar, Straus and Cudahy, 1956.

_____. *Thomas Merton: A Bibliography.* 2d ed. Kent, Ohio: Kent State University Press, 1975.

Griffin, John Howard and Thomas Merton. *A Hidden Wholeness: The Visual World of Thomas Merton.* Photographs by Thomas Merton. Text by John Howard Griffin. Boston: Houghton Mifflin Company, 1970.

Hart, Brother Patrick, O.C.S.O., ed. *Thomas Merton, Monk: A Monastic Tribute.* New York: Sheed and Ward, 1974.

Higgins, John H., S. J. *Merton's Theology of Prayer.* Spencer, Mass.: Cistercian Publications, 1971.

Kelly, Frederick Joseph, S.J. *Man Before God: Thomas Merton on Social Responsibility.* Garden City: Doubleday and Company, Inc., 1974.

_____. "The Social Dimensions of Religious Man in the Writings of Thomas Merton." Ph.D. dissertation, Catholic University.

McInerny, Dennis Q. "Thomas Merton and Society: A Study of the Man and His Thought Against the Background of Contemporary American Culture." Ph.D. dissertation, University of Minnesota, 1969.

_____. *Thomas Merton: The Man and His Work.* Washington: Cistercian Publications, Consortium Press, 1974.

Malits, Elena, C.S.C. "Journey into the Unknown: Thomas Merton's Continuing Conversion." Ph.D. dissertation, Fordham University, 1974.

Nouwen, Henri, J.M. *Pray to Live. Thomas Merton: A Contemplative Critic.* Notre Dame: Fides Publishers, Inc., 1972.

Rice, Edward. *The Man in the Sycamore Tree: The Good Times and Hard Life of Thomas Merton.* New York: Doubleday and Company, Inc., 1970.

Articles and Essays

Andrews, James F. "Was Merton a Critic of Renewal?" *The National Catholic Reporter*, February 1970, Lenten Supplement, pp. 12-15.

Baciu, Stefan. "The Literary Catalyst." *Continuum* 7 (1969): 295-305.

Bamberger, John Eudes, O.C.S.O. "The Cistercian." *Continuum* 7 (1969): 227-41.

Bilski, Nanine. "The Difference He Made." *Continuum* 7 (1969): 320-22.

Bourne, Russell. "The Rain Barrel." *Continuum* 7 (1969): 361-63.

Burke, Herbert C. "The Man of Letters." *Continuum* 7 (1969): 274-85.

Burns, Flavian, O.C.S.O. "Homily at the Mass for Father M. Louis." *Cistercian Studies* 3 (1968): 279-80.

Burton, Naomi. "I Shall Miss Thomas Merton." *Cistercian Studies* 4 (1969): 218-25.

_____. "The Path to Seven Storey Mountain." Condensed from *More Than Sentinels. Catholic Digest* 29 (February 1965): 127.

_____. "Thomas Merton's Mountain." *The Sign* 44 (October 1964): 46-50.

Cameron-Brown, Aldhelm. "Seeking the Rhinoceros: A Tribute to Thomas Merton." *Monastic Studies* 7 (1969): 63-74.

Conner, Tarcisius, O.C.S.O. "Merton, Monastic Exchange and Renewal." *Monastic Exchange* 1 (1969): 1-14.

Connolly, Francis X. "The Complete Twentieth-Century Man." Review of *The Seven Storey Mountain. Thought* 24 (1949): 10-14.

Dumont, Charles, O.C.S.O. "A Contemplative at the Heart of the World." *Lumen Vitae* 24 (1969): 633-46.

Ferry, W. H. "The Difference He Made." *Continuum* 7 (1969): 319-20.

Forest, James. "The Gift of Merton." *Commonweal* 89 (1968-1969): 463-65.

Graham, Aelred, O.S.B. "The Mysticism of Thomas Merton." *Commonweal* 62 (1955): 155-59.

_____. "Thomas Merton, A Modern Man in Reverse." *Atlantic Monthly* 191 (1953): 70-74.

Griffin, John Howard. "Les Grandes Amitiés." *Continuum* 7 (1969): 286-94.

_____. "In Search of Thomas Merton." *Merton Studies Center* 1 (1971): 12-24.

_____. "Merton and His Camera." *The National Catholic Reporter*, November 1970, pp. 6A-7A.

Groves, G. "My Fourteen Years with Thomas Merton." *The Critic* 21 (March 1963): 29-32.

Hart, Patrick, O.C.S.O. "The Ecumenical Concern of Thomas Merton." *The Lamp* 70 (December 1970): 20-23.

_____. "Last Mass in the Hermitage." *Continuum* 7 (1969): 20-23.

_____. "The Merton Publishing Scene." *Monastic Exchange* 4 (Autumn 1972): 67-70.

Hinson, E. Glenn. "Merton's Many Faces." *Religion in Life* 42 (Summer 1973): 153-68.

Kelty, Matthew. "Letter from Gethsemani." *Monastic Exchange* 1 (1969): 86-89.

_____. "Some Reminiscences of Thomas Merton." *Cistercian Studies* 4 (1969): 163-75.

Kountz, Peter. "The Seven Storey Mountain of Thomas Merton." *Thought* 49 (September 1974): 250-67.

Landess, Thomas. "Monastic Life and The Secular City." *The Sewanee Review* 77 (Summer 1969): 530-35.

Lentfoehr, Sister M. Therese, S.D.S. "The Spiritual Writer." *Continuum* 7 (1969): 242-54.

Lester, Julius. "Merton." *Katallagete* 4 (Summer 1973): 21-26.

Lissner, Will. "Toast of the Avant-Garde: A Trappist Poet." *Catholic World* 166 (February 1948): 424-32.

MacCormick, Chalmers. "The Zen Catholicism of Thomas Merton." *Journal of Ecumenical Studies* 9 (Fall 1972): 802-17.

Saword, Anne, O.C.S.O. "Tribute to Thomas Merton." *Cistercian Studies* 3 (1968): 265-78.

Steindl-Rast, David. "Recollections of Thomas Merton's Last Days in the West." *Monastic Studies* 7 (1969): 1-10.

Stevens, Clifford. "Thomas Merton, 1968: A Profile in Memoriam." *American Benedictine Review* 20 (1969): 7-20.

Toelle, Gervase. "Merton and the Critics." *Renascence* 2 (Spring 1950): 139-46.

_____. "Merton: His Problem and a Solution." *Spirit* 16 (July 1949): 84-89.

Van Doren, Mark. "Thomas Merton." *America* 120 (1969): 21-22.
Zahn, Gordon. "The Peacemaker." *Continuum* 7 (1969): 265-73.

SELECTED BACKGROUND TEXTS

Religion, Religious History, Theology, and Spirituality

Aquinas, Thomas. *Summa Theologiae*. Vols. 1 and 2. Garden City: Doubleday and Company, Inc., 1969.

Augustine, Saint. *The Confessions*. Translated by Edward B. Pusey. New York: Washington Square Press, Inc., 1960.

Bernard of Clairvaux, Saint. *De diligendo Deo*. In Ray C. Petry, ed. *Late Medieval Mysticism*. Philadelphia: The Westminster Press, 1957.

Bethge, Eberhard. *Dietrich Bonhoeffer*. New York: Harper & Row, Publishers, 1970.

Bonaventure, Saint. *The Mind's Road to God*. Indianapolis: Bobbs-Merrill Company, Inc., 1953.

Brauer, Jerald C., ed. *Reinterpretation in American Church History*. Chicago: University of Chicago Press, 1968.

Callahan, Daniel. *The Mind of the Catholic Layman*. New York: Charles Scribner's Sons, 1963.

Capps, Donald, and Walter H. Capps, eds. *The Religious Personality*. Belmont, Calif.: Wadsworth Publishing Company, Inc., 1970.

Catholicism in America. A series of articles from *The Commonweal*. New York: Harcourt, Brace and Company, 1953.

Chautard, Jean Baptist, O.C.S.O. *The Soul of the Apostolate*. Translated by Thomas Merton. Trappist, Ky.: The Abbey of Gethsemani, 1946.

Cogley, John. *Catholic America*. Garden City: Doubleday and Company, Inc., 1974.

Cogley, John, ed. *Religion in America*. New York: Meridian Books, Inc., 1958.

Creative Suffering. A series of articles from *The National Catholic Reporter*. Kansas City: The National Catholic Reporter Publishing Company, 1970.

Cross, Robert D. *The Emergence of Liberal Catholicism in America*. Chicago: Quadrangle Books, 1968.

Dunne, John S., C.S.C. *A Search for God in Time and Memory*. New York: The Macmillan Company, 1967.

Ellis, John Tracy. *American Catholicism*. 2d ed. rev. Chicago: University of Chicago Press, 1969.

Ford, George Barry. *A Degree of Difference*. New York: Farrar, Straus and Giroux, 1969.

Francis DeSales, Saint. *Introduction to the Devout Life*. Garden City: Doubleday and Company, Inc., 1955.

Gleason, Philip, ed. *Catholicism in America*. New York: Harper & Row, Publishers, 1970.

Gray, Francine du Plessix. *Divine Disobedience. Profiles in Catholic Radicalism*. New York: Random House, Inc., 1971.

Greeley, Andrew M. *The Catholic Experience*. Garden City: Doubleday and Company, Inc., 1969.

Harnack, Adolph. *What is Christianity?* Translated by Thomas B. Saunders. New York: Harper & Row, Publishers, 1957.

Hudson, Winthrop S. *Religion in America*. New York: Charles Scribner's Sons, 1965.

John of the Cross, Saint. *Ascent of Mount Carmel*. Translated by E. Allison Peers. Garden City: Doubleday and Company, Inc., 1958.

_____. *Dark Night of the Soul*. Translated by E. Allison Peers. Garden City: Doubleday and Company, Inc., 1959.

_____. *Living Flame of Love*. Translated by E. Ellison Peers. Garden City: Doubleday and Company, Inc., 1962.

Johnston, William S.J., ed. *The Cloud of Unknowing*. Garden City: Doubleday and Company, Inc., 1973.

Loyola, Saint Ignatius. *The Spiritual Exercises*. Translated by Anthony Mottola. Garden City: Doubleday and Company, Inc., 1964.

McKenzie, John L. *The Roman Catholic Church*. Garden City: Doubleday and Company, Inc., 1971.

Marty, Martin E. *The Search for a Usable Future*. New York: Harper & Row, 1969.

_____. *Varieties of Unbelief*. Garden City: Doubleday and Company, 1966.

Mead, Sidney E. *The Lively Experiment*. New York: Harper & Row, Publishers, 1963.

O'Brien, David J. *The Renewal of American Catholicism*. New York: Oxford University Press, 1972.

Ong, Walter J., S.J. *American Catholic Crossroads*. New York: Collier Books, 1962.

_____. *Frontiers in American Catholicism.* New York: Macmillan Company, 1964.

Peguy, Charles. *Basic Verities.* Translated by Anne and Julian Green. Chicago: Henry Regnery Company, 1965.

Sertillanges, A.D., O.P. *The Intellectual Life.* Cork: The Mercier Press, 1946.

Thérèse of Lisieux, Saint. *The Story of a Soul.* Translated by John Beevers. Garden City: Doubleday and Company, 1957.

Tillich, Paul. *On the Boundary. An Autobiographical Sketch.* New York: Charles Scribner's Sons, 1966.

_____. *Systematic Theology.* 3 vols. Chicago: University of Chicago Press, 1967.

_____. *Theology of Culture.* New York: Oxford University Press, 1959.

Troeltsch, Ernst. *The Social Teaching of The Christian Churches.* Translated by Olive Wyon. 2 vols. New York: Harper & Row, Publishers, 1960.

Underhill, Evelyn. *Mysticism.* New York: E. P. Dutton and Company, Inc., 1961.

Wills, Garry. *Bare Ruined Choirs: Doubt, Prophecy, and Radical Religion.* Garden City: Doubleday and Company, Inc., 1972.

History, Philosophy of History, Philosophy

Barraclough, Geoffrey. *An Introduction to Contemporary History.* Baltimore: Penguin Books, 1967.

Bloch, Marc. *The Historian's Craft.* New York: Alfred A. Knopf, Publishers, 1953.

Dawson, Christopher. *The Historic Reality of Christian Culture.* New York: Harper & Row, Publishers, 1960.

Dilthey, Wilhelm. *Pattern and Meaning in History: Thoughts on History and Society.* New York: Harper & Row, 1960.

Freidel, Frank. *America in the Twentieth Century.* 3d ed. New York: Alfred A. Knopf, 1970.

Gellner, Ernest. *Thought and Change.* Chicago: University of Chicago Press, 1964.

Goldman, Eric. *The Crucial Decade—And After. America, 1945-1960.* New York: Random House, Inc., 1960.

_____. *Rendezvous With Destiny.* New York: Random House, Inc., 1955.

Gombrich, E. H. *In Search of Cultural History*. Oxford: Clarendon Press, 1969.

Hughes, H. Stuart. *Consciousness and Society*. New York: Random House, Inc., 1958.

_____. *History as Art and as Science. Twin Vistas on the Past*. New York: Harper & Row, Publishers, 1964.

Huizinga, Johan. *America. A Dutch Historian's Vision, From Afar and Near*. New York: Harper & Row, Publishers, 1972.

_____. *Men and Ideas. History, The Middle Ages, The Renaissance*. New York: Meridian Books, Inc., 1959.

Jaspers, Karl. *Man in the Modern Age*. New York: Doubleday and Company, Inc., 1957.

Kohl, Herbert. *The Age of Complexity*. New York: The New American Library, 1965.

Kroeber, A. L., and Clyde Kluckhohn. *Culture: A Critical Review of Concepts and Definitions*. New York: Random House, Inc., 1952.

Lasch, Christopher. *The New Radicalism in America, 1889-1963. The Intellectual as a Social Type*. New York: Random House, Inc., 1965.

Lifton, Robert Jay. *History and Human Survival*. New York: Random House, Inc., 1971.

Marcel, Gabriel. *Man Against Mass Society*. Chicago: Henry Regnery Company, 1962.

_____. *Problematic Man*. New York: Herder and Herder, 1967.

Marcus, Robert D. *A Brief History of the United States Since 1945*. New York: St. Martin's Press, 1975.

Mazlish, Bruce, ed. *Psychoanalysis and History*. Rev. ed. New York: Grosset and Dunlap, 1971.

Mowry, George M. *The Urban Nation: 1920-1960*. New York: Hill and Wang, 1965.

Sklar, Robert, ed. *The Plastic Age: 1917-1930*. New York: George Braziller, 1970.

Stern, Fritz, ed. *The Varieties of History, From Voltaire to the Present*. New York: Meridian Books, 1956.

Susman, Warren, ed. *Culture and Commitment: 1929-1945*. New York: George Braziller, 1973.

Weintraub, Karl J. *Visions of Culture*. Chicago: University of Chicago Press, 1966.

Williams, Raymond. *Culture and Society: 1780-1950*. Garden City: Doubleday and Company, Inc., 1960.

Monasticism and Monastic History

Benedict, Saint. *Rule for Monasteries*. Translated by Leonard J. Doyle. Collegeville, Minn.: The Liturgical Press, 1948.

Bernard of Clairvaux. *Studies presented to Dom Jean Leclercq*. Washington, D.C.: Cistercian Publications, Consortium Press, 1973.

Butler, Cuthbert. *Benedictine Monachism*. 2d ed. Cambridge: Cambridge University Press, 1961.

_____. *Western Mysticism*. 2d ed. London: Constable Publishers, 1951.

Canu, Jean. *Religious Orders of Men*. Translated by P. J. Hepburne-Scott. New York: Hawthorn Books, Inc., 1960.

Chadwick, Owen, ed. *Western Asceticism*. Philadelphia: The Westminster Press, 1957.

Hallier, Amédée, O.C.S.O. *The Monastic Theology of Aelred of Rievaulx*. Shannon: Irish University Press, 1969.

Knowles, David. *Christian Monasticism*. New York: McGraw-Hill Book Company, 1969.

_____. *From Pachomius to Ignatius. A Study in the Constitutional History of Religious Orders*. Oxford: Clarendon Press, 1966.

Leclercq, Jean. *The Love of Learning and the Desire for God*. New York: New American Library, 1961.

Lekai, Louis J., S.O. Cist. *The White Monks*. Okauchee, Wisc.: Our Lady of Spring Bank, 1953.

Pennington, M. Basil, O.C.S.O., ed. *The Cistercian Spirit. A Symposium in Memory of Thomas Merton*. Shannon: Irish University Press, 1970.

Petry, Ray C., ed. *Late Medieval Mysticism*. Philadelphia: The Westminster Press, 1957.

Workman, Herbert B. *The Evolution of the Monastic Ideal*. Boston: The Beacon Press, 1962.

Zarnecki, George. *The Monastic Achievement*. New York: McGraw-Hill Book Company, 1972.

Aesthetics, Art, Art History, Literature, and Writing

Anderson, Sherwood. *A Story Teller's Story.* New York: The Viking Press, 1969.

Bader, A. L., ed. *To the Young Writer.* Ann Arbor: University of Michigan Press, 1965.

Barthes, Roland. *Writing Degree Zero and Elements of Semiology.* Boston: The Beacon Press, 1970.

Berger, John. *The Look of Things.* New York: The Viking Press, 1974.

Brome, Vincent. *Confessions of a Writer.* London: Hutchinson and Company, Publishers, Ltd., 1970.

Cowden, Roy W., ed. *The Writer and His Craft.* Ann Arbor: University of Michigan Press, 1954.

Cowley, Malcolm, ed. *Writers at Work.* The Paris Review *Interviews,* 1st series. New York: The Viking Press, 1959.

Day, Douglas. *Malcolm Lowry, A Biography.* New York: Oxford University Press, 1973.

Dunham, Barrows. *The Artist in Society.* New York: Marzani Munsell, Inc., Publishers, 1960.

Edman, Irwin. *Arts and the Man.* New York: W. W. Norton and Company, Inc., 1939.

Fiedler, Leslie A. *Love and Death in the American Novel.* Rev. ed. New York: The Dell Publishing Company, 1966.

Frye, Northrop. *The Educated Imagination.* Bloomington, Ind.: The Indiana University Press, 1964.

Gombrich, E. H. *Meditations on a Hobby Horse And Other Essays on the Theory of Art.* London: Phaidon Publishers, Inc., 1963.

Hail, James B., and Barry Ulanov, eds. *Modern Culture and the Arts.* 2d ed. New York: McGraw-Hill Book Company, 1972.

Klee, Felix, ed. *The Diaries of Paul Klee: 1898-1918.* Berkeley, Calif.: The University of California Press, 1968.

Langer, Susanne K. *Problems of Art.* New York: Charles Scribner's Sons, 1957.

Maritain, Jacques. *Art and Scholasticism and The Frontiers of Poetry.* Translated by Joseph W. Evans. New York: Charles Scribner's Sons, 1962.

May, Rollo, ed. *Symbolism in Religion and Literature.* New York: George Braziller, Inc., 1960.

Meyer, Leonard B. *Music, The Arts, and Ideas. Patterns and Predictions in Twentieth-Century Culture.* Chicago: University of Chicago Press, 1967.

Moore, Thomas H., ed. *Henry Miller on Writing.* New York: New Directions Publishing Corporation, 1964.

Mumford, Lewis. *Art and Technics.* New York: The Columbia University Press, 1952.

Plimpton, George, ed. *Writers at Work. The* Paris Review *Interviews*, 2d series. New York: The Viking Press, 1963.

_____. *Writers at Work. The* Paris Review *Interviews*, 3d series. New York: The Viking Press, 1968.

Rilke, Rainer Maria. *Letters to a Young Poet.* Translated by M. D. Herter Norton. Rev. ed. New York: W. W. Norton and Company, Inc., 1954.

_____. *The Notebooks of Malte Laurids Brigge.* Translated by M. D. Herter Norton. New York: W. W. Norton and Company, Inc., 1949.

Shahn, Ben. *The Shape of Content.* Cambridge, Mass.: Harvard University Press, 1957.

Sontag, Susan. *Against Interpretation.* New York: The Dell Publishing Company, 1966.

_____. *Styles of Radical Will.* New York: Farrar, Straus and Giroux, 1969.

Sypher, Wylie. *Loss of the Self in Modern Literature and Art.* New York: Random House, Inc., 1962.

Trilling, Lionel. *The Liberal Imagination.* Garden City: Doubleday and Company, Inc., 1953.

Wilson, Edmund. *The Twenties.* Edited by Leon Edel. New York: Farrar, Straus and Giroux, 1975.

Index

"Huxley and the Ethics of Peace," 60
immigrates to America, 3-4
importance of writing to, 113
influences on, 5, 9-10, 12, 13-14, 17, 18, 25, 27-28, 30, 34, 55-57, 58-59, 60-61, 62, 69
journal-keeping practices of, xxii
"Katabolism of an Englishman," 49
The Kingdom of Jesus, 125
The Labyrinth, 36, 79, 84
letters of, xxiii-xxiv
in London, 19, 27-28
love affairs of, 14, 30-31, 34, 184n
Love and Living, xxii-xxiii
A Man in the Divided Sea, 129, 141
and monastic life, 120-22, 123, 124-25, 126, 143-44, 147-48, 148-49
monastic training of, 130-31
and mother's death, 6
My Argument with the Gestapo, xx, 15, 17, 21, 22, 29, 34, 36, 39, 41, 44, 105, 110, 119, 170, 184n, 186n
Mystics and Zen Masters, xxii
"Nature and Art in William Blake," 63-64
"The Necessity of Silence," 167
in New York, 31, 39
on silence and solitude, 157-59, 160-62, 167-69, 173
on writing, 127-28
ordination of, 148-49
"Paris in Chicago," 41
"Perry Street Journal," xxix
"Poetry and the Contemplative Life," 135, 138, 139, 141, 177
poetry of, 77
prepares to enter monastery, 84-85
and priesthood, 71-72, 76, 80-82, 90-91, 92-93
and psychoanalysis, 34-35, 42
receives Catholic instruction, 71
religious epiphanies of, 37-38, 53-54, 72-73, 86-90, 92, 98-99
"religious phase," 21
retreat at Gethsemani, 99-104
retreat at Our Lady of the Valley, 106-7
The Road to Joy, xxiv
Saint Bonaventure Journal, xxix
and Saint Bonaventure's, 63
and sainthood, 78-79

scholarship regarding, xix, xvii, xxiv-xxvii
The School of Charity, xxiv
The School of the Spirit, 147
in Scotland, 21-23
Secular Journal, 85, 97, 106, 112, 119, 185n
Seeds of Contemplation, 141-43, 150
The Seven Storey Mountain, 54, 58, 104, 106, 108, 109, 129, 132-33, 138, 140, 141, 171, 172
The Sign of Jonas, 135-37, 148, 152, 163, 169, 172, 173
"The Silence of the Psalms," 168
The Soul of the Apostolate, 125
The Spirit of Simplicity, 125
"St. Malachy," 141
"The Stroller," 119
studies philosophy, 32-33
The Tears of the Blind Lions, 141
"From the Legend of St. Clement," 141
theology of, 133-34, 139-40, 144-45, 146-47
Thirty Poems, 127, 141
Thomas Merton in Alaska, xxi-xxii
travels, xxi-xxii, 6-7, 13, 14, 35-36, 37-39
use of language, 177
A Vow of Conversation, xxi
The Waters of Siloe, 130, 165
What Are These Wounds?, 165
Woods, Shore, Desert: A Notebook, May 1968, xxi
and World War II, 41
writings of, xix-xxiv, 119-20, 122-23, 125-26, 129, 134-43, 146-47, 150, 152-53, 163, 165-66, 176, 186n
Zen and the Bird of Appetite, xxii
Merton: A Biography (Monica Furlong), xxv
Merton Legacy Trust, xix, xxv
Merton Seasonal, xix
Metaphysics (Aristotle), 84
Metrotone, Terrence, 79
Migne, Jacques Paul
    his *Latin Patrology*, 55, 147
Miller, Henry, 120, 175, 177
Molière, 35
Mont Sainte Victoire (Paul Cézanne), 43
Moore, Father, 71-72, 73, 76
Mott, Michael, xxv-xxvi
Movies, 8, 49

Chicago Studies in the History of American Religion

Editors

JERALD C. BRAUER & MARTIN E. MARTY

(continued, over)